ANANSI

My Heart is Africa

My Heart is Africa

A FLYING ADVENTURE

SCOTT GRIFFIN

ANANSI

Library of Congress Control Number: 2006927140

Quotes on pages 184, 210, and 211 courtesy of *Africa: A Biography of the Continent*
by John Reader. Published in the United States by Alfred A. Knopf © 1997.

Editor: Janice Zawerbny
Cover image: Getty Images
Back cover photograph: George Whiteside
Photo section: Krystyne Griffin and Peter Shark

First published in Canada
by Thomas Allen Publishers.

Published in the United States
by House of Anansi Press Inc.
www.anansi.ca

Distributed by
Publishers Group West
1700 Fourth Street
Berkeley, CA 94710
Toll free tel. 1-800-788-3123

10 09 08 07 06   1 2 3 4 5

Printed and bound in Canada

To Krystyne, wife, companion, and co-pilot

CONTENTS

Acknowledgements xi

PART ONE

Chapter 1
Flight into Darkness 3

Chapter 2
Reaching for Africa 21

PART TWO

Chapter 3
City of Tears 39

Chapter 4
The Hangar 57

Chapter 5
Angels of Mercy 75

Chapter 6
The Poisoned Spear 89

Chapter 7
Repairs and Reconciliation   113

Chapter 8
Life in Nairobi   125

Chapter 9
Weekend Safaris   147

PART THREE

Chapter 10
Captive in Tanzania   159

Chapter 11
Wings of Sunlight   177

Chapter 12
South Africa   191

Chapter 13
Diamonds and Blood   207

PART FOUR

Chapter 14
Waiting for Twilight   235

Chapter 15
Tangier   261

Epilogue   269

Glossary   271

ACKNOWLEDGEMENTS

A writer's first book is an expedition through unmapped territory; greatly aided by the generosity of those who point out the inevitable pitfalls along the route and, in doing so, give of their time and interest.

I spent two months writing it in Mexico, overlooking the Pacific Ocean at "Cuachalala," generously provided by Maria Cristina and Wojtek Stebelski. Ramsay Derry spent hours meticulously editing the early stages of the book, and Ruth Smith, my assistant, typed endless drafts. Jim Gifford of Toronto and Nicky Blundell Brown of Kenya offered useful advice. Patricia Kennedy and Janice Zawerbny, my editors, and Patrick Crean, my publisher, were patient and generous beyond measure. Others including family members who know the author only too well offered insights—mostly positive. Special mention of my father, Tony, and brother, Tim, is affectionately noted.

This book is a true account of my flight to Africa and the two years spent in Nairobi with my wife, Krystyne, working with the Flying Doctors Service there. The book is an accurate record as seen from a personal perspective; only the mission flights have been constructed in a dramatic format as a story to hold the reader's interest.

I have abandoned any attempt to disguise names, with a few exceptions, since it would be too easy for those featured in the book to identify themselves. I accept responsibility and offer apologies to anyone who believes they have been misrepresented—the intention, in every case, was to portray Africa's characters, who are legion, as accurately as possible; seen, of course, through my own eyes. I continue to hold feelings of warmth and affection for all those in AMREF, the Flying Doctors Service, and for those I met over our two and a half-year period in Africa.

Finally, I owe, as most writers do, an enormous debt to my wife, Krystyne, who not only features as an impressive person in this book, but has provided both the patience and the support to ensure that it was written.

Scott Griffin
Toronto

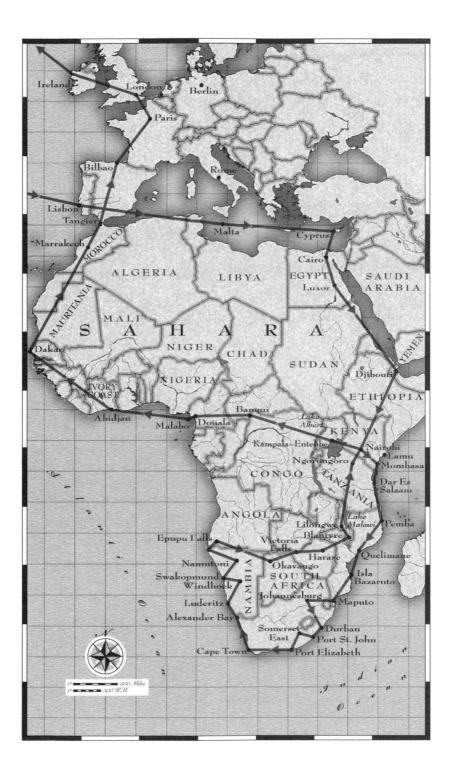

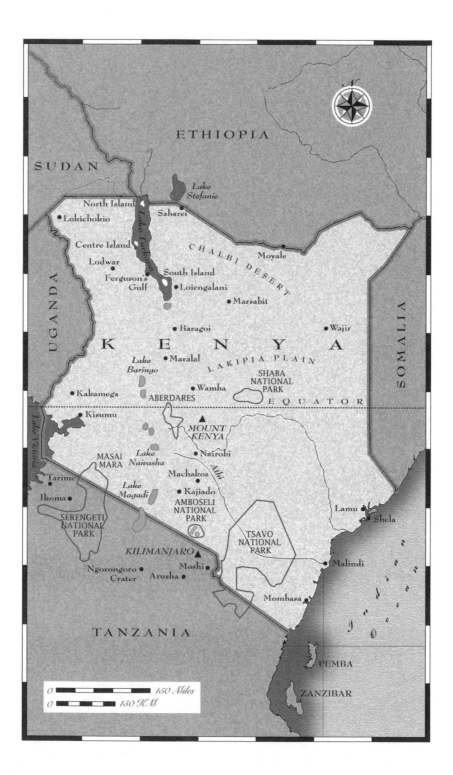

Ex Africa semper aliquid novi.
Africa always brings something new.

— PLINY

PART ONE

1

Flight into Darkness

THE NIGHT was Bible-black, cold and forbidding. Sea and sky were fused into a huge, inky void. Outside my Cessna 180, the darkness held no earth, no stars, no departure point, no feeling of movement—a world suspended. Only the warm glow of the instrument lights and the throb of the engine gave hint of the plane's small progress through the slow heartbeat of space. I was reaching into the unknown, a mere speck over the cold Atlantic. It was the first time I ever sensed vertigo.

The cockpit was crammed tight, like the inside of a space capsule, fragile and claustrophobic. My breath quickened, firing the imagination. Extrication in the event of an emergency would be impossible. Squeezed into a rubber survival suit and strapped into my seat with the doors locked, I was flying in a coffin with no means of escape. Streams of digital information curved over the Perspex windscreen: altitudes, airspeeds, nautical waypoints, reflecting my fear with split-second precision, shooting it deep into the starless night.

It was 2:10 a.m. The Newfoundland coast slipped beneath my right wing, inducing a sense of panic as I struck out over open water. I was losing my nerve. I fought for a legitimate reason to bank the plane and return to the safety of St. John's airport. A navigational miscalculation, an operational error or misjudgment from this point forward could lead to fuel exhaustion, mechanical failure, or loss of direction, forcing me to ditch into a fearsome sea. Somehow, in spite of all the careful planning, all the preparation, I was not yet ready to penetrate the night, to fly solo over fourteen hundred miles of ocean to the Azores. How to explain this sudden loss of nerve? With every passing minute I slipped, inch by inch, farther out over the ice-cold water, deeper into a private world of fear.

The coast was my lifeline. Like a drowning man I watched the faint outline of the shore receding into darkness. It was my last chance to turn back to safety. If I pressed on, I would lose the ability to investigate a snapping cable torn loose from the controls, an insidious airlock in the fuel line, an unexpected illumination of the alternator light, sudden loss of communication, or worst of all, catastrophic engine failure. Minutes drained away, inexorably, into the night. I had an overwhelming need to rest, just for a moment, to collect myself, to take stock, before pushing forward. Demons of doubt crowded in on me. Was this not foolhardy, courting unwarranted danger? Was it fair to my wife, Krystyne, anxiously waiting for news? Should I not turn around while I was within reach of the coast? I wavered. Then suddenly, from somewhere deep inside, a certain resolve took hold and I knew that my course was set. I was committed to trying to reach the Azores, the first leg of my solo flight from Toronto to Africa, whatever the risk.

It was 1996, and I was beginning a two-year mission with the Flying Doctors Service of Africa. I had decided to fly my own plane from Toronto to Nairobi, Kenya. I knew that flying a single-engine plane solo across the Atlantic left little room for error. On the other hand, once there, flying my own plane in Africa would make the experience unforgettable. It was a calculated risk, one I felt I could manage.

———————

St. John's airport tower transmitted final instructions over the radio and signed off. At 5:00 a.m., two hours from the coast, I had passed beyond normal VHF (very high frequency) radio range. I tried contacting Gander via HF (high frequency) radio, a long-distance radio used for transoceanic flights, without success. Perplexed as to why I was unable to make contact, I fiddled half-heartedly with the knobs for another five minutes and then gave up. There would be time later to concentrate on communications; I needed to turn my attention to navigation.

I planned to navigate across the ocean by hand, calculating my position hourly by dead reckoning and not relying solely on the GPS (global positioning system) instrument in the unlikely event it should fail. Manual calculations involved interpreting direction and strength of the wind to determine how far the plane would be blown off course. Gander provided St. John's with detailed forecasts of upper winds, which were printed for pilots an hour prior to departure. In daylight, wind force and direction were verifiable by sighting the size and angle of the waves relative to the plane's heading; at night, one had to rely on forecasts. In addition, hourly course adjustments were necessary, based on magnetic variation. I dutifully recorded my calculations and the GPS instrument times and positions on my aviation map, comparing the two: they were remarkably close over the first five hours.

I had virtually no room in the cockpit. Behind the front seat the large spare tank known as a ferry tank held 120 gallons of extra fuel, leaving almost no space for storing gear. The co-pilot's seat held the life raft on top of which was the HF radio. The fuel pump for the ferry tank occupied the floor of the cockpit. Where to store the flashlight, the emergency flares, the fresh-water container, the EPIRB (emergency position indicating radio beacon), the hand-held radio, and the thermos? More importantly, I needed space for the navigational charts, plotting charts, calculator, protractor, ruler, pencils, along with reference lists for HF radio frequencies, reporting positions and ETA (estimated time of arrival) calculations; the Jeppeson flight supplement; approach plates; emergency reading glasses. They all had to be within immediate reach. Having no autopilot, wing leveller, or co-pilot meant that I could not just abandon the controls to search for some vital piece of equipment or information.

Three hours and twenty minutes out of St. John's I encountered my first serious problem. I was flying through thick cloud with no visibility outside the cockpit, not a star nor horizon to rely on. Flashes of light reflected off the murk of cloud from the plane's navigation lights. The engine rumbled over a range of harmonics as the plane laboured through increasing turbulence. Suddenly, the LED (light-emitting diode) of my number-one radio blanked out. Presumably, the radio still worked, but it was utterly useless if I could not read the frequency numbers. LEDs are illuminated by gas-emitting diodes, normally reliable. This was an unexpected development, hard to fathom. Particularly worrisome was the prospect of having to rely on my number-two radio, a twenty-three-year-old vintage Cessna 120 model. Its limited range was useful around airports only. My HF radio, of course, was designed for transoceanic radio communications over long distances, but it had not worked since I left St. John's. The prospect of having to rely on a hand-held emergency radio of limited range all the way to the Azores was unnerving.

Should I turn back or continue flying for another eleven hours, unable to communicate? St. John's would assume I was proceeding across the ocean with all equipment functioning, since I had left their control zone. Gander, on the other hand, handled all trans-Atlantic flights; they would be waiting for me to establish contact.

I remembered reading in an avionics journal that diodes were affected by pressure changes; perhaps it was worth changing altitude. I descended from eleven thousand feet to nine thousand feet, noting the last frequency on my plotting chart before turning my attention back to the HF radio.

The HF radio raised different questions. Were the HF receiver and antenna system incorrectly installed, or was the problem caused by my inability to manipulate the latest interlocking features of the Kenwood receiver? I felt like a novice facing the complexities of a computer for the first time—only I was flying an airplane, at night, over water, with no reference points or horizon. Five hundred miles off the coast of Newfoundland, unable to raise Gander, Halifax, or any other station, I had to concede that if I continued on to the Azores it would be without communication with the outside world.

Thickening banks of cumulus cloud reduced all visibility to the wing tips. Turbulence increased from light to moderate. Flying became more difficult, requiring my full concentration. The GPS instrument silently recorded an accumulating bank of nautical miles off the North American continent. I had become a tiny speck inching farther and farther out over the Atlantic, alone and vulnerable.

Still, I had faith in my plane and ultimately in my own ability to reach the Azores and then Africa. It was blind faith, perhaps, but enough to hold me on course. Surely, I mused, the idea of faith was blind, more akin to instinct, and subtle in that respect. Faith in God, faith in yourself; you either possessed it or you did not. For me it provided comfort. Not that I could ask God to look after me, only that He not abandon me. The parable of the lost sheep was intriguing: the lamb never alone in its lost-ness was infinitely more reassuring than the lamb rescued. Faith embodied so much more than fate. I knew God's mercy paid no heed to merit, had no court of justice. And I never thought of God as determining the outcome of my flight. There was more to it than that. Faith provided the strength to endure, to survive the consequences, whatever they might be. Faith kept me flying with hope, and hope knew no boundaries.

Suddenly, without warning, the sky cleared. The planet Jupiter hung under the soft light of a lambent moon. My spirits lifted and, flying into a star-filled night, I rejoiced at my refusal to turn back. The Milky Way spread across the sky like a jewelled carpet reflecting a path over the silver ocean. First-magnitude stars wheeled on their prescribed passages across the firmament, like a giant clock recording the slow passing of the night. How many navigators, I wondered, over how many centuries, had put their faith on sightings from these selfsame stars? Ancient seafarers, desert nomads, Arctic explorers, even modern-day astronauts all relied upon these heavenly waypoints. The celestial chart, a construction of the first order, exquisitely beautiful, mathematically precise, utterly divine, held for me the reconciliation of faith and the secular world of science.

The LED display on my number-one VHF radio flickered and came alive again, filling the cockpit with its orange glow—the change in altitude worked. VHF (very high frequency) radio operates on line of sight and with the curvature of the earth its range is limited, while HF (high frequency) radio waves bounce off the ionosphere and their range is virtually unlimited, although the signal degrades with distance and atmospheric interference. So, while I remained without communication with a defective or inoperable HF at least within range of the Azores, I would be able to transmit and receive on my VHF radio. I offered a silent prayer of thanks, eased the plane back to my assigned altitude of eleven thousand feet, and willed the LED numbers to hold firm.

It was now five-thirty in the morning, three and a half hours into the flight, time to switch to the left tank and to start pumping reserve fuel from the ferry tank behind my seat up to the starboard wing. As I turned on the electric fuel pump, eyes glued to the fuel gauges, I thought of Dave McDevitt, my mechanic in Toronto. Dave had helped me prepare for the trip; it was his installation—this was his moment. He was probably asleep, no doubt confident that his workmanship could be relied upon. Sure enough, as if his thick, stubby fingers were pushing the fuel gauges, the needles crawled up to the full mark. The wing tanks would require two more replenishments before I reached the Azores. Dave's insistence that "fuel and engine—them's the only things that count out there" reverberated through my mind like a mantra.

Dawn broke, spilling light under my port wing. A sleepy grey sky drew a veil of cirrus cloud across the promise of morning. The last shades of night slipped over the plane's tail and my spirits rose. At that moment, I could think of nowhere else I'd rather be than alone in the cockpit, hundreds of miles out over the Atlantic, within range of the Azores, reaching for Africa. I poured myself a cup of coffee and watched the sun inch over the razor-thin horizon, cutting sea and sky, ten thousand feet below. I never felt more alive.

It was the first time since leaving St. John's in the dark that I felt in control of my destiny, reassured by my decision to fly to Africa; a moment of calm, to reflect on why I was here, midway across the Atlantic, flying solo in a single-engine plane.

For years I had been caught up in the business and personal ambitions of life in Toronto. Toronto was like that: money, career, power, and who you knew; it all seemed so important. I was never really interested or particularly successful in making money, in spite of repeated efforts to set some aside, enough to be independent. I was president of a small public company, well paid and secure. By 1995, though, the company, Meridian Technologies Inc., had grown in size and prospects, with two large international shareholders struggling to gain control. This eventually led to a boardroom tussle, which I lost. Although proper financial arrangements were provided, it was a painful ouster, with a sudden withdrawal of support from those on whom I thought I could count. In December 1995, I was out of a job, and from this low point the faint murmurings of Africa beckoned.

I had always been intrigued by the idea of Africa. Africa conjured up all that was fundamental, raw, and powerful with a deep undercurrent of mystery. The heavy beat of dark African nights suggested incarnate desire, danger, and fear. Africa was part of my romantic inventory. I had visited it once earlier in my life and I always said I would return: now was the time.

Still, there was more to it really than just revisiting Africa. I was well along in my business career and yet I remained restless. For years, I had dreamed of breaking away from business into something completely different—combining adventure with an altruistic pursuit in an underdeveloped country. But somehow life had held me prisoner in a world too comfortable. I aspired for something nobler, something more than just making money; something was tugging at my soul. Was it a mid-life crisis or was it an honourable escape from the reality of a world I knew? Hard to say, but for the first time in many years a challenge lay squarely in front of me. While I could hardly afford a sabbatical, I was free of domestic responsibilities— my three children from a first marriage were grown up, and my fourth, a daughter, was at Concordia University, Montreal. If ever I was going to realize the dream of breaking away from a business career, it was now.

I had contacted a number of non-governmental organizations (NGOs): Action Aid, CARE, Médecins Sans Frontières, and World Vision, but they were understandably focused in their desire to en-list employees with specific skills, none of which I possessed. They had no room for a retired president from the business world.

Luckily, I stumbled upon the African Medical and Research Foundation (AMREF), an African-based organization with headquar-ters in Nairobi, which owned and ran the Flying Doctors Service of East Africa. Their work seemed like a noble cause; more importantly, they needed someone to help reorganize their small entrepreneurial Flying Doctors Service division into a more stable self-sustaining organization and they felt I had the requisite skills.

By chance, the director general of AMREF, Dr. Michael Gerber, had arrived in Toronto in September 1996. We met over breakfast and hit it off immediately. He said he could use my help, but the Flying Doctors Service could not afford to pay me a salary, although out-of-pocket expenses would be covered. I was familiar enough with charitable organizations to understand this, so I signed up for two years. I informed him that I would fly my single-engine plane to Nairobi, arriving in Kenya in approximately a month's time. He agreed that having a plane would provide enormous opportunities to explore East Africa, but he expressed concern at my proposal to fly there alone.

Later that day my wife and I walked through the neighbour-hood park together. Krystyne was supportive—even sympathetic—

to pulling up stakes and spending two years in Nairobi, providing she did not have to fly the Atlantic with me. She was giving up more than I was. Her life was in order and she was content. She had a successful career as a fashion-design consultant and here was I suggesting we leave our comfortable Toronto life of the last twenty years for what could easily be a dead end. In our late fifties we were no longer youngsters, and we had no pensions. Was this a wise move? I shall never forget that day: walking in silence along the edge of the ravine, hand in hand, minds racing; a soft drizzle falling into the fading light of a September afternoon. The first hint of autumn had thrown a chill into the air. Doubts crowded in on the muted promise of adventure. Was the excitement of Africa sufficiently strong to make us overthrow our lives in Toronto? I glanced at her, smiling, as her hand tightened on mine, and with that it was decided.

Seven hours into the flight and the engine gauges were holding in the green. Daylight had ushered in a sense of confidence. The cockpit had expanded into the wider world of morning light; the dove-grey sea lay calm under a thin veil of cirrus over a milky sky. There was no human sign within sight and no sound apart from the vibrating drone of the motor.

Suddenly, to my amazement, I heard a voice come over the VHF emergency frequency 121.5. It was Jerry Childers, a professional pilot I'd met in St. John's the night before my departure. He was flying a plane that was sixty knots faster than mine and, although he had left three hours later, he was now overtaking me. While it was comforting to have another soul somewhere out there in that endless reach of sea and sky, given his speed, our radio link would not last more than two hours. So my only contact with the outside world was now through Jerry, who relayed my position back to Gander, indicating that my HF radio was defective.

Jerry and his partner were in an old twin-engine Nordo that had no air pressurization and no heat, which made flying at fifteen thousand feet uncomfortable—but they needed the altitude to maximize fuel efficiency and to maintain speed. Their discomfort was compensated by less flying time to the Azores. It was November and they wanted to make a quick crossing; the weather was holding, but at that time of year it would not last long.

The hours slipped through the day. Gradually, the sky darkened into threatening weather. Waves of incoming cloud gathered into soft, undulating swirls of grey wool, masking the white-tipped waves below. Soon, a thicker blanket of stratus, charcoal and ominous, drew nearer. Off in the distance, a reef of cirrus cloud imprisoned a band of yellow sky. The afternoon slid into premature evening, the precursor of an approaching storm. Enormous cumulonimbus clouds, heavy with moisture, induced a light skimming of rime ice that slowly accumulated on the leading edges of the propeller and wings. The sky coiled in on itself with increasing intensity. Sudden spectacular flashes of lightning illuminated the outside markings of the fuselage. Unrelenting rain beat against the windscreen.

I radioed Jerry requesting that he seek Gander's permission for me to fly at a higher altitude, so that I could rise above the bad weather. "Don't wait for permission, go up," he volunteered useful but unnecessary advice. I struggled to gain altitude above thirteen thousand feet; however, the extra weight of fuel and the rapid accumulation of ice on the fuselage were dragging me down. In addition, the engine repeatedly misfired, indicating icing in the carburetor. Turbulence made holding a course, even controlling the plane, increasingly difficult. The thought of Jerry riding above the weather while I was doomed to penetrate the brunt of the storm had me envious. I would have gladly sacrificed heat for altitude.

"Jerry, I can't get higher. I need to go lower to melt the ice off the airframe." Turbulence made it difficult even to hold the transmit button of the radio.

"You're breaking up, I can't read you," was all I got from Jerry; the rest was garbled. Descending at a thousand feet a minute, I lost radio contact. I was back on my own.

The next hour required my full concentration to hold a steady course. Turbulence increased from moderate to severe; I cinched the seat belt and shoulder strap tight across my chest. Sudden vicious jolts to the plane were so violent I could no longer turn the dials of the radio or navigational instruments for fear of snapping the knobs off the panel. The instrument gauges spiked up and down in a crazy manner, rendering me nauseous. Any semblance of order in the cockpit vanished. Loose gear shifted out of position and catapulted about the cabin as if possessed.

Unable to communicate, alone in the dark, I realized that I might be forced to ditch. Could the plane withstand the stress of such relentless pounding? I had visions of a wing tearing free of the fuselage, the plane in a sickening stall, tripping over into a spin, and then plunging through the darkness into the roaring maw of the sea below. Amazingly, I viewed the prospect with calm, knowing there was little I could do beyond trying to steer with the pedals while leaving the ailerons free to find their own equilibrium.

I suddenly felt an overwhelming sense of regret over my cavalier parting with Krystyne; we had not said a proper goodbye. Leaving Toronto in a blush of self-confidence and eager to get started on my flight to Africa, I had thought it a bad omen to dwell on the possibility of ditching, wrong to invite the unthinkable.

Lightning flashed incandescent through cloud, each electrical discharge spraying the storm-scope with a myriad of small crosses. There was a sudden, shocking, pistol-like report. A lightning strike slammed into the cockpit, knocking out the ADF (automatic direction finding) instrument and firing the cockpit with an acrid smell of burnt electronics. A thin curl of blue smoke rose from under the instrument panel to settle beneath the concave hood of the windscreen. I was more surprised than frightened. The storm's ferocity seemed out of proportion to the neatly defined cold front recorded on Gander's seven-hundred-millibar weather chart prepared nine hours earlier. High over the Atlantic those same small, thinly spaced isobars had translated themselves into forces of nature that threatened to pull me down into a raging ocean with little chance of survival.

I descended to an altitude of four thousand feet, searching for higher temperatures that would herald the melting point. A thick accumulation of ice on the plane gradually turned soft and began to run. Large chunks of ice, thrown by the prop, struck the fuselage with a terrifying noise, like the spray of machine-gun bullets. The warmer temperatures drove sheets of rain onto the plane, so thick I thought the engine air intake might choke with water. The windshield became a river, like being trapped in the underside of a waterfall.

I had passed the point of no return with not enough fuel to make it back to Newfoundland. I was committed to reaching the Azores or ditching into the Atlantic. Proper navigation had now given way to mere survival. I needed to punch through the cold front, ride out the turbulence while trying to maintain control of the airplane. In the meantime the satellite-directed GPS instrument continued faithfully to record my progress from North America, seemingly unperturbed by the surrounding chaos. I was ten degrees to the left of my course, three hours away from the Azores.

My shoulders ached. I longed for relief. The relentless struggle to control the plane had become a series of linked crises. It was important to maintain a light touch on the controls, since I feared the cables might snap under the stress of increasing turbulence. Technically, there comes a point when it is better to give the plane its "head," minimize corrections, and fly with the rudder pedals only. The plane pitched and climbed in such an erratic manner I feared I might involuntarily enter a high-speed stall. I battled on, thrown sideways, rolling first onto one wing and then violently back onto the other, nerves on edge, hoping, praying for a change in the weather.

Three-quarters of an hour later I broke into still air and an unreal calm took hold. Suddenly, it was as if I were suspended, floating through space, like some orbiting planet. Only the drone of the engine gave a hint of movement. The first peeping stars and a three-quarter moon emerged from the remaining wisps of cloud—the storm's spent traces departing gracefully like the beat of angels' wings.

Too tired to sort out the mess in the cockpit I simply sat there staring at the instruments, relishing the calm as the last of the day tumbled into darkness. A sense of peace descended over my small world. The familiarity of my surroundings, the instruments, the competent sounds of the motor, even the rush of wind through the fuselage provided me with a renewed sense of confidence. I was comfortable in my plane, having flown her thousands of miles; I knew her idiosyncrasies by heart and by instinct, which manoeuvres she could handle, the safe limits of her performance. And she almost certainly knew my personal flying characteristics both good and bad. There was a bond that had us relying one upon the other.

My heart leapt as I sighted, far in the distance, tiny pinpricks of light. It was certain to be Flores, the first of the small islands of the Azores. I had only three hundred miles to go before reaching the most eastward island, Santa Maria. I marvelled that body, soul, and engine, flying non-stop thirteen and a half hours over the vast expanse of ocean through mixed weather, had found these small islands in the middle of the Atlantic. Weariness overwhelmed me; still, I could rejoice. I had completed the first leg of a seven-thousand-mile flight to Africa. The relief was palpable.

Santa Maria coordinates: latitude, north 36 degrees, 58 minutes, 04 seconds; longitude, west 025 degrees, 10 minutes, 03 seconds—how could I ever forget them? Pilots for over fifty years had concentrated their wits and physical endurance on this waypoint, the refuelling crossroads for piston-engine airplanes crossing the Atlantic: America to Europe, Europe to South America, and vice versa. For the first half of the twentieth century, this remote little group of volcanic islands in the middle of the Atlantic grew in importance along with the expansion of air travel. No other refuelling stop lay within a thousand miles. Not until the arrival of the jet engine in the 1950s and the introduction of non-stop transatlantic flights did the Azores lose their strategic importance.

Having landed at Santa Maria, I walked over to the airport office to clear customs and pay landing fees. The captain sitting behind an old-fashioned oak desk, chin resting on a hammock of laced fingers, looked dignified and intelligent. He read my papers and then twisted the ends of his moustache. "We don't see many planes coming through here any more," he said, thoughtfully, in perfect English. His ice-blue eyes, fine features, and quiet demeanour gave him a natural air of authority. "May I buy you a drink?" he added, closing his desk drawer, pushing back the chair, and rising to his feet. My arrival had coincided with the end of his workday. I hesitated, surprised at the unexpectedly generous offer. "Perhaps you are tired and wish to retire."

"No, it would be a pleasure," I replied, "but first I should register at the hotel and wash up."

"Yes, of course, you have had a long flight. I'll wait for you downstairs in the bar. Please, take your time. No hurry."

I had met Captain Helder Fernando da Silva Borges Pimental, head of airport operations. His career was bound to the Santa Maria airport, as controller, immigration officer, and now captain of operations. Over the years he had seen many pilots pass through theAzores.

After I checked into the hotel and washed up I wandered down to the bar to find Helder crouched over a whisky. I joined him, ordered a beer, and asked him to tell me about flying into the Azores. He related the story of Clarke Wood—everyone called him Woody—a great pilot. Woody was an American, a professional ferry pilot, transporting other people's planes across the Atlantic for a living—a risky business. He had gone down two hundred miles off the Azores in a Lake Amphibian nine months before. It had been a wild night, and the waves were twenty feet high: no chance in that kind of sea. Helder was the controller on duty when Woody radioed through that he was having engine problems and that he could not maintain altitude. That was at 18:00 hours. Then mysteriously, the engine settled and Woody indicated that operations were back to normal. Could it have been carburetor icing? Twenty minutes later, the trouble recurred and this time he had to ditch. He radioed his latitude and longitude and then silence.

I shuddered. Sad to think of Woody hanging on out there in the middle of the night, hoping to beat the odds. Helder told me he had sent two planes out to look for him, hoping to see a light near his reported position, but it was a storm-swept night, pitch black—making rescue impossible. In the morning, reconnaissance planes sighted the ferry tanks floating just below the surface, and bits of wreckage scattered near his reported position. No sign of Woody. There was no doubt in Helder's mind that Woody had died in the crash. A Lake Amphibian with all that fuel and the engine mounted above the fuselage is a tough airplane to glide into a stormy sea. He probably didn't even see the water before he struck the first wave, like hitting cement.

One drink and my head was swimming. I needed sleep. Helder insisted we meet again, the next day. I agreed, said good-night, and stumbled towards my hotel room. I placed a call to Krystyne who sounded relieved to hear my voice, though she seemed distant—on the far side of a dream. I told her the remainder of my flight to Africa was without danger, but her instincts said otherwise, and so our thoughts remained hanging. Minutes later, I fell into sleep and immediately began to climb through cloud, rudder and ailerons guiding me through a tangle of dreams.

Dawn broke, uncertain, through a pearl haze of light. A twenty-knot wind funnelled down Santa Maria Runway 36. The tarmac stretched three thousand feet to the north, ending abruptly in a fifty-foot cliff overlooking a cobalt sea. The plane's nose pointed upwards, ready for takeoff, the engine idling, the two-bladed prop describing a blurred arc against a worried sky. A sweep of clouds raced before the north wind.

I had tried for an earlier start, but the hotel was empty and the old night watchman's eyesight was unable to handle the checkout. In future I vowed to settle accounts the evening before departure. Helder had found me a technician to help repair my HF transoceanic radio—a functioning HF radio was absolutely mandatory flying into Europe. It turned out that there was a hairline break in the antenna lead where it joined the HF receiver. The repair was simple. A further delay was caused by the chaotic state of the cockpit from the previous flight and the struggle to squeeze into my oversized rubber survival suit. I was now two hours behind schedule. Mine was the only airplane on the island, and yet the clearance seemed to take forever.

Flying over open water in daylight was a good deal more comforting than the 3:00 a.m. plunge into darkness off the coast of Newfoundland. Although my departure was delayed, I estimated arrival in Lisbon, Portugal, before nightfall. A light tailwind was forecast to last the day and then gradually dissipate near the European coast. I expected a trouble-free flight.

Navigating the second half of the flight across the Atlantic, from the Azores to Portugal, was considered easy compared to flying from St. John's to Santa Maria. Unlike the first leg, navigating to small islands in the middle of the ocean, all one had to do was maintain an easterly heading and you were bound to land somewhere in Europe. Nevertheless, eight hundred miles of ocean and nine hours of flying to Portugal are not to be taken lightly; anything can happen and usually does flying an airplane. The radio airwaves would be thick with North American flights arriving in Europe, as pilots reported positions to the oceanic controllers whose job it was to coordinate hundreds of airliners crossing the Atlantic twice daily. I would be slotted into the traffic at a lower altitude.

Ten miles out from Santa Maria the controller's voice came over the HF radio—a distinctive HF burble, as if the sound was passing through a tube under water. I exulted in my good fortune at having befriended Helder. My plane, with the call sign CF-WMJ (Charlie Foxtrot Whisky Mike Juliet), was trimmed for a long, slow climb, managing only two hundred feet altitude per minute with the extra weight of fuel and gear. Flying at a thousand pounds over gross legal weight meant I had to keep a close eye on the manifold and oil temperatures and manoeuvre gently until the first two or three hours of fuel had burned away.

Hours passed without incident. Imperceptible changes in the weather, in line with the forecast, drew thin wisps of cloud across the sky with the occasional non-threatening rain showers between the shafts of sunlight reflecting off the waves below. Operating routines were, by now, familiar: pumping fuel up to the wing tanks, plotting dead-reckoning positions, communicating with the controllers, calculating speed, drift, and estimated time of arrival.

Six hours into the flight the first loom of landfall came within sight: the European coastline. Transoceanic control transferred me over to the Portuguese traffic controllers responsible for merging streams of air traffic into the country's major airports. Clipped voices relayed instructions in rapid bursts over the radio. The mix of nationalities speaking English—the international language of aviation—required professional radio procedure and military-like execution of instructions.

The weather deteriorated rapidly as I approached the coast. Late-afternoon convective activity over the warm land swelled into a solid mass of cloud, embedded with thunderstorms. Controllers tried to accommodate repeated requests from commercial airlines to divert around bad weather. At my lower altitude I had no choice but to fly through thick cloud and turbulence. The ferry tank occasionally expanded with the change in air pressure, making a loud bang. It was unnerving. Each time, I thought I had lost part of the plane's fuselage.

Rain streamed over the windscreen and pummelled the plane, increasing the noise level in the cabin. Turbulence made hand flying increasingly difficult. Commercial airliners at the higher altitudes were also finding it uncomfortable, judging by the number of diversions requested of controllers. Bad flying weather was solid up to thirty thousand feet, far beyond my plane's climbing capability.

I was vectored into a five-minute holding position while a number of jumbo jets were slotted into final approach for Lisbon International Airport. I sensed the controller was having difficulty finding enough space to accommodate my slower speed. Flying IFR (instrument flight rules), in a holding pattern with no visibility, after nine hours over the ocean seemed unreasonable. I was on the verge of complaining when I received my instructions to pick up the localizer and hold the centre line of the runway; then execute an instrument landing onto Runway 21.

I touched down and, to my amazement, found no response in the left brake. My plane, a tail dragger, can be steered on the ground only by using the brakes. Swerving farther and farther off the runway I fought to maintain directional control, without success. The plane barely avoided a ground loop, hit a grass bank, and slid down a gentle incline to the right of the runway into a flaming carpet of wild poppies.

Recovering, I immediately realized the oversized rubber foot of my survival suit had wedged itself under the brake pedal, rendering it inoperative. Somewhat sheepishly, I applied maximum power and managed to re-enter the runway under the urgent instructions of the controller to proceed immediately to the taxiway in order to make way for a Boeing 747 on final approach.

I was worn thin with exhaustion. Plans to tour the old city of Lisbon faded as I made for the nearest hotel. The smoke-filled warmth of a crowded restaurant had me aching for sleep. Still, I could enjoy the taste of triumph. After all, I had crossed the Atlantic. Now Africa was within reach.

2

Reaching for Africa

ORNING BROKE with rain sheeting the sixteenth-century roofs of the old city of Lisbon. Water poured from the terra cotta eaves, sloshed along the gutters of the narrow cobble-stoned streets, and swirled into the small, grilled openings of the city's drains. Pedestrians hurried past ancient doorways, weaving through a field of black umbrellas, grim-faced people on their way to work. What concern had they about flying weather? Under Lisbon's dreary skies their focus was on getting to the office. We inhabited different worlds.

Peering out the small attic window of my hotel room, I estimated the freezing levels to be somewhere close to five thousand feet, perhaps higher. A nervous wind lashed the wooden shutters which tugged at their pintles. Clouds tumbled over the city skyline. The day argued for staying in bed or reading a book by the fire. I speculated that my proposed route, south over Algeria to Malta, would permit me to fly low enough to avoid picking up ice, and presumably the weather would clear farther south. It was worth going out to the airport to get a detailed weather report.

It turned out that Lisbon International Airport had little time for a private pilot's deliberation over weather. Jet airplanes fly in bad weather. Pilots and passengers may have an uncomfortable ten-minute climb after takeoff in a commercial jet, but soon after that it breaks out at thirty thousand feet and all is calm. A propeller-driven plane, in contrast, has no choice but to fly through the bad weather at five thousand or seven thousand feet in order to stay below the freezing level and escape the deadly potential of ice.

Nevertheless, I decided to fly. Predictably, within minutes of takeoff I flew into turbulence and zero visibility and immediately regretted my decision. I was tired from the accumulation of hours flown over the previous two days and I toyed with asking Lisbon for permission to return, but that would have required explanations and a full instrument approach; it seemed easier just to maintain course. Two hours later, jolted and buffeted, nerves weary with strain, the plane sluggish under a full load of fuel, I burst without warning into clear skies over the expansive blue of the Mediterranean Sea.

Small-plane flying with its lurking potential for danger is addictive. An irresistible urge draws pilots back into the cockpit again and again to experience the sweet thrill of speed. The power at one's fingertips is physically pleasing, sensual, and never more so than when a plane explodes from dense cloud into clear blue sky. The close confinement of the cockpit bursts open into the blue to describe parabolic arcs of bank, loops, and spins, defying the laws of gravity and balance. The dream of unrestricted flight—the early flyers, daredevils swooping under bridges, barnstorming stunt flyers and World War II ace fighter pilots understood it, flying their unsafe machines with giddy recklessness. The seduction lies in the freedom of the sky, where only a hint of hubris can reduce a pilot to mortality.

The Spanish controller suddenly interrupted my thoughts with an instruction to change frequency and register with Algerian control. I was leaving Spanish airspace. I tried contacting the Algerians repeatedly. No joy. I was probably too low in altitude and therefore unable to make radio contact, so I continued flying, on course, out of communication with both the Spanish and the Algerian controllers.

Ten minutes later I attempted contact again and this time the Algerian controller responded. My first contact with Africa sounded unfriendly, demanding my flight-clearance number, authorizing me to fly over Algerian airspace. I did not have one. He asked if I was aware of my current position, and told me to evacuate Algerian airspace immediately or be shot down.

I made a quick calculation. To avoid Algerian airspace would mean flying an additional four hundred miles north and east around Algeria to Malta. A diversion of this magnitude would add another two and half hours to my flight. I thought of appealing; however, the controller sounded uncompromising. I quickly dismissed a fleeting temptation to fly low, hoping to avoid radar detection. The thought of being shot down or interrogated in an Algerian prison argued in favour of diversion.

The flight around Algeria's northern airspace seemed endless. The border extended beyond Africa's most northern peninsula, almost to the Italian island of Pantelleria in the Sicilian Channel. I rankled at the controller's mindless adherence to nationalistic and bureaucratic regulations, but at least I was favoured with a sixty-knot tailwind off the starboard quarter.

Late afternoon gradually slipped into an apricot-coloured sunset that took fire. The Mediterranean lay mirrored below, awash in orange and pink ribbons of light. The faint, recumbent outline of Malta emerged on the horizon, its western end bathed in gold from the setting sun. I entered a left-hand downwind visual approach for Luka Airport, touching down as nightfall blanketed the island in darkness.

I had one more flight to reach Africa. The next morning I clambered into the cockpit and set about the familiar routines for the twelve-hour flight to Luxor, Egypt. The sun rose rapidly over the table-flat horizon of the Mediterranean as I started the long slow climb to ten thousand feet. A slight headwind added an hour to my estimated time of arrival in Luxor. I had fuel for over seventeen hours of flying time, easily enough for this leg of the flight. Dependent on winds, travelling at approximately 120 knots, I could fly nearly three thousand miles without stopping.

I was now more than halfway to Nairobi from Toronto; the navigation and flying had become routine. Although exhausted by three consecutive long-distance flights, I was increasingly familiar with the workings of the cockpit and excited by the slow countdown of the instruments, drawing me closer and closer to the African continent.

Gazing through the pilot's-side window I sighted an old freighter bucking a stiff sea, ten thousand feet below on a southwesterly heading—probably making for Alexandria. My thoughts drifted into every pilot's nightmare: what to do in the event of an engine failure over water. Procedures unfold according to a prescribed order: reconfigure the flight controls; trim the plane for a glide; circle the freighter several times; lose altitude while not losing sight of the chance for rescue; cross the freighter's bow fifty feet above the water; contact control by radio and transmit my latitude and longitude; prepare to ditch into the sea—one has to get it right.

Suddenly, the controller's voice from far off sifted into my consciousness, momentarily confusing me. He repeated instructions to switch over to Cairo control. I was approaching the coast of Africa, entering Egyptian airspace. The hours had slipped by unnoticed and the freighter, my one chance of rescue in the event of a crash, was plunging through mountainous seas now four hundred miles behind me.

A reddish haze lay indistinct, barely discernible below. I was flying over Africa at last. The ancient city of Alexandria emerged through the liquid haze of noon. The languid, flowing Nile meandered through its enormous delta, disgorging silt and history into the Mediterranean.

I flew due south over the undulating desert to the sprawl of Cairo which sat like an enormous blister enveloping the smoky haze of the slums, industrial plants, warehouses, and railways. The green Nile twisted like a serpent over the sand to the desert city of Luxor where I needed to refuel.

Luxor sat, desiccated by the sun, enveloped in the stink of dust. I shut down the engine and heard the muezzin's wailing call to prayer. In the town the chaotic clatter of buses belched diesel fumes into the air, mixed with the smells of urine and rotting garbage. Men in white flowing djellabas gathered in the cool doorways, women in black bui-buis scuttled like crows through the narrow streets; electrical wires and lines of laundry looped overhead; donkeys, carts, and street urchins pushed between the sweet-smelling spices, ochre, green, and blood-red mounds piled in woven baskets; vendors cried out for buyers, voices ululating over the din; the daily commerce of the Nile remained timeless and unchanging.

I walked along the riverbank. Flotillas of "bateaux-mouche," garishly lit, poorly maintained, lay moored alongside the quay, muscling aside the elegant Nile feluccas, older than history. Luxor, it seemed, had embraced the shoddy commerce of mass tourism. Only in the back alleys, beyond the street vendors and the neon-lit food stalls, into the Moslem quarter, where the dilapidated multi-storeyed buildings pressed against the narrow streets, did one discover the human cry of that impoverished city.

I crossed to the west side of the Nile: the Valley of the Kings and the smaller Valley of the Queens, where the hills shimmered in the translucent heat of the desert, magnificently still. There, the dead haunt the living. Only time bore witness to the passage of civilizations: the Phoenicians, the Syrians, the Greeks, the Romans under Caesar, the Turks, the Mamelukes, the French under Napoleon, the English under Kitchener; they all came and fell under the spell of this royal burial ground.

On the east side of the Nile stood the temples of Luxor, ancient city of Thebes: Karnak, Dendora, and Kom Ombo. Enormous blocks of pink granite, exquisite, massive in stature and grace, towered above the tourists, guides, and beggars. Statues of Hatshepsut and Ramses gaze across the river; seamless links to the past. Ancient Egypt remains eternal.

And yet, even more impressive is the night sky over the desert at Luxor. It fires the imagination. The sun sinks below the western hills of the city in a conflagration of red and orange, painting the desert. Suddenly, a fall of midnight-blue ushers in the first magnitude stars—the early arrivals. A curtain of darkness spreads over the sky, hosting a crowd of lesser stars, the smaller stitches of heaven. One by one the constellations rise over the horizon, tracing their arcs across the heavens, a nightly procession across the firmament.

The desert cools. The camels are fresh, capable of great distances at night. Tents are folded and the barking and mewling of departure signals the start of the caravans on their long trek across the sand. Nomadic tribes, wanderers of the desert, depart on well-footed tracks over an ocean of undulating dunes. Overhead, the stars serve as way stations, constant companions, intensely personal, guiding the camel drivers through the darkness. The telling of stories passes from father to son, generation to generation. Under a starlit vault these wanderers of the desert grow older, edging closer and closer to God.

Shortly after dawn, I got into a clapped-out old Ford taxi, which inched its way out of town, passing donkeys, camels, and buses bound for the chaotic bustle of the market. I had hoped to be airborne within three hours of waking—too optimistic a goal for Egypt. Interminable delays plagued my departure; officials thumped their stamps on my passport, exit visa, declaration of entry, landing and navigation clearances. Two hours of painstaking procedures led me through the depressing halls of the airport. Authorities sat like spiders spinning their bureaucratic web of ordinances, waiting for under-the-table payments.

By nine in the morning, the sun was burning the desert. High above the hills east of Luxor the cyanic blue of a cloudless sky beckoned. I was late, and a long flight remained ahead of me. I had decided to avoid flying over Sudan, the largest country in Africa, because of the ongoing civil war in the south and the extortionate overflight fees demanded by Khartoum. Instead, I would fly across Egypt's eastern desert and south along the Red Sea to Djibouti.

The temperature had climbed to forty-nine degrees centigrade on the ground. My electronics, rated for temperatures far lower, were inoperative, leaving me without navigational instruments or communications. I climbed for one and a half hours after takeoff, dead reckoning on the compass, before reaching a cruising altitude of eleven thousand feet—and cooler temperatures which revived the instruments.

The plane's controls felt unresponsive with the weight of full tanks in the thin hot air. I was buffeted by hot-air thermals rising eighteen thousand feet above the desert. I flew out of Luxor's air-space without communication. Only the drone of the engine and the occasional bang of the ferry tank expanding under altitude pressure punctuated my progress over hundreds of miles of empty desert.

I watched the plane trace its shadow on the sand below. Slowly a few scattered veins of black and red lava rock coursed their way into the eastern foothills of Kosseir. There was no sign of human exis-tence anywhere.

In the distance, dark, threatening clouds walled the western banks of the Red Sea. Electrical discharges sprouted tiny crosses of warning on the green-lit screen of my storm scope. The approaching cloud bank gradually turned black and yellowish-green. The warm air of the desert clashed with the cooler air over the sea to form light-ning with repeated flashes over the fuselage.

I diverted from a southerly course to avoid entering the massive storm clouds. Thunderheads, powered by the heat of the desert, created dangerous updraughts capable of tearing the wings off the plane. Since I didn't have permission to fly over Saudi Arabian airspace and Sudan was also out of bounds, I had little room to manoeuvre between the thunderstorms that spread over the Red Sea before reaching the latitude of Port Sudan.

By five-thirty the setting sun had thrown a shadow over my port wing. The faint tinge of the instrument lights marked the end of day.

The cockpit gradually evolved into the warm glow of numbers and gauges as I plunged deeper into the night. The GPS indicated four more flying hours to Djibouti. I had not communicated on the radio for nine hours. My body ached with stiffness from the lack of movement. I needed to rest.

Two hours later I detected small pinpricks of light on the horizon from the Eritrean coast north of Djibouti. The contour map indicated a coast that was ringed with steep mountains; I needed to gain altitude immediately.

The coastal mountains of Eritrea, majestic and rugged, rise dramatically from the sea to form the eastern wall of the Great Rift Valley. This valley is part of an enormous geological fault that extends from the island of Madagascar through East Africa and Ethiopia to the Red Sea; the spine of Africa, massive in scope and beauty.

Moist warm air from the Red Sea pushes up the sides of these Eritrean mountains, cooling the moisture into thick cumulus cloud, which produces turbulence and potential for icing. Soon the plane's running lights reflected a halo of light off the first bank of cloud, which obscured all visibility. I climbed higher, well above thirteen thousand feet, to safely cross the mountain range north of Djibouti. The plane laboured under the constant buffeting of air currents and thick cloud. Sharp, short jolts jerked the plane's control cables, which alternated from slack to tense with a snap. Flying became more and more challenging.

Suddenly, the engine faltered. Its familiar, constant vibration and tonal pitch stuttered, threatening to stop altogether. For an instant I was transfixed, paralyzed, in total disbelief. Every nerve jangled, every muscle tensed, as I focused on this life-threatening and unexpected development. I pulled on the carburetor-icing knob. The engine continued to stumble, dangerously close to a stall. There had been no icing all day, so instinctively I dismissed icing as the cause of the problem. The engine coughed again, caught once more in a valiant attempt, and then fell silent—leaving only the sound of rushing wind through the airframe. It was startling the way the silence broke in.

I quickly set the controls into a glide, watching the altimeter unwind at a rate of eight hundred feet per minute. I could scarcely believe it. This was no practice drill, no routine exercise. Alone, no communication, no visibility, dropping into an unfamiliar, uninhabited mountain range at night. This was a flying nightmare—as bad as it gets.

My mind raced over the available options and there were precious few. Crashing into a remote set of mountains in the dark with no visibility meant the chances of survival were negligible. I was struck by a sudden overwhelming sense of weariness that dulled the threat of impending disaster. A sense of resignation took hold, the end was unavoidable. I was so close to completing the trip. All the effort, the calculation of risk, the preparation, the hours of flying—to have it end like this was so utterly futile. I thought of Krystyne. How would she ever know what had happened? A wave of regret washed over me at the unfairness of it all. Was this really taking place?

I forced myself to get a grip, to concentrate, to do everything possible until the last second before the plane slammed into the mountainside. There are prescribed procedures for engine failures, starting with a review of instruments and gauges, one by one, starting left to right. I methodically went through the routines, conscious of the pressure of depleting time and altitude.

The port fuel tank gauge read empty. The fuel selector valve pointed to the left tank . . . "God Almighty, I forgot to switch over to the starboard fuel tank. I've run out of fuel. How could that have happened?" Switching to the full fuel tank, I reset the mixture to restart the engine. The Cessna Continental 047J engine is susceptible to flooding when hot; it needs careful coaxing. "Please God, let it start." Fully anticipating a flash of mountainside to suddenly fill the windscreen as the plane continued its downward plunge into darkness, I reached for the ignition.

The engine restarted. I eased the stick back in an effort to regain the thirty-five hundred feet I had lost over the previous four minutes. I was below the highest mountain peaks, in danger of flying blindly at full power into the side of one of several mountains that towered nine thousand feet into the night. I set the controls to maximum power and pitch for the steepest climb speed, waiting with bated breath during the three minutes of climb it took to reach eleven thousand feet and safe clearance. It was long enough to dwell on my oversight, a sure sign of fatigue. I badly needed to reach Djibouti, to get my feet on the ground.

An hour later, I started the descent into Djibouti through a corridor of mountains. Minimum navigational aids into Djibouti made the approach tricky, one any pilot would prefer to make in daylight. With a renewed sense of concentration I entered into the instrument approach, passed the directional beacon outbound, and a minute later circled into a teardrop turn, back across the beacon inbound on the final descent, breaking through cloud three hundred feet above the runway lights that shone like a diamond bracelet directly before me.

Safe on the ground at last, I shambled across the tarmac, glanced back at my plane, sitting with its nose in the air, and reflected on what could have been our last flight. We had flown so many hours together, she and I, as faithful companions. How could I have endangered us in such a slipshod way? I turned away, documents in hand, and headed over to the airport tower encircled by barbed wire.

The whole airport at Djibouti was abandoned save for a lone controller, locked in the airport tower along with his Second World War instruments and a small sleeping cot. It was ten-thirty at night, and there were no officials, no taxis, and nowhere to go. Resigned to spending the night on an airport bench, bitten by mosquitoes, I was nevertheless grateful to be alive. Neon lights hanging from the ceiling cast a greenish, funereal glow over the vast hall as they buzzed and flickered. A driving thirst had me drinking tap water that smelled and tasted polluted. I had completed thirteen and a half hours of difficult flying, only to end up sleeping on an airport bench. Still, I was safe, and my final destination, Nairobi, was now only one more long-distance flight away.

An hour later, a car drove up to the airport. After protracted negotiations, I was able to convince its driver to take me into town to the Hotel du Ciel. Too tired to find food, I fell into bed reflecting on my good fortune to be alive in Djibouti, Africa.

Djibouti is an unlikely country. Tucked within the folds of overlapping mountain ranges it guards the western portal of the strait, Bab Al Mandeb (Gate of Tears), the narrow entrance at the southern end of the Red Sea, which sits at the base of the Horn of Africa. Only thirty-five miles separate this part of Africa from Arabia and both sides are visible on a clear day.

Djibouti is really a city state, a border town between North and sub-Saharan Africa, where Islam and the Christian Coptic religions meet. The Jewish community has virtually disappeared. North African Arabs rub shoulders with black Africans, exchanging goods and services in Arabic, French, and Swahili. The restaurants, mostly empty, still produce good food, influenced by the French. Ethiopian girls in brightly coloured skirts have a saucy look in their eyes, fully prepared to meet you later in a bar. Prostitution is rife, but the lack of paying customers a problem. The occasional out-of-place European youth wanders lost and dirty along the broken sidewalks of the main street. Djibouti, it seems, is a cosmopolitan dumping ground of human misery.

Historically, the city has been one of the principal gateways into Africa. Arab dhows loaded with merchandise arrive with the monsoon, seeking trade. Times are tough and trading thin. Nevertheless, enormous quantities of cheap goods from as far as China pass from trader to trader before reaching Djibouti's sprawling open-air market. Prices rise and fall with the monsoon, like so much else along the Indian Ocean coast. Arrivals and departures, fortune and misery, seem dependent on the trade winds.

The city stirred before dawn. I wandered through the back alleys surrounding the massive open-air market where Ethiopians, Somalis, and Arabs struggle to eke out a meagre living in a world of sellers with no buyers. Men sat cross-legged, pencil thin, behind piles of wood, corrugated iron, hardware, electrical supplies, pots and pans, and plastic trinkets. Women with carefully arranged pyramids of oranges, dates, limes, spices, and nuts; colours and shapes, designed to appeal, were crammed into ridiculously small stalls. Liquid doe-like eyes peered out from above the ubiquitous veils. The market sprawled as far as the eye could see, a teeming mass of humanity.

A soft rain fell, turning the red earth into rivers of mud. I tracked through the slippery narrow passages between stalls, surveying the array of goods on offer. Vendors silently endured the trickle of water dripping from old umbrellas and bits of plastic covering their wares. The lack of buyers said it all. Djibouti is a small and desperate world on its own, forgotten by its former colonial masters, the French—a country no longer of use or concern to the world.

My ancient Renault taxi sloshed along the main road to the airport. The car's radio wailed Arabic songs, while beads and pompoms hanging from the mirror danced drunkenly across the driver's line of vision. As the car pulled up under a regal line of tall and graceful doum palm trees fronting the Djibouti Airport, rainwater spurted from the open crevices of the old cement building. Pools of brown muddy water swirled over the *murram* (mud) road into swollen ditches. The humid air was suffocating. I was anxious to leave Djibouti, to be airborne again.

The airport administration office was cluttered with files, damp and smelling of mildew. Two soldiers slouched in swivel chairs, smoking and talking, guns across their thighs. They eyed me vacantly as I tried to open one locked door after another in an attempt to reach my plane. Unhelpful and sullen, they shrugged their shoulders at my inquiries. "*Le capitaine vient bientôt. Il faut l'attendre.*" I settled down to wait.

It took self-discipline and patience to wait three-quarters of an hour for the captain's arrival. Eventually, a pompous little man with short-cropped hair and a self-important moustache burst through the door and strode directly into his office, without glancing to either side. Five minutes later, unable to contain myself any longer, I knocked on his door and requested a clearance to fly to Nairobi. I was informed he had important business to attend to and that I must wait. Fuming, I returned to my seat, contemplating revenge. Twenty minutes passed without development.

Two Swedish pilots and a Canadian Forces lieutenant joined the queue. The Swedes, flying a King Air, were on their way to Mogadishu, while the Canadian was attempting to make arrangements for refuelling a Hercules 130 that was due to land later that day. I now understood why pilots hated flying into Djibouti, wrestling with police, immigration, and airport officials. The four of us decided to join forces and take the captain on.

We marched into his office, refusing to leave until he processed our clearances. He immediately called for his soldiers, who shambled in through the door and appeared startled by the apoplectic look on their captain's face. We stood our ground, refusing to leave. The captain's options were limited; he could shoot us or find some face-saving compromise. Finally, he assigned one of his illiterate soldiers to our needs, so that he might continue with important military matters. We ended up processing the forms ourselves.

On the ramp, I discovered a fuel cap was missing and my wing tanks had been drained of fuel. In a fury, I returned to remonstrate with the captain, who smiled with enormous satisfaction at my misfortune. He took great delight in directing me to the east-side hangar where I could buy replacement fuel, pumped from unsealed drums at a cost of $1.75 a litre—more than three times the cost of fuel in Luxor. I was probably repurchasing my own fuel, but I had no choice but to pay the price and cast a special curse on Djibouti.

Shortly after takeoff I was instructed to fly at flight level 140 (fourteen thousand feet), as high as the plane, fully loaded, could climb. I circled for an hour before reaching my designated altitude; anything lower was not permissible south of Djibouti under instrument flight rules. I soon understood why as I caught a glimpse of the mountainous terrain through broken cloud less than four thousand feet below me.

The Ethiopian mountains rose in spectacular ridges up to ten thousand feet from sea level along that section and I was amazed to see telltale signs of cultivation on their upper reaches, almost always in cloud. What kind of people lived at those high altitudes?

The same impenetrable terrain was traversed by Sir Charles Napier, the British general, with an army of thirty-two thousand men in 1868. Under Queen Victoria's directive, General Napier had been sent to defeat Emperor Theodore, the Abyssinian warrior king, whose outrageous defiance of the British Empire and her Sovereign Queen was considered intolerable. General Napier's trek, complete with fifty-five thousand animals, including elephants shipped from India, took him across those mountain ridges below me, surely some of the world's most inhospitable terrain.

A British emissary, Charles Cameron, held hostage by Emperor Theodore for five years, was the *casus belli* for that incredible expedition. Napier's route from the coastal town of Magdala into central Ethiopia took almost six months, but the battle that followed lasted less than twenty minutes. Emperor Theodore lost the battle, his kingdom, and his life. The British recovered their emissary, their honour, and their reputation, leaving Ethiopia to sort out its own future through tribal warfare and natural anarchy—at a time before airplanes had even been invented.

At Mandera I flew into Kenyan airspace. After ten hours of flying I was closing in on my destination. Shards of sunlight pierced the towering clouds of cotton wool. The ground fell away from the mountains into forest clearings, spotted with thatched *makutis* (roofs) and the smoke of cooking fires whose wisps of smoke curled into the bluish haze of an African sky. The number of settlements multiplied, laced by red earthen paths through a patchwork of small farms with their *bomas* (thorn-bush corrals for herding goats). Corrugated tin roofs glinted in the sunlight, through the emerald-green baize of tea and coffee plantations. In the distance, the city of Nairobi rose faint against the murk of a polluted skyline. My heart beat faster.

———————————

The instrument approach into Wilson Airport, the smaller of the two airports servicing Nairobi, is linked to that of the larger, Kenyatta International Airport. Instructions on the approach plate for landing are confusing: midway through the procedure for Kenyatta Airport, the pilot is expected to break away and enter the approach for Wilson Airport—a most unusual arrangement and a lot to ask of a pilot after ten hours of flying at fourteen thousand feet.

My head ached from dehydration and the lack of oxygen. I had to rely on the controller's limited patience as I stumbled through his instructions and eventually touched down on Wilson Airport's Runway 07. I taxied the length of the field, crossed Runway 14 and pulled up in front of the Flying Doctors Service hangar.

A number of Flying Doctors Service pilots had gathered outside the hangar to watch as I cut the engine and swung out of the cockpit. Tousled, dirty, and lacking in sleep I could hardly make my legs work as they were stiffened from so many hours of flying. I approached the pilots, who were waiting at a respectful distance from the plane. So this was the consultant, come to help reorganize the Flying Doctors Service. At least they were impressed by my having flown from North America to Africa in a single-engine plane. That was a good start.

We shook hands and, after a brief discussion, I informed them that I needed food and sleep; their questions would have to wait for morning. They understood, offered to place my plane in the hangar, and helped me call a cab.

As the taxi careered and swayed along Milimani Road towards the city, my driver, who introduced himself as Michael, talked nonstop. He persuaded me to stay at the Nairobi Club, a perfect club for a gentleman from Canada, he claimed. He would vouch for it and for me—I had only to leave everything to him. What's more, he would meet me the next morning in order to show me the city.

I gazed abstractly out the window at Nairobi, large and bustling under the white gold of a setting sun, and all very peaceful. I had flown eight thousand miles from Toronto to Nairobi in seventy-six hours' flying time. The excitement of flying solo to Kenya to work on an aid project in Africa suddenly seemed less romantic, even mundane—but then I was tired, very tired. I needed sleep. Tomorrow, I thought, would be time to rekindle my spirits, to seek adventure in Africa, and whatever else lay ahead, over the next two years.

PART TWO

3

City of Tears

I REMEMBER the jacaranda trees. They formed my first impression of Nairobi—dotting the hills like puffs of blue smoke, presaging the rainy season—delicate blossoms, like fallen tanzanites sprinkling the blood-red earth every morning. The city sits five degrees south of the equator, a mile above sea level, basking under a brilliant sun by day, blanketed in liquid coolness at night. How can I ever forget those early-morning sunrises, the magnificent variegations of an African sky, spilling light across the city, or the majestic wash of violet when the sun falls into the Rift Valley at the close of day?

Nairobi must have been a beautiful city in its time. By the time I arrived, sadly, everything about Kenya's capital required patience and charity. The city's infrastructure had crumbled; roads, telephones, and government services had become unreliable, subject to sudden breakdown. Giant potholes pockmarked the crowded and dangerous roads. Poorly paid bureaucrats, dispirited and helpless, no longer maintained even the pretence of public service. Civil responsibility seemed a thing of the past, long forgotten. At night the downtown streets remained unlit; an invitation to loiterers, shifting gangs of hoodlums, prostitutes, and the homeless. Mounting heaps of refuse lay uncollected, a permanent part of the landscape. It was depressing to see this once-lovely city fallen into such neglect and decay.

Michael, my taxi-driver friend, had suggested I stay at the Nairobi Club the first night, and not having anywhere else in mind, I simply followed his lead. We pulled up to a large, rambling, grey, stone, white-pillared building sitting on ten acres of beautiful grounds on one of the seven hills of Nairobi. The club had been founded and built in 1921 by tradesmen, in opposition to the exclusive up-country white settlers' Muthaiga Club on the other side of town. The two clubs represented separate classes during colonial rule, a strictly observed division that gave rise to much sneering and disapproval from both sides.

As I would discover, the Muthaiga Club was always the more chic of the two, with its golf course, squash courts, croquet lawns, pools, and ballroom. Built by Indian artisans from large blocks of stone, and with small Doric columns, it possessed a façade of grandeur. Polished floors and deep, soft armchairs covered in flowered chintz provided an air of English gentility that disguised the prejudices, scandals, and internecine squabbles of its members over some eighty years. Sunday lunches of curry and roast beef remained an enduring tradition. Members still behaved as if the British Empire existed and nothing was ever likely to change.

The Nairobi Club, in contrast, was worn and shabby. Its membership was 95 per cent black African, many of whom were associated with Kenya's ruling party. The high-ceilinged rooms of the club were in need of a coat of paint, the carpets threadbare. Members were notoriously lax about the payment of bills; the staff, routinely cursed and cajoled, provided mediocre service in return. While the Nairobi Club had squash and tennis courts (no golf) and many of the same facilities as the Muthaiga Club, it remained the poor cousin. Only the Nairobi Club's cricket field was superior; lovingly cared for by groundsmen who devoted their lives to a perfect crease and the resounding thwack of a willow bat on a leather-covered ball.

I was struck by the informality of the Nairobi Club and the fact that its members had long ago shunned the expatriate European community. The room I selected had windows looking out onto the cricket pitch. It was simple, furnished with a double bed, armchair, and small desk. The only luxury was a small bathroom with a six-foot bath, the hot water supplied by a wood-fired furnace located in a shed next to the club.

My first day at sundown, I watched as the flags overlooking the terrace were ceremoniously lowered, a signal that the tea room and the dining room required proper evening dress: jacket and tie for men and dresses for women. The club's flag, with a yellow sun and the words "Light and Liberty" (taken from the crest of the Imperial British East Africa Company), was treated with regimental pride. Payment for food and drink was transacted on various coloured chits, an antiquated inheritance from the British, whose customs remained unquestioned by Africans long after these traditions had disappeared from Britain.

At the top of the grand, wood-panelled staircase I found a musty old library, a treasure house of seven thousand books, including African titles, many of which were long out of print. The library listed 170 members; however, not more than ten members seemed to make use of it during our two-year stay there. The full-time African librarian, Stephen Mukuna, whose love and knowledge of books on Africa was remarkable, sat reading under the lead-framed windows behind his desk. Day after day, like an aging prophet, imprisoned in shafts of sunlight and the motes of ancient dust, he devoured the written word.

The perimeter of the Nairobi Club was patrolled by *askaris*, or guards, who were on duty all night. These poor souls were paid less than KS 1,300 per month (approximately $250) for remaining outside shivering in the cold and the rain. The *askaris* were forbidden to light fires for warmth, and their clothing consisted of rags, layers of cotton or wool discards they found or stole. It gave them a wraith-like appearance in the dark.

Michael, the taxi driver, was my first friend in Nairobi. On reflection, I realize he probably adopted me as *his* friend. A newly arrived *muzungu*, or white man, in this part of the world spelled opportunity. That was fine by me. I knew few people in Nairobi, and without Krystyne I welcomed the attention. During my first week in Nairobi I agreed to employ Michael as a personal chauffeur. He was expensive by African standards at $20 a day—but for me it was a bargain.

Michael's cab was in pretty bad shape, but, at the age of twenty-two, owning his own taxi made him a star among his envious friends. The cost of running a car with only a few customers left him chronically short of cash. His standard greeting, "Hello, Scott. Give me something," was outrageous; however, his unabashed delight at receiving a pen or a cheap pair of sunglasses was endearing—at first. It wore thin over time. However, we remained loyal friends long after I bought my own car and no longer needed his services.

My first day in Nairobi was a Sunday and most of the Flying Doctors Service staff had the day off. I had decided to walk downtown and meet Michael in the afternoon at the Stanley Hotel, half expecting him not to show up. But Michael was there, slouching against the newsstand at the corner of the hotel, a large grin on his face. He swung his arm in a wide arc culminating in an African handshake—a clasp of hands, the holding of thumbs, followed by a second handshake. His boyish round face under a New York Yankees baseball cap advertised a warm and gentle disposition. Michael was a Kikuyu, the largest of the forty-eight tribes of Kenya. He was easygoing, perennially on the lookout for an extra shilling, particularly if it required little or no effort on his part.

"Ah, man, where you been?" he inquired with an indolent shrug.

Nairobi was teeming with people like Michael who came in from the country desperate for work. Over 55 per cent of Nairobi's population lived in slums that occupied less than 16 per cent of the city. These slums were truly appalling, crowded, filthy, and unsanitary. Michael had a brother, Isaiah, who lived in Kibera, the largest slum, not far from Wilson Airport. Michael offered to take me there and introduce me to his brother since it was unwise for a *muzungu* to go unaccompanied. I wanted to see for myself what constituted an African slum, so I agreed to go.

Kibera held almost a million people, packed into tiny mud hovels. The press of humanity was suffocating to the outsider. Open sewage ran along narrow passageways with hardly enough space for people to pass. Rank smells of burning dung, garbage, and rot permeated the fetid air. We left the car and I found myself holding on to Michael's jacket, fighting claustrophobia, pushing through the jostling throng, wading through rivers of muck and feces.

Isaiah lived with five other men, all of whom shared a hut furnished with two cots and a chair in a space no larger than a walk-in closet. Half the occupants worked the night shift, which allowed the others to rotate every two hours between a chair and two cots—four hours sleeping, one hour sitting. Isaiah made a great fuss over our arrival.

"Come in, come in, you are welcome to my home," he said, enthusiastically. The smoke-filled hut was completely devoid of light. The smell of stale sweat and dirty feet was overpowering. Isaiah unceremoniously roused his roommates from their cots and ushered them, dazed and shuffling, out the doorway to provide space for us to sit.

"Get out, get out. Can't you see I have guests?" he said, as they slouched uncomplaining into the blinding light of day. He then set about serving us a syrupy sweet tea in tin mugs.

"You shouldn't have disturbed your mates," I interjected, embarrassed at the fuss he made over our visit.

"Don't worry about them," Isaiah said quickly. "It's not every day we have a *muzungu* visit us in Kibera." Isaiah and Michael laughed and immediately switched to speaking Kikuyu. Michael did most of the talking, while Isaiah repeated, "Ahaa, ahaa" every few seconds.

I cast my eyes around the room, slowly adjusting to the lack of light. The mud walls were bare except for a cracked, unframed mirror and a calendar featuring a girl pulling on a pair of stockings.

I speculated absent-mindedly that Michael and Isaiah were discussing whether or not I had money. I decided it didn't matter. I simply sat there drinking tea, trying to imagine how six full-grown men could live month after month in such restricted quarters.

Eventually, I interrupted their conversation. "What do you do for work, Isaiah?" I asked. Both brothers turned, as if surprised that I was still present.

"Oh, I'm not working at the moment, *bwana*. Between jobs," Isaiah volunteered. Michael quickly added that it was very hard to find work living in Kibera. I could see the conversation was heading towards a request for money so I ignored Michael's remark and addressed Isaiah again.

"Do you have a family?"

"Oh yes, he has a family living in Nakuru," said Michael, determined to steer the conversation back to himself. "It's very hard for my brother. He must send money to his family every month."

A loud whistle from the train travelling from western Kenya to Mombasa interrupted our conversation. The train passed right through the middle of Kibera between the press of people and the racks of cheap clothes hanging from poles on either side of the tracks.

Resigned now to the inevitable request for money, I asked Isaiah how it was possible to send money to his family if he had no job. Unfazed, Michael rose to the occasion, while Isaiah sat silently, anticipating rejection.

"Isaiah lost his job from Asian boss in Biashara. He closed his shop and refused to pay last week's wages. Now my brother can't pay his rent. It's a very bad situation, you understand, Scott." Michael's persistence was relentless.

"How much is rent?" I said, incredulous that rent could be collected for such a place. That was it; the trap was sprung.

Triumphant, Michael announced, "Rent is 1,800 Kenyan shillings a month. Isaiah must pay his share, 300 Kenyan shillings, by this evening. Only 300 Kenyan shillings, Scott. Can you help him?"

I pulled out my wallet and passed the money to Isaiah who appeared stunned at this miraculous event. He accepted the money without saying a word. Michael quickly added, "God bless you and your family, Scott." Turning to his brother, he added something in Kikuyu that sounded like a rebuke. Isaiah remained silent. The business over, it was time to go. Isaiah's roommates had gathered round the doorway, anxious to return to their sleeping quarters. We made our way out into the press of people, towards the eastern end of the slum, where Michael had left his car.

There was something impressive about Kibera. In spite of the dirt, poverty, and unsanitary conditions, there was a social order that I found extraordinary. The intensity and vibrancy of close quarters, shared hardships, and the mix of generations gave Kibera a sense of community. This enormous congregation of people, mired in pollution, without police or government, had a commonality of purpose which focused on day-to-day survival. It was unlike anything else I witnessed in Nairobi during my two-year stay there.

Sometime later, I learned from friends in Westlands, a well-to-do suburb, that their African staff, living in separate quarters palatial by comparison to Kibera, became lonely, missing the life in Kibera, depressed by the material comforts of Westlands but devoid of human contact. Similarly, aid agencies such as the Flying Doctors Service spoke of refugees who were loath to abandon the intense social life of the massive refugee camps, no matter how bad the conditions, for the less human prospects of resettlement.

Michael and I made our way along the railway tracks that bordered the slum. Mounds of rotting garbage piled several stories high redefined the landscape. I could see first one, then two, and soon over half a dozen children, picking and sorting their way through the slime, in search of anything of value they might possibly turn to a shilling. Their eyes darting, alert to danger and opportunity, the scavengers were totally unaware of our presence.

Monday morning, November 18, 1996, I walked up the laterite path that led in from the main road to Wilson Airport, to an area where a collection of attractive bungalow-style buildings butted up against a nondescript office block. A large nandi flame tree had dropped its gold-laced, reddish flowers on the dark earth. There, under the leafy shade of a parking lot, dappled in sunlight, I found the main reception of the African Medical and Research Foundation (AMREF) headquarters. I was pleasantly surprised. Inside, the atmosphere was professional and efficient. The corridors buzzed with activity; doctors, nurses, secretaries, and messengers were striding purposefully from office to office, sheaves of paper in hand, intent on AMREF business. A small group of Africans waited patiently for news about a sick relative or a job application. The phones never stopped ringing. On closer examination, the buildings required minor repairs and a lick of new paint but, for an NGO (non-governmental organization), dependent on private funding, headquartered in Africa, the place scored high on first impression.

The African Medical and Research Foundation was the brainchild of plastic surgeon Sir Michael Wood, who was knighted for his work in Africa. He was born in 1919, educated at Winchester, and interned at the Middlesex Hospital in England. He and his wife, Susan, immigrated to East Africa after the Second World War. Two other plastic surgeons, Sir Archibald McIndoe, a New Zealander, and Dr. Thomas Rees, an American, arrived in Nairobi in 1957. All three met and together founded AMREF; however, it was Sir Michael Wood as director general who continued to be the driving force of AMREF until his premature death in 1987.

Sir Michael Wood, a man of charismatic charm and imagination, was also a pilot and larger than life. He realized that in Africa it was impossible for the sick to reach the large hospitals in major centres such as Nairobi and that medical help should be delivered to the outlying areas where people lived—a concept later endorsed by the Declaration of Alma Ata at a World Health Conference in Kazakhstan in 1977. He initially organized AMREF with trucks equipped with an operating theatre, dispensary, and radios, but he quickly discovered that these vehicles were cumbersome and impractical given the impassable roads in Africa, particularly during the rainy season.

Small planes were the answer: planes equipped with HF radios that could fly in and out of dirt strips. And so, the Flying Doctors Service was formed as a division of AMREF. Michael Wood's personal plane, a Cherokee 180, and a twin-engine Piper Aztec donated by Arthur Godfrey (the 1950s host of *The Arthur Godfrey Show* on ABC television) formed the Flying Doctors Service's first fleet of airplanes.

Years of hard, selfless work followed, building countless dirt airstrips, installing an expansive HF long-distance radio network, constructing outreach clinics, and raising donations from Europe and North America. Forty years later, the Flying Doctors Service had become a critical part of Kenya's medical infrastructure.

I knocked on Dr. Michael Gerber's door. His second-floor office was a large room, nicely appointed with black-and-white photos of doctors and nurses dispensing aid to black women and their children—typical NGO advertising, designed to tug at the donor's purse strings. I found Michael Gerber at his desk, hunched over a computer from which he directed a seven-hundred-employee organization, responsible for training and operating clinical outreach programs for the whole of Kenya and much of East Africa as well as the Flying Doctors, who provided medical evacuation services.

Right from the start, Gerber made me his confidant, unloading his private thoughts and frustrations without seeming to worry about the political consequences of such indiscretion. Over the next two years, our regular weekly meetings would cover subjects that went far beyond my assignment to reorganize the Flying Doctors Service. Gerber's concerns included the composition of the AMREF board, governance, and personnel issues—all political minefields that were driving him to distraction.

That first day, though, we spoke only of my assignment. He launched into it almost before I had a chance to sit down.

"Scott, I've got a hell of a problem with the Flying Doctors Service. It's badly run, losing money, and draining resources from the organization. My board members are upset. They insist I do something about it."

Gerber had inherited an awkward corporate structure that complicated the reorganization of the Flying Doctors Service, which was legally owned and operated by AMREF. The Flying Doctors Service's revenue came from funds raised by the Flying Doctors Society, referred to as the "Society," a separate legal organization whose sole purpose was to raise money for the Flying Doctors Service.

The Society was made up of volunteer ladies, most of whom were well meaning but completely out of touch with the operating requirements of the Flying Doctors. The Society's constitutional mandate was to raise money for the Flying Doctors Service by selling annual memberships to the Society for KS 30,500 or $65 per member. Membership entitled a member to a free emergency medical evacuation from any swamp, mountain, or desert in East Africa, by the Flying Doctors Service. It was an excellent fundraising idea, popular with travel agents and tourists visiting the game parks. The only problem was that the Society jealously guarded the funds it raised and had no legal obligation to hand the money over immediately to the Flying Doctors Service. The Society's board believed their first obligation was to Society members to ensure that monies raised were properly spent.

The Society had lost confidence in Mike Gerber, and because they felt that the Flying Doctors Service was poorly run, the Society's board felt justified in withholding funds. While there was some justification for their complaints, no one on the board had a clue about the operations of an emergency medical flight evacuation unit, and this led to ferocious arguments and much bitterness.

Since the Society had few expenses and no obligations, it had accumulated substantial amounts of cash. Its board met infrequently to review its bank account and members debated whether or not to make a "donation" to the Flying Doctors Service, usually amounts that were pitifully small and bore no relationship to the actual costs of operation. To make matters worse, the Society did a lamentable job selling memberships; they had little incentive with so much cash in their bank account. Meanwhile, the Flying Doctors Service, carrying all the expenses of running the medical-evacuation service, was cash-starved and hounded by outraged creditors who threatened to close them down.

Gerber's frustration over this impossible situation and his uneasy relationship with his own board had him pacing the room. Part of his problem lay in the fact that AMREF was still living under the shadow of his predecessors, Sir Michael Wood, whose reputation had taken on mythical proportions, and his younger brother, Christopher Wood. Sir Michael's charismatic personality had been universally attractive to all those connected with AMREF, making him a tough act for Mike to follow.

Mike Gerber was an American who had grown up in New York City, received his doctorate in Asian studies from New York University, and then became a professional aid worker. He had spent a number of years in the Philippines and India before joining AMREF's national US office in New York. Tall, warm, and gregarious, he seemed nevertheless out of place at AMREF. It was generally agreed that he was the complete opposite of the legendary Sir Michael Wood.

Over the years the Flying Doctors Service focused on emergency medical evacuations, employing professional pilots and nurses, sometimes accompanied by doctors. Seriously ill patients were flown from outlying areas to Nairobi to be treated by doctors at one of the major hospitals. Since most emergency evacuations involved Africans who had no money, the Flying Doctors Service division, without access to the Society's cash, eventually became a financial drain on its parent, AMREF—a drain that AMREF could ill afford. My assignment was to free Gerber to concentrate on AMREF and to reorganize the Flying Doctors Service, making it more efficient, providing it with a renewed sense of purpose, and, more important, reversing its financial losses.

Mike Gerber and I quickly agreed that I should spend a few weeks at the Flying Doctors Service hangar to assess the operation, produce an initial set of recommendations, discuss and agree on a business plan, and then submit it to the board for approval.

"Well, that's fine, Scott," he said. "It's wonderful to have you with us. I really need your help and I look forward to your recommendations."

Suddenly, he seemed to realize that he hadn't made the proper polite inquiries about how and when I had arrived in Nairobi and whether I had a suitable place to stay. We took another few minutes on the subject, following which he insisted that I join him and his wife for dinner. By the end of the evening, I realized that I could be of real help to Mike. His daily routine had become a struggle, made difficult by a political board and a recalcitrant Society. I sensed he was looking forward to early retirement.

The next day, I bought a second-hand Nissan sedan, and soon discovered that driving in Nairobi is a blood sport. It is not so much that drivers drive too fast, which they do, but that virtually all cars on the road are unsafe, wrecks held together by a grotesque patchwork of metal and body filler. No matter how old or damaged cars appear, however, they remain a potential target for thieves. The manufacture of security devices ranges from enormous links of chain to bars inserted through the steering wheel and red-blinking lights that warn of electronic sirens—mostly non-operational. The sale of security systems was and still is a thriving industry in Nairobi. Popular bumper stickers read "This car is protected by the blood of Jesus." Expensive Land Cruisers and Mercedes-Benzes usually carry the added protection of a chauffeur armed with a billy club or a pistol, the use of which is never really in question.

The roads in and around Nairobi when I was there were a disaster. Potholes were so numerous they served as speed bumps or what some called "sleeping policemen." On occasion, I would bring my

Nissan to an abrupt stop as the frame rested on the edge of a hole, leaving a front wheel hanging suspended in mid-air. Extrication from one of these craters entailed commandeering a gang of youths to lift the car bodily out of the hole, and then enduring the inevitable haggle over payment.

Driving at night with no streetlights, behind billowing clouds of black exhaust and defective headlights was nerve-racking. Rules of the road were simply guidelines. Assuming safe passage through a green light could be as dangerous as running a red light. High beams were used as a weapon and passing was considered a competition.

Matatus, or privately operated small buses, are now regulated, but during our stay in Africa they were not, and merely added to the confusion. *Matatu* drivers—usually young men in their twenties—were paid by the number of passengers they transported over a ten-hour day. Passengers were packed like sardines inside a *matatu* by "touts," or encouraged to hang from the sides, roof, windows, and bumpers—wherever a hand- or foot-hold could be found. Once passengers were on board the *matatu*, the driver and the "tout boy" assumed no responsibility for safety.

Matatus, although fast and frequent compared to the lumbering, unreliable public buses, were dangerous. They competed for riders by using moronic-sounding horns, neon lights, psychedelic paint jobs, and trendy names: Muscat Candy, The Undertaker, Shaggy by Nature, The Smasher, Brown Baby, Bad Manners, Fly Baby Fly.

Matatu accidents were frequent and horrific. A typical Monday-morning article in the Kenyan newspaper *The Nation* reported that a *matatu*, with a legal limit of sixteen passengers, had broken through the barrier of a bridge and plunged into the Athi River, killing the driver and all forty-three passengers.

My poor old Nissan sedan took incredible punishment over the two years in Nairobi. Aggressive driving seemed mandatory and I entered the fray with unabashed enthusiasm. On one occasion, I was trapped in a full-scale downtown riot caused by the political tensions over the 1997 elections. Surrounded by an angry mob throwing stones and bottles, I realized I might have to abandon the car. Tear gas and policemen wielding clubs had worked the crowd into a frenzy. The street was blocked at both ends. Drivers had deserted their cars and were running for cover. I swung the steering wheel hard over, drove up onto the curb, and, with a fearful bang to the under pan, drove over a flower bed between the trees bordering Uhuru Park, and raced across the grass to the Haile Selassie intersection. I escaped with only a slow, thin leak of oil that traced my whereabouts in and around Nairobi for the next thirteen months.

By November, the rainy season had ended, leaving Nairobi caparisoned in fresh flowers. Krystyne was still in Canada and I anxiously awaited her arrival. I had negotiated a long-term rental of our room in the Nairobi Club, and made a few exploratory forays beyond Nairobi to the districts of Thika and Karen. I was beginning to get the feel of things, know my way around Nairobi, make a few friends, and assess the size and extent of my assignment at the Flying Doctors Service.

David Huntington, an Englishman in his late forties, attractive and intelligent, had become a special friend. He was in Kenya on a three-year assignment with the United Nations. He loved Africa and was hoping to stay on indefinitely, perhaps even to settle permanently in Kenya. His young wife, Amanda, however, found life in Nairobi difficult. She was clearly homesick for England. It had become an issue between them. David and I had met at a United Nations–sponsored conference in Nairobi on aid. He took me under his wing and helped me learn the ropes in and around the city.

David had developed a healthy disdain for those in the aid business who he felt profited from Africa's misery. Nairobi served as a base for a proliferation of aid agencies, most with headquarters in Europe and the United States. The United Nations had its own private, fenced-in compound situated in northwest Nairobi, with its own modern supermarkets, theatres, sports facilities, and schools. A large expatriate community lived there in relative comfort, with tax-free salaries, free housing and schools, expensive four-wheel-drive vehicles, and special discounts at designated expatriate stores beyond the reach of Africans. One had to question whether these agencies were organized for the benefit of the aid receivers or the aid givers. David had strong views on the subject and over time he struck a sympathetic, though less cynical, chord in me on the complicated business of providing aid to underdeveloped countries. David would become a close friend to whom I could turn for advice concerning the restructuring of the Flying Doctors Service.

The evening of Krystyne's arrival, December 10, I was stuck in rush-hour traffic on my way to meet her at Kenyatta International Airport. The length of Kenyatta Avenue was blocked solid. Waves of pedestrians streamed between my Nissan and the line of cars stalled in traffic. A haze of suffocating exhaust hung over Kenyatta Avenue like a dirty blanket. Stoplights in Nairobi took forever to change, causing frustration for drivers who sat immobile, staring grim-faced in the heat and pollution.

Without warning a loud bang interrupted my daydreaming as a beaten-up Ford Opel sedan struck me from behind. Both my tail lights were smashed and the trunk acquired an ugly hump. The driver of the Opel, an older African, and his terrified wife were shouting excitedly in Kikuyu, while he waved his arms and pointed to the empty space in front of my car. Apparently, he felt I was to blame for not having advanced quickly enough. It was a hopeless argument. I re-entered my car and resumed the frustrating crawl towards the roundabout, cursing.

A small boy in rags ran in front of the car and around to the driver's-side window, "Please, Mister, give me something," he held out his hand pleading. I kept a bag of sweets in the glove compartment for such occasions; within seconds the car was surrounded by a band of urchins, brown eyes imploring, fingers tapping the window, eager for treasure.

Begging in Nairobi is an art form. Mothers supervise their daughters from a distance as they work the street. Six-year-old girls dressed in rags with *totos* (small babies) on their backs are trained to run into the thick of traffic to secure a shilling from white female drivers waiting at a stoplight. The boys are more aggressive, working in packs, waiting for an open car window so that they can grab whatever is lying on the back seat or snatch a watch off a wrist, or earrings, sunglasses, or even necklaces from unsuspecting drivers. The older ones ply the traffic lanes, selling newspapers, magazines, and articles ranging from full-length mirrors to cosmetics, toasters, hammers, and toilet paper, most of which have been stolen during the previous night's escapade. The jumble of traffic and frenetic market activity along the street provides an exciting sense of energy; everyone is hustling, hands and eyes active, never missing a trick.

Finally breaking free of the jam, I circled the roundabout and bounced along the Valley Road to the Mombasa Highway against the piercing headlights of oncoming traffic. My excitement mounted as I turned into a parking space and headed for the international terminal building to meet Krystyne.

Krystyne, tall and regal (a shade under six feet), stood apart from the bustle of tourists and Africans scrambling to extract their bags from the luggage belt. She looked lovely, dressed in linen, standing under the garish neon light of the arrivals terminal. I slipped past the guard into the baggage claim area. We met over a pile of luggage— our first embrace in Africa.

Night fell with a thud over the Nairobi plateau. We emerged from the glare of the airport into the unlit parking lot. The crumpled trunk of my Nissan refused to open. I loaded Krystyne's bags into the back seat and we headed into the chaotic rumble of traffic towards Nairobi. Krystyne gripped the armrest, bracing herself against potential accidents as cars careened towards us like alien meteorites off a video screen. The drive had her guarded and nervous as she related home news. It was only when we entered the Nairobi Club that I realized how incredibly shabby the place looked, paint peeling from the ceilings, leather chairs disgorging parts of their interior, carpets threadbare and unable to hide the creaking, wax-caked wooden floors.

We made our way up to our small room and squeezed into the small space available between the bed, the chintz-covered armchair, and the small writing table. For Krystyne it was a stark change from the comforts of Toronto, where the luxury of space and a garden were taken for granted.

"Think of it as a cabin on board ship," I said enthusiastically. "You'll see, space is relative," I added optimistically. "Did you know that Nelson, after a year of chasing the French back and forth across the Atlantic, refused to disembark in Toulon, preferring to remain in his small cabin?" Krystyne let this pass without comment. Sure enough, our little room soon became a real home. In a curious way, it drew us closer together; closer than we ever could have imagined that evening, her first in Africa.

4

The Hangar

TUESDAY MORNING, following my first meeting with Gerber, I entered the Flying Doctors Service hangar and found it a mess. Surplus equipment lay abandoned in every corner. Damaged propellers hung from the walls, old engine blocks gathered dust in the back corners of the stock room, and tools were scattered everywhere. More than half the hangar floor was occupied by two "hangar queens"—partially dismantled planes that were a permanent feature of the hangar but had not flown in years and were not even owned by the Flying Doctors Service. Aircraft wings, parts of airplane fuselage, spare seats, damaged instrument panels, the list went on and on. Parts were piled high to the ceiling. A pack-rat mentality prevailed, understandable in Africa, where spare parts were almost impossible to obtain. The place had not been properly cleaned in years.

On the mezzanine floor I toured the offices of the manager, the chief pilot, and the dispatcher, as well as the pilots' common room. At the far end of the corridor I found the flight records squeezed in alongside the HF radio set. Space was at a premium, and here, too, nothing was ever thrown out. Loose papers and files bulged from filing-cabinet drawers and shelves sagged under the weight of aviation operating and regulation manuals.

Engineering and maintenance departments were housed on the hangar floor, with their own set of records and a sizable inventory of spare parts. Aviation legislation required detailed records, which added to the duplication of paper, spare parts, and tools. It was all an invitation to waste, inefficiency, and loss of money.

The magnitude of the task of transforming the Flying Doctors Service into an efficient, self-sustaining operation hit me like a ball-peen hammer. The clean-up alone would be monumental, let alone the necessary change in attitudes among the personnel. Suddenly, the idea of coming to Africa on such a project seemed ridiculous. This assignment had the sag of hopelessness about it.

Even so, I felt confident I could assist the Flying Doctors Service. I had had considerable experience running small entrepreneurial companies. The challenges facing an expanding business almost always fell into a familiar pattern, and the Flying Doctors Service was no different. However, this was Africa, and I was there as a consultant, not the president responsible for the organization—two significant differences. I needed to win over the managers and those on the hangar floor before making recommendations. So I spent my first days listening to complaints and recommendations, which flooded in from every direction.

Disorganization in the hangar placed inordinate demands on employees, who were expected to work long hours with little pay. Employee disgruntlement permeated the place, occasionally erupting into a crisis that brought activity to a stop. Jim Heather Hayes, manager of the Flying Doctors Service, had threatened to fire the lot countless times. The subsequent impasse inevitably ended in the granting of minor concessions that still left workers underpaid and overworked.

Jim Heather Hayes in his youth had been rakish and handsome. He had a well-established rally-driving reputation and a special talent for flying airplanes. In his day, he had been the closest thing in

Africa to an American barnstorming stunt flyer. His acrobatic exploits were legendary: landing on the roof of a moving Land Rover,
hydroplaning on water, flying under hydro wires, and setting down
on the front lawn of a safari lodge in front of startled tourists. These
days, though, Jim was a harried man. He spent hours on the phone
tucked in a small corner office under the sloping roof of the hangar,
chain-smoking, trying to resolve a cascading number of problems.
He was big and gruff, with sandy-blond hair and a ruddy face
blotched from sunburn and repeated attacks of malaria. I felt he was
unfairly criticized as manager of the Flying Doctors Service by both
the Society and by AMREF. The Flying Doctors Service had become
a convenient dumping ground for most of AMREF's unwanted problems. He had taken on responsibility for the maintenance of the
organization's 150 vehicles on the basis that he used to be one of East
Africa's premier rally drivers. However, the operation of a garage at
the back of the hangar not only encroached on Jim's time and attention, it was also a money-loser and took up valuable space, diverting
resources from the Flying Doctors Service.

"What does vehicle maintenance have to do with the Flying Doctors Service?" I asked.

"Who else is going to take it on?" Jim replied with a look of pride.
"Besides, it's extra revenue for the Flying Doctors Service." This
typical entrepreneurial approach, while admirable, led to organiza-
tional chaos. The back of the hangar had become a dirty oil-soaked
garage, where old cars and spare parts occupied the turning space
that ambulances required to access the rear of the hangar. Jim's tendency to focus on his current problem, at the expense of long-term
solutions, meant that his office groaned under mountains of unre-
turned phone messages and defective airplane and car parts, all of
which required immediate attention.

As manager of the Flying Doctors Service, Jim was responsible
for the pilots, the planes, the radio network, and the maintenance of
aircraft in the hangar—all the operational details of a small airline.
The Service owned seven different types of aircraft, each one with a
different manual, different parts, and different flying characteristics.

The updating of the charts of landing strips and radio frequencies for Kenya, Ethiopia, Sudan, Somalia, Uganda, Tanzania, Rwanda, and Burundi required a sizable database of current information. The workload was punishing.

Jim's close friend, Colin Davies, was the flight engineer, and he exercised absolute rule over the hangar floor. Colin never really trusted me, and it was not until much later that I got to understand and like him. He viewed my arrival as an intrusion by a starry-eyed North American, naively optimistic over possibly changing the Flying Doctors Service.

Colin was tough, rugged, down on his luck, with a chip on his shoulder. He was personally shy and publicly aggressive, constantly digging himself out of problems of his own making—and irritated by his string of misfortunes. He was short and pugnacious, and yet still retained a vestige of his former good looks, the kind of man that could break a woman's heart if she fell for him—and many did years ago. He was a true white-African character. He attributed his problems to Kenya's general decline following the country's independence in 1963, and he was quick to point out that his misfortunes coincided with President Moi's accession to power and the country's subsequent descent into corruption.

It was easy to be dismissive of white-Kenyan types like Colin, but they were born in the country and considered themselves part of Africa, emotionally committed. They accepted that blacks, democratically elected, should run the government, as long as it was based on parliamentary traditions and the rule of law. Every year, though, they witnessed more corruption, increasing crime, and outright prejudice towards the Asian and white minorities. This they bitterly resented. It was too late for them to leave the country, to start up elsewhere. Life was slipping by, and they were swept reluctantly into what they saw as Kenya's accelerating slide into chaos.

Colin was a genius around airplanes. I have never seen anything quite like it. His instincts were uncanny. He understood planes—their design, construction, and operation—even though he'd never learnt to fly one. He would stride around the hangar in short pants, chin thrust out, eyes glaring, yelling one expletive after another at the incompetent hangar staff. Without warning, he could suddenly ground an aircraft just as the pilot was taxiing off the ramp. David Mutava, the chief mechanic, or his assistant, Stanley Gakure, would be instructed to have the pilot shut down the engine if Colin didn't like the sound of the motor. Sure enough, a problem would be discovered and Colin's instincts would be vindicated. He ruled the hangar floor like a dictator; no one dared cross him, not even Jim.

Colin's ability to improvise temporary repairs on a plane that had crashed in the bush was also legendary. He and Jim, in partnership, could rescue any plane, no matter where it came down; no pilot's carelessness had yet defeated them. Jim, of course, would fly the plane once Colin had jury-rigged the wreckage back into some kind of flying shape. The wall of Colin's office was covered with photographs of rescued aircraft that had been hauled out of the jungle by Land Rover or winched out of a sand dune. There was even one that had been transported over water by a raft of dugout canoes.

Jim relied heavily on his chief pilot, Benoit Wangermez, who was professional and demanding of the pilots reporting to him. Benoit was an enigma to most people in the Flying Doctors Service. No one really knew much about his background except that he had been in the French Foreign Legion and had spent time in North and West Africa. A man of few words, he refused to talk about his past, which only added mystique to his appearance in Nairobi in 1984, when he came looking for a flying assignment. There were not many pilots certified to fly DC3 airplanes, so he easily got his certification and a job at Air Kenya, and soon became a fixture around Wilson Airport.

In 1986, Jim hired him as a pilot for the Flying Doctors Service and it soon became obvious that Benoit should be the chief pilot. A good-looking bachelor, elusive and pensive, he lived alone. His proclivity for married women had rumours circulating that he had left his mistress in Algiers in a hurry, but no one really knew about Benoit's private life. As chief pilot he was good at his job, well organized, and a stickler for the rules. His penchant for detail was prodigious; he built a valuable database for the Flying Doctors Service, which listed the coordinates and details of thousands of landing strips that covered the whole of East Africa. He was an excellent flyer and commanded the respect of all pilots flying out of Wilson, not just pilots working for the Flying Doctors Service.

I got on famously with Benoit. He considered me an ally who was genuinely concerned with implementing badly needed changes to the Flying Doctors Service. His caustic sense of humour had him mimicking the Québec "joual." I was sure he viewed my flying exploits with suspicion, but since I was not one of his pilots, he was discreet enough to keep those thoughts to himself.

Almost all Benoit's pilots were young, enthusiastic, and romantic: Grégoire Tallot, also French, only twenty-five years old, good-looking and keen for any assignment, the more challenging the better; Trevor Jones, laid-back, a good pilot, always weighing the risk, erring on the side of caution; Ahmed Ali, a Somali, older, more experienced, with more hours in his logbook than the others, the brother of the famous fashion model Iman, although he remained quiet about that.

On missions, the pilots were supported by nurses—the backbone of the Flying Doctors Service. They were supervised by Bettina Vadera, a young, attractive, blond German-born doctor, who was dedicated to her nurses, never demanding from them anything she was not prepared to take on herself. All the nurses were African, well trained, and capable. Among them were Rose, the oldest, a single mother, wise and competent; Judy, her inseparable friend, the supervisor in charge of training the new arrivals from nursing school; and Rebecca, whose quiet dignity, grace, and gentleness exemplified all that was noble about the vocation of nursing.

The nurses supervised the twenty-four-hour emergency HF radio station housed at AMREF headquarters, a medical radio link that covered all of East Africa and served as a reliable backup for the army when their communication system failed. The Flying Doctors Service delivered medical services to many in East Africa who otherwise would never have seen a doctor or nurse in their lifetime.

In spite of the cash-flow difficulties and the political intrigues typical of most volunteer-based organizations, the Flying Doctors Service was viewed as a first-class organization of vital importance to Kenya. Employees believed they served a higher cause, which nurtured heroic performances by both pilots and nurses that often went unnoticed by the outside world.

On the hangar floor David Mutava, the chief mechanic, was in charge of the men; he was devoted to Jim Heather Hayes, having flown with him in years past. He would point a gnarled finger to his head, saying, "See this white hair? How do you think I got that? Flying with Jim." David relished telling tales of Jim's flying exploits. "He was an uncanny pilot, knew the plane's capabilities, always pushing the envelope. He used to scare the shit out of me."

David served as mediator between the men and Colin's wild ranting on the hangar floor. The men trusted David. He had the instincts of an older African—wisdom acquired from years of watching and adapting to the *muzungu*'s, white man's, ways, without losing his natural instinct and cunning.

David and his men gathered regularly for tea breaks. They drank a mixture of hot milk and tea, a leftover from English colonialism, in the lunch room, where the language was Swahili and corporate politics were viewed from the perspective of the hangar floor. The place was off limits to senior management, a custom even Colin observed.

After lunch, men and supervisors would saunter out onto the ramp to lie under the wings of the Flying Doctors Service aircraft. Cool breezes blew across the open airfield as they watched the airline hostesses walk by on their way to the Air Kenya terminal two hangars east. There was much informal banter as well as hard work, and in this sense, life in the hangar was like living in a large family.

In many respects the whole of Wilson Airport was similar. It was a close-knit community of flyers, charter operators, mechanics, electronics shops, and flight-training schools. The private companies were owned exclusively by white Kenyans or Asians. Black Africans served as employees, rarely rising to a level above that of mechanic.

There was no animosity, no conscious reference to colour or class; that was the pecking order. The British had bequeathed a class system that was firmly entrenched on the airfield. It was just accepted.

Most of the aviation companies teetered on the edge of bankruptcy. Owners spent their days grappling with the lack of spare parts and chronic shortages of cash. It was a tight community in continuous crisis; everyone owed someone else a spare part, money, or a service of some kind. The reconciliation of accounts when an outfit went bust left a wave of recriminations and the licking of wounds.

———————————

On the mezzanine floor of the Flying Doctors Service hangar, the pilots' common room was squeezed between dust-covered offices. The walls sported pin-up pictures of girls, cartoons, and a giant topographical map of Kenya spotted with coloured flags identifying hundreds of landing strips across the country. Distances were measured with a length of string affixed to Nairobi, on the free end of which swung an old nail. The spare HF radio squawked and wheezed in the corner next to the window. A battered, food-stained sofa thrown against the wall was usually occupied by a couple of slouching pilots, drinking coffee and grousing about the latest flight regulations promulgated by the Kenyan Ministry of Transport. The air, thick with cigarette smoke and exaggerated tales of flying, remained permanently stale and unhealthy.

One morning I entered the room to hear the pilot Trevor Jones ask, "How about we go to the Aero Club for breakfast?" There were no flights scheduled that morning and pilots could always be reached on a beeper by the radio room, provided they remained within ten miles of the airport. Breakfast at the Aero Club seemed a good suggestion, far better than moping around the hangar waiting for an emergency. I had the accounts-receivable ledger to review with Stephen Mugungo, the accountant, later that morning, but the idea of joining Trevor and Grégoire proved irresistible.

We piled into Trevor's Range Rover and took off down the airport road, past the charter aircraft companies, the aviation-parts supply depots, and the jumble of signs strategically placed among the bougainvillea bushes growing along the airport fencing.

The Aero Club of East Africa, founded in 1927, is the second-oldest active flying club in the world, after the Aero Club de France, which was originally formed outside Paris for balloonists. The clubhouse, a white-stucco-and-clapboard building, consisted of a large saloon, a dining room, offices, and an attractive wood-panelled bar. Adjacent to the clubhouse were squash courts, a small swimming pool, and overnight quarters for visiting pilots flying in from remote areas of the country.

The bar room, the main attraction of the club, sported black-and-white photographs and memorabilia of early African flyers, many of them women: Florence Kerr Wilson, Beryl Markham, Connie Johnston, and Maia Carberry (killed in an airplane crash in 1928) standing next to their magnificent flying machines. The room was filled with a sense of romance and history, characteristic of those early flying years in East Africa. A huge, beautifully preserved, wood-spliced, two-bladed propeller hung over the bar. Here, club members exercised their notorious, enduring, and ongoing reputation for outrageous behaviour. Although planes were more risky to fly in the early days of the club, the same nonchalance and devil-may-care attitudes of independence still permeated it, especially on Friday evenings, when beer flowed like water.

I noticed Sir Malin Sosbie's photograph hanging over the entrance to the dining room. He was a member of the Royal Canadian Mounted Police who later joined Imperial Airways. During the Second World War he flew fighter aircraft from Takoradi in West Africa to Cairo over the Western Desert, stopping at Khartoum to refuel from drums transported by camel.

Trevor ordered eggs, bacon, and bangers and mash. Grégoire and I settled for a Coke. We were alone in the dining room except for a couple of bored waiters relieved that the morning rush of breakfast guests had departed. The other two lit up cigarettes, while I shifted my chair to avoid the curl of smoke drifting my way. The steady roar of planes taking off from Runway 07 behind the club drowned out most of the conversation about hang-gliding and water-skiing at Lake Baringo, subjects of little interest to me.

I stared at the coloured photograph of Sir Michael Wood that hung on the wall directly in front of me. His aquiline features, deep blue eyes, and warm smile conveyed a sympathetic and vital man of action. I wished I had met him. His wife, Susan, a woman of considerable stature in her own right, whose energy and support were critical to his success, was still living in Karen. She had been born in a mud hut in the Congo, the first white baby born in the Congo jungle.

We were suddenly startled by the ring of Trevor's beeper. The hangar was calling for the pilot on duty to pick up a tourist who had been gored by an elephant in Tsavo East National Park. We paid, rushed back to the hangar, and reported in to the dispatcher, who had been searching for Trevor. Jim was standing with one foot on the railing of the mezzanine, furious, muttering that in future pilots on duty were not to leave their post without indicating their whereabouts.

Bettina had arrived from AMREF headquarters fifteen minutes earlier to help Judy load the Cessna Caravan with medicine, oxygen, and blood supplies. Reports had come in over the safari-camp radio that the patient would require immediate blood transfusions, and Bettina decided to accompany Judy on the flight in case field surgery was necessary. Trevor concentrated on preparing for the flight, collecting strip cards for landing information, completing the flight plan, and performing the pre-flight aircraft checks. Once on board Trevor gave the thumbs-up to the ramp man, who removed the auxiliary power. The turbo engines slowly turned, then caught, and wound up into a high-pitched whine. Two minutes later, the Caravan lifted off the runway and headed southeast on a mission that would save another person's life.

Only one doctor remained active from the original cast of characters that had formed the Flying Doctors Service back in 1959. She was Dr. Anne Spoerry, known by the Africans as "Mama Daktari." She had joined the founders as a junior member but, now in her eighties, she was still flying her Piper Cherokee Lance PA-32 single-engine plane to remote areas of Kenya, dispensing medicine, and performing consultations for remote tribes that had no other possible access to medical help, in exactly the same tradition as that practised by Sir Michael Wood.

Born in 1918 in Cannes, France, to parents from Alsace, Spoerry was the great-granddaughter of Henry Schlumberger, founder of a major French textile firm. She was educated in England and France, graduating in medicine shortly before the outbreak of the Second World War. She and her brother worked in the French Resistance. She was betrayed, caught, and sent to Ravensbruck, the notorious Nazi concentration camp. Psychologically marked by the experience, she left her friends and family in Europe for Africa and, after a brief stint in Yemen, dedicated the rest of her life to Africa as a flying doctor. She wrote a memoir entitled *They Call Me Mama Daktari* a few years before she died in 1999.

I was determined to befriend her and enlist her support for amalgamating the Society with the Flying Doctors Service, for I knew her approval as a senior doctor would have an effect on the Society's board. When she agreed to meet me, suggesting that I fly with her on a mission north of Lodwar near Lake Turkana, I readily accepted.

The morning of our rendezvous the sky was burdened with clouds, racing low over the horizon. The wind veered and backed nervously through a full quadrant of the compass, unsure where to settle. Flight conditions were far from ideal. Waiting on the ramp in front of the hangar, I wondered if she had cancelled and forgotten to inform me. She was in her eighties, after all, and inclined to overlook certain details she considered unimportant. A year earlier the Flying Doctors Service had insisted that she fly with a co-pilot, which threw her into a rage; she finally acquiesced and engaged a student pilot, who was instructed to sit in the co-pilot's seat and not say a word.

I recognized her lumpy gait as she approached the hangar. Disdaining the Flying Doctors Service uniform, she wore an old blue jumpsuit and a Toronto Blue Jays baseball cap given to her on a recent goodwill fundraising trip to Canada.

"You're a pilot, are you not?" she demanded as she approached me. When I indicated that I was, she added, "In that case we need not take the boy with us. Get in while I check the plane." I was unfamiliar with her aircraft and I had no idea where we were headed. I thought of voicing an objection, but her intimidating manner argued for silence. She started up the motor and we took off, her seat pushed so far back from the controls she could barely see out the windscreen. I watched her every move carefully and realized that, while her reactions were slow and methodical, flying was as familiar to her as driving a car. I began to relax.

Once beyond Nairobi control, we headed northwest high above the Rift Valley. I inquired as to our destination.

"Marsabit," she said, "southeast of Lake Turkana," which was familiar to me. She looked straight ahead, refusing to turn her head in my direction when she spoke, as if a glance sideways might send the plane into a tailspin. Our flight east of the Rift, past Isiolo and over the Losai National Reserve, was long and uneventful. We opted for silence—it was easier. She was slightly deaf and the noise-cancelling intercom filled with static when either of us spoke.

"Anne, how much farther?" I inquired eventually, risking her displeasure by calling her Anne. "We're nearly there," she said, adding, "Rendille country down below. Wonderful people, the Rendille." She adjusted the trim for a gradual descent. "The strip's a mile north of town." I vaguely wondered how we would get into town, but I soon found out that she planned to conduct her consultations right beside the airstrip, under a *mugumu*, or fig tree. The Bantu considered the *mugumu* a place of worship and healing.

Anne was a no-nonsense character who treated her patients in a deft, common-sense manner based on unwavering conviction and absolute authority. Underneath her gruff exterior, though, was a kindness that won her a following of loyal supporters, particularly black Africans whom she had treated over the years. Some of them she supported financially, three she had even legally adopted.

She and Sir Michael Wood both had enormous respect for African traditions. Many Bantu tribes still paid heed to these ancient traditions, including the ancestral spirit Ngoma who wielded influence over a patient's recovery. Many of the local cures held validity, and anyway, strong beliefs were a powerful antidote against illness and a salve for rapid recovery. Wood and Spoerry were also prepared to work with the *m'ganga*, or witch doctor—the traditional African healer. The *m'ganga* held obvious power over the patient's mind and Dr. Anne Spoerry claimed in her book that while "her medical attention was far more efficacious in treating bodily symptoms . . . the *m'ganga* put the patient into a relaxed state. . . . beneficial for both the patient and her treatment." The flying doctor's medicine almost always cured the patient while the *m'ganga* claimed the credit, and that was a perfectly good arrangement as far as Anne was concerned.

The airstrip lay directly ahead, a visible scar on the parched land, knobbled with loose rock. A gathering of African patients waited for the *ndege* (Swahili for bird and plane) to arrive. Anne was approaching too fast, and my feet instinctively pressed against the firewall to slow us down. We hit the ground and bounced down the runway in one of the roughest landings I'd experienced in fifteen years of flying. I wiped the sweat from my brow, expecting an apology or an explanation from her, but without a word she swung her legs out of the cockpit and ordered the erection of a table and camp stool, which I proceeded to haul out of the baggage compartment. Speaking Swahili, she greeted people by name and although I understood little, I could see that she was a revered figure in their midst.

"*Jambo, jambo, Mama Daktari, karibu sana.*" ("Hello, hello, Mother Doctor, welcome.") The patients quickly formed a line, eager to receive her ministrations. Anne methodically inspected each, providing medicine or inoculations, peering down throats and into ears, and on one occasion instructing a man to lower his trousers so that she could inspect his private parts. Flies and dust competed with the thermals that blew the leaves of the *mugumu* tree like schools of silver fish back and forth through the swaying branches. The sun beat down hard on the patients seeking relief, resigned to the fate of Mama Daktari's medicine. I sat under the wing of the plane, poleaxed by the heat, counting the hours that stretched on into the afternoon.

Suddenly jolted out of my hazy reverie, I heard Anne call me for assistance. Towering above her was a man, thin as a stick, with a pained expression on his puffy face. He had an abscessed tooth which needed pulling. Anne rose from her camp stool and instructed the man to sit in her place. I was to kneel behind him, wrap my arms around his skinny chest, and hold him firmly to the chair. Anne lifted herself up onto the table, inserted what looked like a large pair of pliers around the infected tooth, raised both her legs, placing a foot on each of the man's shoulders, and then started to pull with both her arms outstretched. There was a fearful yowling that came from the poor man as Anne pulled and twisted with all her might, but the tooth, stubborn as a tree trunk, refused to give way.

By now the line of patients had disintegrated into a mob of interested bystanders fascinated by this strange tug-of-war. Every time she twisted the pliers, the man's head twisted in response in an effort to alleviate excruciating pain. Exasperated, she commandeered the nearest male patient to hold his head in an arm lock and set about her task again, feet on his shoulders and me pinning the poor man to the chair. Suddenly, the tooth gave way, and a jet of blood spurted in an arc from his mouth over Anne's jumpsuit. The relief was immediate and the man burst into a hideous grin, blood and mucus running down his jaw and across his chest.

"*Asante sana, asante sana, Mama Daktari*," ("Thank you, thank you, Mother Doctor") he yelled, jumping up and down as if possessed by the devil. Then he turned and took off at a run through the acacia bushes in the direction of his home to show his family the happy result, released at last from the purgatory of pain.

The first shadows of grey fingered the Marsabit hills signalling the end of day, but the line of patients remained as long as when we first arrived. The heat, even this late in the afternoon, remained stifling. Huge sweat marks ringed the armpits of Anne's jumpsuit. She was visibly drained from the relentless stream of patients she attended, the details of each treatment recorded in her tiny neat script in a notebook.

All of a sudden she stood up, declaring that her visit was over but that she would return in two weeks' time. Visible disappointment spread across the long line of faces of those unattended, but she remained unmoved. We proceeded to pack up her medical supplies, the consulting table and chair, as a crowd gathered around the plane. And then unannounced, there was a spontaneous outbreak of singing, a chorus of chanting, in celebration of Mama Daktari's visit. She stopped and listened, hands hanging by her sides, visibly moved at the warm outpouring of affection. She looked tired but pleased, and it was then that I first noticed the faint traces of beauty in her face which had lingered from her youth.

On the long flight back to Nairobi, I reflected on Anne Spoerry's time in Africa and the incredible life she had led flying her own plane and ministering to the sick in remote parts of the country in the fifty years she was there. She was a holdover from a romantic era when individual characters made all the difference. It was sad to see older doctors like her, larger than life, rendered less effective now. However, population explosion demanded change. The population of Kenya had exploded from six million at Independence in 1963 to sixty million projected by 2010. Organizations like the Flying Doctors Service had to transform themselves from entrepreneurial individuals into professional organizations to make an impact. The old characters like Spoerry, Wood, Rees, and McIndoe had served Africa well in their day, but their time was past. They could no longer do the job alone.

I liked my weekly visits to Mike Gerber's office in AMREF's headquarters. It was a civilized break from the noise and dust of the hangar.

The quiet hum of computers, the muffled double ring of telephones, and the air-conditioning conveyed an atmosphere of sanity lacking at the hangar. His secretary, Margaret, served us tea and took all calls. I viewed these meetings as delicious interludes.

"Sit down, sit down," Mike said during one of them, gesturing to the sofa. "I want to raise an important issue, something that has to be dealt with immediately." He launched into an account of a conflict of interest involving Jim Heather Hayes and Colin Davies.

The two had surreptitiously formed a separate aircraft maintenance company, located next to the Aero Club. Jim, apparently, was only a shareholder; Colin ran the new enterprise. Colin spent his day racing back and forth between the two hangars serving as flight engineer for the Flying Doctors Service and president of the new company, exchanging parts and services between the two operations, and creating an accounting nightmare and a mountain of unpaid bills.

"Scott, these guys are long-term employees, collecting salaries from the Flying Doctors Service and running a private business on the side. It's an outrageous conflict of interest!" Mike was apoplectic and it was easy to sympathize. "This unacceptable behaviour has been brought to my attention by two of my directors, providing proof positive that the Flying Doctors Service is completely out of control."

I had to admit I was taken by surprise. What's more, it made the recommendations I was about to propose to Mike a tough sell.

"Listen, Mike," I said, "I can assure you of one thing, Jim is honest—of that I'm certain. I don't know about Colin." I had made a point of getting to know Jim over the previous three weeks, and I was confident of my assessment. Colin was more remote, a tough guy to get close to, but my instincts said he too was honest—more naive, perhaps, but honest. Still, they were both clearly in a conflict-of-interest situation, even if there was no outright dishonesty.

Not quite sure how to reply, I ventured, "Mike, leave it with me for twenty-four hours, and I'll come back to you with some answers." I wanted a chance to talk to Jim first. Mike agreed in the interest of taking the problem off his desk. A scowl clouded his face at what he considered to be Jim's and Colin's betrayal.

"Mike," I said, trying to introduce my recommendations, "I have been at the hangar for three weeks now, flown on a couple of missions, talked to the pilots, worked with the mechanics, and reviewed the financial accounts." Mike peered at me from his seat, which provided him with the advantage of height.

"The Flying Doctors Service has problems, we both know that, Mike, but there are good people over there working hard. The problem, in my opinion, is the awkward reporting structure." Mike listened without saying a word. "The Flying Doctors Service will never become financially self-sufficient unless the various services—doctors, nurses, clinic, radios, pilots, planes, and the Society—are collected under one roof directed by one manager, and run as a separate cost centre. This is what I'm recommending." Mike looked skeptical, but I went on: "Prior to producing a business plan, though, I need to know that I have your support, and we must agree on the choice of manager. I believe Jim can do the job given the right support."

Mike's face indicated he could scarcely believe what he was hearing. I continued before he could interrupt. "Jim's current position, without control of his revenues, unable to pay his bills, and saddled with the vehicle maintenance, makes his job impossible."

At this point Mike, exasperated, cut me off. "Scott, isn't it Jim that's got us into this mess in the first place?" Mike's undisguised frustration exploded at the direction I was heading. He was astute enough to see that backing Jim would cause him difficulties with his board. I, in turn, was in danger of losing Mike's confidence.

We spent an hour discussing the subject. In the end I gained Mike's grudging commitment to back Jim, on the basis that, within six months following the restructuring, it would become obvious whether or not Jim should remain in charge. He suggested I proceed with the business plan and present it to the directors at the February board meeting in two months' time. It was a victory of sorts.

Having gained approval in principle from Mike Gerber, it was now important for me to seek endorsement from the Society. It made no sense for them to remain apart from the Flying Doctors Service. Both organizations had the same purpose: to provide medical evacuations for those who did not have access to a hospital and to provide transportation for doctors and nurses to the clinical outreach programs. Mike agreed that in future the Flying Doctors Service would manage its own bank account and operate as a separate cost centre. Assuming the Flying Doctors Service could gain access to the revenues controlled by the Society, it stood a chance of gaining financial independence.

The Society, though, guarded its fundraising role jealously, convinced that the Flying Doctors Service was eager just to grab the funds; both organizations felt they were entitled to control the money. Clearly, it would be a challenge to persuade them to consolidate their activities under Jim Heather Hayes.

I was destined over the next year to spend long, fruitless hours with the Society, listening to harangues over the inept operation of the Flying Doctors Service: Jim's mismanagement and Mike Gerber's ulterior motives. The scars of past disagreements were deep and the two sides' positions seemingly irreconcilable. I tried to reason with the Society's board on more than one occasion, but they would have none of it. They simply did not trust the Flying Doctors Service, Mike Gerber, or Jim Heather Hayes. And so, before my two years in Africa came to an end, I had to concede defeat. The amalgamation of the Society into the Flying Doctors Service would have to wait until some future day; the hardest-fought campaigns do not always lead to victory.

I recommended to Mike that we implement the rest of the plan anyway in the forlorn hope that we might find a way to break through the Society's intransigence prior to the next board meeting. Gerber's frustration, even greater than mine, made him sympathetic to the idea, and his tentative acquiescence was all I needed to proceed.

5

Angels of Mercy

WHAT STRUCK ME MOST about working at the hangar was the dedication of the Flying Doctors Service employees. They earned pitifully low salaries and could expect no personal gain from their extraordinary efforts, their desire to help others. Somehow, it reawakened my faith in mankind; here was a higher order of morality, one understood and practised by the African nurses, the mechanics, and the ambulance drivers.

Day after day, calls came in over the radio to the Flying Doctors Service from people desperate for help: ghastly car accidents, with victims dying on the side of the road; children feverish with falciparum, the killer malaria; the dreaded dengue, known as "break bone fever"; Bancroftian filariasis or elephantiasis; AIDS. It was endless. People living in remote areas had nowhere else to turn when tragedy and illness struck. The Flying Doctors Service never refused a call, even when patients had no hope of paying. I resolved to remain a supporter for as long as I could be of some use to them.

The success ratio of the Flying Doctors Service missions was unusually high. In spite of the disorganization of the hangar and the separate location of nurses, radios, pilots, and clinical services, the Service was able to build and maintain an outstanding reputation of selfless care throughout East Africa.

I remember being told the story of a mission that took place before my arrival to Africa, for which the pilot almost lost his job. It is a story that typifies the difficulties experienced by Flying Doctors Service pilots, and illustrates the dedication of staff and their unselfish desire to help those in serious need.

As it was related to me it was a Saturday afternoon and the hangar was quiet. Requests for medical evacuations were unpredictable; the radios produced only long hours of static. Nevertheless, they had to be monitored night and day—a tedious chore assigned to the nurses. Suddenly, the number-one radio crackled, "Foundation, Foundation, Sabarei police station, how do you read?" (The Flying Doctors Service was also known as "Foundation," a shorter nomenclature used for radio procedures.) The transmission was barely comprehensible through the static. Rose, the nurse on duty, leaned over the 1950s radio set that had long ago lost its calibrated markings and concentrated on the caller's message. Tweaking the squelch button, she cradled the apparatus close to her bosom, as if to protect her voice before sending it through the hand-held microphone.

"Sabarei, this is Foundation, reading you three by three, go ahead please, over." The radio room held an eerie glow from the greenish overhead neon light. The room was stuffy. She had been on duty for six hours. Her shoulders ached and she worried about her son, Moses, who was in Kenyatta Hospital following an appendix operation. Kenyatta Hospital was a bad place to leave a patient; too many scandals circulated about the lack of care, the unsanitary conditions, the horrendous inefficiencies, the ghastly mistakes. The government had appointed a commission of inquiry recently to investigate the alarming number of unexpected deaths in the hospital, but of course, nothing came of it.

"Foundation, we have a young woman hemorrhaging badly after giving birth. We need assistance, she's losing a lot of blood . . . over." The last part of the message was garbled, as the strength of the signal kept fading in and out of phase.

Rose struggled for more information, but there was confusion at the other end and that, combined with the inferior quality of the reception, meant the remainder of the transmission was lost. At four o'clock there was little daylight time left for flying. She decided to cut the communication short and call Michel, the pilot on duty. Sabarei was up near the Ethiopian border, and it was debatable whether a Flying Doctors Service plane could get there from Nairobi before dark.

Michel reached for the beeper hanging on his belt. It was wedged under the seat belt of his red, second-hand Suzuki and only retrievable after a contorted twist that almost had him off the side of the road. He was on his way to his girlfriend's apartment in Karen on the outskirts of Nairobi, but well within the mandatory ten miles of Wilson Airport—beyond which he could not go while on duty. The Suzuki, fresh out of the body shop after a major repair, shuddered and vibrated as it made its way along the N'gong Road; both the frame and the wheels were badly out of alignment. He had rolled it three weeks before, trying to negotiate a roundabout at full speed, blind drunk, an event that had him concerned for his job. After all, he was still intent on proving to Benoit that he was mature enough to fly with the other Flying Doctors Service pilots who were at least ten years older. He really didn't have to worry too much; they all thought it was pretty funny.

Michel, handsome, looking younger than his years, had the face and enthusiasm of a boy. He was clean-shaven, and his light blue eyes and blond hair perfected an air of innocence that, mixed with Gallic charm, was irresistible. His shyness masked a quiet determination and strength of character that was not immediately evident and was often underrated at first meeting. Dressed in a pilot's uniform, though, he was postcard-perfect and turned heads wherever he went. He was universally liked, even though his circle of friends and acquaintances was limited.

Michel stepped on the gas. He decided to wait and call the Flying Doctors Service from his girlfriend's apartment. He was no more than twenty minutes away. It was probably the instructions for tomorrow's flight to Kilimanjaro, he thought. Once a month he flew a medical team to the outreach clinic at the foot of the mountain to service a remote community with no other access to medical support. Tomorrow would be a long day sitting under the wing of the plane while the doctor and nurse ministered to an unending stream of ailments. Still, he loved his job. At only twenty-five years old to be flying airplanes for medical-emergency rescue work in East Africa—how could you beat that?

Michel was lucky—and lucky to be French. Benoit Wangermez was also French, and that was the break Michel had needed; it had got him in the door for an interview, and the rest he had won on his own merit, especially when it came to his flight test. He was a good pilot; he knew that; Benoit was too tough to let nationalist sentiment influence whom he might hire. Nevertheless, the other pilots secretly felt that Michel got the job because of his nationality.

Rose, in the meantime, was waiting for Michel to call and wondering how it was that fate would have the junior pilot, just two months on the job, on duty that night. She knew it would be difficult flying if the pilot's decision was to go. The overhead clock ticked on relentlessly, inviting the first long shadows of late afternoon. Why didn't he call? She couldn't help thinking that, if one of the older pilots had been on duty, she would have had her instructions by now and be preparing her medical supplies. At that moment the phone rang and Michel's unmistakable accent came through, bright and chipper. She explained to him that, according to the Sabarei police chief, the woman was bleeding a lot and they were afraid she might die. Sabarei had no facilities beyond a first-aid kit and the local *m'ganga*.

"Well, Rose, we'll go. I'll be there in fifteen minutes, okay?" Michel was out of breath, but never for a second did he consider not going. "Tell Sabarei to line the runway with fires, every hundred feet, both sides, not big ones. We'll take the Cessna 206." Rose looked up at the clock and made a mental note of the time, 15:55; the sun set at 18:30. They wouldn't get airborne for another hour and it was a two-hour flight. Yes, they would be landing in the dark. It was the organization's policy to avoid dirt strips at night, but one did not question the pilot, who could always refuse to land. She was secretly pleased with Michel's decision to go. She knew that most of the other pilots would have followed regulations. Maybe the junior pilot was the right choice after all. God worked in wondrous ways, and she had faith in His divine will.

Rose handed the radios over to Judy. They had both been with the Flying Doctors for over ten years and could follow the routine blindfolded: a call to the hangar to get the plane ready; check off the list of medical supplies; call Bettina and inform her of the mission. Bettina insisted on participating in the decision as to who was to go on a mission, and more often than not she would accompany the nurses, not only to help, but also to provide leadership to her team. In this case though, with the Cessna 206 being tight for space and with so little information, Bettina asked Rose if she felt okay going alone. She suspected that Michel would get out to the Sabarei strip only to find it impossible to land and would return without completing the mission. Bettina had no wish to endure a four-hour round trip for nothing; instead, she promised herself she would go out on tomorrow's flight to Kilimanjaro.

Daniel Lomoni, the ambulance driver, had the hangar doors open, and the stretcher, pillows, and blankets all piled beside the airplane by the time Michel burst through the back door adjusting his Flying Doctors wings to his shirt pocket. Running up the stairs he gave instructions to load up the plane while he pulled the "strip card" with the Sabarei landing information—he could read the instructions on the flight. Right now he had to file his flight plan. Then he dashed downstairs to do the pre-flight checks on the plane and supervise the loading of gear. Rose had brought what seemed like a whole hospital of supplies, including blood for transfusions and boxes of surgical equipment. He wondered how they would get it all in the plane.

The Cessna 206, identified as "5Y FDS," was the Flying Doctors Service's oldest single-engine plane. The back seats had been removed to make room for a stretcher. They clambered aboard and Michel took off from Wilson Airport at 17:00, banked into a left turn from Runway 14, and headed into the northeast corridor that skirted the large Kenyatta International Airport just as the sun plunged over the N'gong Hills. At the northeast boundary of Kenyatta's control zone he signed off with Nairobi control, switched over to frequency 118.2, and started the long, slow climb to twelve thousand feet. He and Rose were on their own, flying along the east side of Mount Kenya over the Lakipia Plain towards the Kaisut Desert.

Darkness fell. In this part of Africa, smack on the equator, night dropped like a curtain, black as soot. Michel stared out the side window of the cockpit at the scattered pinpricks of cooking fires far below. There was no other hint of human habitation. Rose was still fussing with the stretcher and the boxes of her equipment in the back of the plane. She eventually crawled forward and settled herself into the co-pilot's seat beside him. He didn't know her very well, even though they saw each other almost every day; it was strictly a working relationship. The nurses, the clinic, and the radio room were in different buildings, far from the pilots' common room. This was a problem, causing delays in the response time to emergency evacuations. As a result neither group fully appreciated the stress of the other's job. Little communication existed between pilots and nurses except when they were on a mission.

Michel had done one previous evacuation with Rose, but Bettina had accompanied them sitting in the co-pilot's seat and so he had literally not said more than a few words to Rose. But Rose rarely spoke anyway, unless spoken to. She was a modest, unassuming woman in her late thirties, though she looked older. A devout Baptist, she spent virtually all her waking hours doing good works for others. Her impenetrable eyes had a faraway look that carried all the signs of a hard life: tribal parents; convent life as a young girl; a husband long gone; and a son who lay seriously sick in the hospital with appendicitis. Now here she was at twelve thousand feet over the Lakipia Plain, staring out into the night, sick with worry, alone with her thoughts. She longed to be home.

The next hour and a half droned on without a word spoken. The old Cessna 206 rattled and shuddered under the pounding noise of the Continental 260 horsepower engine that had clocked more than ten thousand hours under harsh African flying conditions. Both the engine and the plane seemed destined to go on forever. Assuming proper maintenance, no one really knew how long a plane like this could be flown. In this part of the world, a plane's life expectancy was usually dictated by a crash. The cost of repairs and how much cash was available determined whether or not it should be consigned to the graveyard. Until that time came, it was always capable of at least one more flight.

Michel glanced over at the GPS instrument flashing twenty miles to go to the Sabarei strip. He set the elevator for a gradual descent into the pitch-black void below and took another quick look at the strip card describing the landing conditions at Sabarei. The information was not reassuring: there was a dirt landing strip, described as short and soft, particularly at the south end. The runway butted up against a steep hill at the north end, which meant it could only be approached from the south, and if an overshoot were necessary it would be tricky to execute. Benoit's distinctive, precise handwriting indicated "exercise extreme caution; downdraughts can be severe on approach; first half of the runway is often under water." Had Michel taken the time to read this back in Nairobi he might have had second thoughts about landing at Sabarei at night, but now he kept his thoughts to himself. He always had the option to turn back. Only, how then to explain the cost of the flight to Benoit the next day? It was a nagging worry. A tight knot formed in his stomach as the moment of decision drew closer.

Within minutes, the GPS indicated they were over the strip and, sure enough, he sighted three or four fires directly below. However, they seemed haphazardly placed, not in line with the runway. He flew as low as he dared with the landing lights on, but they only obscured the visibility below. He pulled up, switched off the lights, and prepared to make a second pass. Banking into a left turn he lowered the flaps to maximum and reduced the speed before descending to within two hundred feet of the ground. Now he could make out the direction of the strip and see the shadows of people huddled around the south end. Depth perception was difficult and he was dangerously close to a stall. Flying at such low altitude at night was risky.

He had to land or pull up immediately. His emotions were running in all directions. There was a woman dying two hundred feet below him. Landing a plane under these conditions was an enormous risk. On the other hand, the cost of the flight would require explanation if he returned empty. He glanced over at Rose, who sat immobile, staring out the window, waiting.

"We're going in," he said, flicking the lights back on. She had flown on far more evacuations than he had, and she knew this one was dangerous. Her instincts were to protest, but her job was on the ground and not to question the pilot's decision to land. Staring out the window, she prayed to Jesus to watch over them and to look after her boy back in Nairobi. She tried to think of a suitable sacrifice she might offer if her prayers were answered, but there was no time left. The plane was on short final approach and the wheels were about to touch down.

Suddenly, Michel saw the landing lights reflecting off the surface of water. "*Merde*, we're landing on water!" he exclaimed. The main wheels hit the water and immediately the Cessna 206 began to hydroplane. It was impossible to maintain directional stability. Michel pulled back on the stick with all his might in an effort to keep the nose wheel in the air; once it touched the water it would dig in and flip the plane onto its back. Halfway down the strip, the plane's wheels sloshed over a mixture of soft mud and puddles of black water. The brakes were locked, totally ineffective. They slid through mud as if it were grease, with the end of the strip fast approaching. There was no possible way the plane could stop in time.

Michel hit the left brake and instinctively threw the stick over to the same side, hoping the ailerons would somehow swing the plane sideways and create more braking action. Rose cried out in alarm as the plane bounced, slid, and came to an abrupt stop fifteen feet past the end of the runway, nestled amongst a large clump of acacia bushes. The engine shuddered and stopped. No one spoke. At least they were down and safe.

Michel wiped the sweat from his face, vaguely aware of the noise of the gyros winding down as he sat immobile in the pilot's seat. People were running through the night towards the plane. He was trembling as he recognized just how close he had come to a complete disaster. He needed time to recover. How the hell was he going to get out of here? Should he even try? The safe thing would be to sit tight and wait for daylight. How was he ever going to explain this to Benoit? It had been safe enough to land, but too dangerous to take off? Then why land?

Excited voices closed in on him, adding to the general confusion. Rose had climbed out and had organized the men to carry the patient from the other end of the runway to the plane. They were expected momentarily.

Michel sprang into action. He grabbed his flashlight and proceeded to pace off the strip in order to determine the length of usable runway available for takeoff—maximum nine hundred feet. Not much, even for a Cessna 206, the bush plane of Africa. And they would have the weight of another passenger.

Rose met him returning to the plane. "She's just a girl, not more than fifteen years old. The baby's dead. We've got to get her to Nairobi, fast. I'm not sure we have enough blood here. She's bleeding badly." Any thought of spending the night on the ground vanished; the girl was already being loaded into the plane. Rose began setting up the equipment to give her a blood transfusion.

Michel, with the help of others, swung the plane around by leaning their weight on the tail and lifting the nose wheel off the ground, so that it pointed north. Rose supervised the transfer of the girl's small body onto the stretcher at the rear of the plane. Michel glanced quickly at the girl's terrified face, and then resumed his check of the instruments.

The plane was completely covered in mud. Michel had to wipe the outside of the front windshield with the sleeve of his flying jacket in order to see out of the cockpit.

"Rose, this is going to be tight, there's not much of the strip that's dry," he said. He realized he was seeking her support on whether or not to take off, but she was totally engrossed in ministering to her patient and didn't answer. The girl's pulse was so weak it seemed at times as if she had already expired. Rose struggled to stem the flow of blood, but most of the bleeding was internal. A transfusion would buy time, but not much. The delay in takeoff seemed an eternity to Rose when every minute was critical. She looked into the young girl's lost and frightened eyes. Poor thing, she had never been out of her village, let alone in an airplane. The noise of the engine, too powerful to resist, seemed to push her into unconsciousness, as if it were an unknown force controlling her will to live.

Rose tried to make contact with her, speaking in Swahili, even though she was Gabbra and could not understand. She uttered soft pleading words of comfort, anything to keep her from slipping away. It was an exhausting process, cradling the girl's head, stroking her forehead, coaxing her back again and again from the edge of unconsciousness. The slightest relaxation and the girl's dark brown eyes retreated into a faraway look that spelled danger.

Michel pulled on twenty degrees of flap and raced the engines up to 2,850 revolutions per minute before releasing the brakes. The plane skewed and skidded down the runway, gaining speed as it neared the thick mud and water at the far end. The wheels hit the water at eighty knots—enough to hydroplane. He pulled the stick back, lifting the wheels from the surface tension of the water. The plane soared into the star-filled night, leaving the Sabarei hills far below.

Michel levelled the plane at twelve thousand feet and radioed Foundation to inform them the patient was on board and that all flight operations were normal. He was alone in the cockpit. Rose was in the back, sitting alongside her patient. He gradually began to unwind, knowing he was lucky to have pulled off such a risky exercise. But having done so, could he not afford to congratulate himself? Sure, it was close, damn close, but he was a bloody good pilot and had he not saved the girl's life? Satisfied he had made the right decision, he understood what the Flying Doctors Service was all about. There were bound to be risks saving lives. Still, he knew he had to rehearse his story carefully before meeting with Benoit on Monday morning. Benoit would demand a detailed explanation and he was a stickler for the rules.

The higher altitude increased the patient's heart rate, and with it her rate of internal bleeding. Rose applied more pressure bandages to the girl's genitalia; the swollen purple scars of circumcision indicated that the crude operation was recent and badly performed, leading to infection. Giving birth so soon after the operation had been disastrous for both mother and child.

Rose didn't question the subject of female circumcision. It was a fact of tribal life in the villages; both her mother and older sister were circumcised. Rose's family resented her refusal to undergo the ordeal herself. They believed she had come under the misguided influence of the missionary convent, but all that was in the past now. Her mother was proud that she was a nurse and Rose's father welcomed the money she sent him. It gave him important status amongst the village elders.

The plane rattled on through the night, a small, self-contained world of its own. Michel, not fully aware of the life struggle taking place three feet behind him, let his mind wander. He enjoyed flying at night. In Africa you are on your own, with no controllers, no other planes in communication, only a night sky filled with stars and below everything pitch black except for the occasional bonfire. Before the rainy season people set fire to the grass, and fires are left to burn out of control—sometimes a whole mountainside could be covered in flames—a spectacular sight, even though ecologically it was a poor way to manage the land. Michel decided he would go and see his girlfriend, Margie, once he landed. He couldn't just go home after a flight like this one—he'd be pacing around his flat like a caged lion all night.

Two hours on, the lights of Nairobi glowed in the distance. Wilson Airport was closed after 16:00 hours, which meant flying into Kenyatta International. The Flying Doctors Service's ambulance would meet them there, take the patient to the hospital, and transfer all the gear to the hangar at Wilson. Monday, he would have to go back out to Kenyatta International, get the plane, and fly it back to Wilson Airport, a five-minute flight that would take him all morning dealing with the bureaucratic arrangements of filing flight plans. Michel turned around to inform Rose of the change in plan and saw her sitting motionless, staring vacantly at the young girl.

"Rose," he had to yell over the noise of the engine, as she was not wearing her headset. "Rose, we'll have to go in to Kenyatta. I've told Foundation to have the ambulance ready." Rose didn't say anything. The young girl had died. Rose was sitting beside the body, with the girl's hand still resting on her lap.

Rose was so terribly tired. Every part of her body ached, and with it came the renewed worry about her son. Here she was, sitting beside a girl she had never seen before, whose life she had been unable to save, while her own son was alone in Kenyatta Hospital in critical condition. It was all she could do not to panic.

Daniel, the driver, was at Kenyatta International with the ambulance standing by, and they loaded the girl's body into the ambulance without saying a word. Her death underlined the apparent futility of the risky landing at Sabarei. Their efforts had been reduced to no more than a thankless job, subject to criticism, a dereliction of duty in which clear rules had been broken. Michel felt increasingly uneasy about his meeting with Benoit. He realized that flying the Cessna 206 into Wilson Airport on Monday morning would mean that everyone at the Flying Doctors Service hangar would see the plane covered in mud and that alone would demand a pretty detailed explanation.

No one spoke as the old Flying Doctors Service ambulance bumped and swayed down the Mombasa Highway. The blinding lights of oncoming traffic made driving hazardous, but Daniel had driven the route a thousand times before; he knew every pothole and how best to avoid them. He dropped Michel off at the hangar. There was the bang of car doors closing and a perfunctory goodnight as Michel set off to meet his girlfriend.

Daniel and Rose drove on to the morgue with the girl's body. It was only then that Rose realized she didn't even know the girl's name.

She would have to return the next morning to sign the papers. Obviously, no one could afford the expense of transporting the body back to her village, so it would be left here in the N'gong morgue. There would be no funeral, no burial. Her body would be disposed of as if it was mere garbage.

Daniel could see that Rose was utterly exhausted. They had worked together for years, and he was one of the few who knew her son was seriously ill. He offered to drive her home, but instead she opted to go straight to the hospital. He turned onto Haile Selassie Avenue and drove up the hill to N'gong Road and into Hospital Road. Although he had been on duty for fifteen hours, he told her he would wait for her, but she intended to spend the night at the hospital. Too tired to say more than good night, they parted. Daniel walked back to the ambulance, sat in the cab, and lit a cigarette.

A low cloud cover with light rain shrouded the hospital's imposing structure. The blaze of neon directed onto the parking lot threw a cold light against the black night. Inside, the hospital showed all the signs of neglect—burnt-out light bulbs, paint peeling off the walls, and tiles lifting from the cracked concrete floors. No money had been spent on maintenance for years. People shuffled along the dimly lit corridors; at times it was difficult to tell the difference between staff and patients. Kenyatta Hospital had, back in the 1960s, boasted an international reputation as Africa's finest hospital, but that was long ago. Now, its reputation was in tatters. The hospital was an eyesore, like so much else in Kenya.

Rose turned down the corridor towards her son's room, moving slowly past the surgical recovery rooms, the intensive care unit, and on to the main ward. A slow, sinking feeling in the pit of her stomach turned into a rush of dizziness as she spied the empty bed where Moses had lain that morning. "Mother of God, please, where is my son?" She found herself running from patient to patient, cot to cot, demanding, pleading with them to tell her what happened. No one moved, no one volunteered a word or even seemed to care. Desperate for information, she ran down the hall, hysterical, looking for a doctor, a nurse, anyone to give her news of her son.

Suddenly, she saw Judy from AMREF walking towards her and she knew without having to be told. She knew everything. Judy could be at the hospital at this hour for only one reason. She let out a barely audible cry, a cry that was less than a whimper. So much hurt welled up inside her, hurt that had accumulated over fifteen years, the result of too much caring, too many heartbreaks. Judy took and held Rose close to her and waited, waited for the first tentative cries to break into sobs, and then the unrestrained wailing of the aggrieved.

The two women stood locked together, swaying. Judy almost lost her balance. She was vaguely aware that Rose was covered in dried blood and smelled of death. Slowly, the two nurses, entwined in an embrace, slumped in a heap to the floor. The ululating cries began in earnest while, at the far end of the corridor, a man in dirty overalls pushed a cart of soiled linen through the set of swinging doors.

6

The Poisoned Spear

OUR FIRST CHRISTMAS in Africa, December 1996, had us thinking of home. Strange for us to imagine the cold, the snow, and those short winter days in Canada with crowds bustling in and out of stores to finish last-minute Christmas shopping. We missed the season's exhausting parties in Toronto before the scramble to pack up gear and drive to the Laurentians for the holidays. It all seemed so far away now.

Nairobi, by contrast, was in flower, the weather gloriously pristine following the big rains. Those who could afford it were leaving the city to go "up country" to spend Christmas with their families, travel that could take several days in crowded *matatus* over impossible roads. These migrations to parents, family, clan, and tribe were considered obligatory.

Krystyne and I decided to leave Nairobi and fly in our plane to Lake Turkana, situated in the Northern Frontier District, on the southern edge of the desert next to the Ethiopian border, a part of Kenya that was geographically cut off and politically hostile. The Turkana tribe was considered lawless, and the region so remote it was difficult for the government to exercise control. Still, the area was fascinating from a geographical and sociological point of view, although not for the timid. It was our first extensive "air safari" out of Nairobi since my arrival in Africa three months earlier.

A two-hour flight from Shaba took us over the Ndoto Mountains, the Korante Plain, and down into the lava moonscape of Lake Turkana, a large, mysterious lake lying in the middle of the northern desert, the object of fascination for a long list of late-nineteenth-century white-African explorers.

Lake Turkana, formerly Lake Rudolf, was originally named after the Hapsburg Crown Prince Rudolf of Austria in 1888, by Count Samuel Teleki de Szek and his companion Lieutenant Ritter Ludwig von Hohnel, the first white explorers to travel into this sparsely inhabited part of Africa. A unique body of water, Lake Turkana was haunted by the prehistoric ghosts of man's past. Alistair Graham, in the book he co-authored with Peter Beard, *Eyelids of Morning*, described it as "a one hundred and eighty mile long trough, six to thirty miles wide, of slippery green water, brackish enough to make you vomit and vindictive enough to make one hate. It can look innocently beautiful, glistening seductively in the morning sunlight; or ominous, like a huge brown slug aestivating in the crippling afternoon heat when even the flies are torpid." Lake Turkana, sinister for the unsuspecting, evil for the timid, contains one of the largest concentrations of crocodiles in the world.

It was here, on the eastern shores of Lake Turkana at Koobi Fora, that Louis and Mary Leakey in the early 1970s found amongst the oldest rocks in the world the skull of *Homo habilis*, a three-million-year-old Austropelithicus, whom they named Lucy. Turkana was the ossuary of mankind at that time; the earliest-known habitat of man's ancestors was found in this desolate and inhospitable part of the world.

Lake Turkana lies on the borders of the Chalbi and Kasuit Deserts, and the lake remains an important source of water for people who live in these deserts. Wandering nomads and tribal settlements dot its shores: the neighbouring Samburu, Rendille, Turkana, El Molo, Gabbra, Boran, and Dasenech tribes, whose Nilotic and Cushitic antecedents conspire to make uneasy relationships that regularly erupt into cattle raiding and tribal warfare.

Survival in these parts is a full-time occupation, requiring specializations that have evolved over millennia. The sun washes out the blue of an overexposed sky, pulverizing the earth's crust into swirling sand and dust. Only the foolhardy dare enter this blast furnace on foot. Some say the Turkana wandering these deserts are deranged—certainly lawless.

Farther south lies semi-desert, sprinkled with isolated oases where doum palms, spike grass, and scrub brush seek a hint of moisture from the wisps of cloud blowing in warm from the Rift Valley. Here the yellow hairs of desert grass blow silly under the hot thermals that sweep the scorched land. Moisture is sucked from every crevice, and the earth cracks open into giant fissures like gaping wounds. There is no escape, no relief from this burning hell. The dry season is endless, punishing; there is only resignation and waiting, interminable waiting, for the rains.

Cattle go down first, in an agonizing struggle. Circling the dried watering holes, they bay at the retreating smell of moisture. Resignation sinks to a slow and awful end. Days pass, one by one. The merciless sun blasts the porcelain sky. Only the few, driven by preternatural instinct, set out on the long trek across the burning sand to Lake Turkana, the last remaining hope. Bleached bones litter the route, grim evidence of decisions made too late.

The sight of Lake Turkana from the air was like a mirage of water folded into a desert where the hot, dry winds swept small dust devils, from a sea of drifting sand. The landscape resembled a burnt-out battlefield. Round boulders of lava lay strewn on the sand, like old cannonballs, the forgotten remnants of some ancient campaign.

We settled the plane down on the rough tarmac strip at Loiengalani, an oasis that sat partway up the eastern shore of the lake. The place once boasted a military fort built by the British, but now Loiengalani was a sparsely outfitted safari lodge run by an eccentric German called Wolfgang Dechter. The punishing heat of the desert, the impossible trek through the mountains, and the lack of facilities discouraged all but the intrepid or eccentric to visit Loiengalani; tourists rarely ventured so far north unless by chartered plane.

The sound of our arrival had Wolfgang sensing captive trade. He sent his right-hand man, Miglia, in a beaten-up old Land Rover down the runway to transport us to his lodge, where he served us drinks under a large, open *makuti*, or grass-roofed porch, overlooking the lake. The main lodge was pleasant enough; however, the dismal sleeping quarters, small *bandas*, or cabins, were badly in need of repair.

Wolfgang was a dreamer and a drinker. He spent his days in a dirty undershirt and shorts, unshaven, a quart of warm Tusker (the Kenyan beer) always within arm's reach. He ordered his unpaid staff about in a domineering Teutonic manner that had bred into them infinite patience and quiet resentment. At night he operated a ham radio, holding conversations with lonely voices undulating in and out of phase through the crackling static of the ionosphere. He almost never slept.

I had heard that Wolfgang had bought the lodge ten years before, in 1986, from an Italian, following a murder and bankruptcy that plunged the place into a private scandal. He had persuaded his young, stunningly beautiful wife—a German model called Margit— and their baby daughter to live with him in this remote part of Africa. However, the marriage was doomed, and he was left, bitter and lonely, hanging on to broken dreams and a dying enterprise. His aristocratic German mother visited him occasionally, only to suffer enormously from the heat, the flies, and his persistent requests for money.

We spent Christmas Day at Loiengalani. The air seared our throats, making it difficult to breathe. The land, dizzy with drought, was dying around us. I walked along the lava track from the lodge to my plane which sat alone shimmering on the tarmac. Hot winds blew into the plane's stall-warning horn, sounding a mournful whine, like a wounded animal. A nineteen-year-old Samburu warrior walked at my side, anxious to sell me his spear.

"This spear has killed five lions. It carries the strength and bravery of my father. You can buy it for special price." I made no reply. "I have fifteen brothers," he continued. "You can be my brother too. It would be an honour for me to say you are my brother. My name is Kipsoi. I am your friend and your brother."

High overhead, Nubian vultures soared in lazy figure eights, seeking death.

"A thousand shillings is too expensive for a spear," I said. "Besides, there are no lions here any more."

Kipsoi remained undeterred. "How much you pay then?" His eyes peered into my face, searching. "This is a very old spear, given to me by my father when I was a boy. I would be honoured for you to have it."

I wanted the spear, but tried not to show it.

We approached the plane. Keys in hand, I opened the pilot's door and rustled through my flight bag in search of the folded topographical map of Lake Turkana. Kipsoi peered over my left shoulder, staring in wonder at the inside of the cockpit. His interest gave me an idea.

"What about a ride in the plane in exchange for the spear?" I suggested. Krystyne and I were contemplating a short flight to the southern end of the lake to view Teleki's crater from the air—taking him along would be no hardship. A large, childish grin spread across his face. A ride in an *ndege* was beyond the dream and envy of his friends. We had a deal.

A few minutes later Krystyne joined us, and we took off into the hot, dry wind towards the lake, Krystyne in the co-pilot's seat wearing a bathing suit with a light sarong around her waist. Kipsoi, smelling of fermented goat's milk and blood, sat silent, ramrod stiff, in the back seat, holding his dismantled spear. The sun, an orange fireball, rode low over the Loriu Hills, casting afternoon light like spilled diamonds onto the green-watered waves of the lake below.

We flew to the south end of Lake Turkana and circled the gaping mouth of Teleki's crater. I remember vividly the strange sensation of skimming over that ancient geological landscape, our Samburu warrior staring, unblinking, at the electronic instruments, which flashed digital information across the front panel of the cockpit.

Lengthening shadows held the remnants of day. It was time to fly back up the lake to Loiengalani. It is easy to miscalculate the sudden fall of night in these parts and Loiengalani had no runway lights. Kipsoi remained immobile, silent, registering neither fear nor excitement, as if a wrong move on his part might cause the inexplicable magic of flight to end in disaster.

Directly ahead lay the recumbent shape of South Island, uninhabited, dangerous, and remote, bathed in the golden wash of the setting sun. A barren volcanic island, it sits majestically in the middle of the southern part of Lake Turkana. I knew of its reputation.

South Island was designated a park in 1972 under the supervised authority of the Kenya Wildlife Service. Its eerie landscape of black lava, devoid of all life except for crocodiles lining the shore, resembled a moonscape. Several white explorers had disappeared mysteriously from South Island, their fate the probable result of sudden and ferocious katabatic winds that funnelled down the lake from the towering walls of the Rift Valley. These winds, without warning, could rise to incredible force, whipping the lake into a storm within minutes and capsizing the large wooden and fibreglass canoes commonly used in central and eastern Africa.

South Island's sinister reputation intrigued me. I knew of only one pilot, Jamie Roberts, who had ever landed a plane on South Island. He considered it his own private romantic domain for camping with female friends.

Jamie was a regular flyer into Wilson Airport with a reputation of being a wild man with an eye for the girls. He was also an excellent pilot. The owner of a small local air-charter and safari business, he attracted well-heeled North Americans looking for excitement in East Africa. Jamie was the guy to provide it. He specialized in taking his clients to out-of-the-ordinary places, which included South Island, Mount Kenya (a narrow airstrip at ten thousand feet altitude), and isolated parts of the Masa Mara. The archetypal Kenyan cowboy

(KC), he was attractive, daring, and naughty. Jamie had often spoken to me of the haunting beauty of South Island, and here it was lying directly on our course back to Loiengalani.

We had time to circumnavigate the island, looking for the place where Jamie landed. The island is almost entirely mountainous with uneven stretches of lava rock. On the west side I sighted a narrow strip of black lava beach, and speculated that this was where he landed. I circled a hundred feet above the water. On the second pass, I impulsively decided to touch down. A slight crosswind complicated the final approach and I floated onto the soft, fine-grained, black lava beach. The plane's wheels sank into the sand. Too late, I realized, I was in trouble. I pulled hard on the stick, trying to hold the plane's tail from rising, but as the front tires dug deeper into the sand, the nose pitched forward, planting itself firmly into the beach.

Kipsoi, spear in hand, hurtled into the front cockpit, along with a loose assortment of gear. The tail of the plane ended up pointing straight into the sky, while the three of us, bodies in somersault positions, were pressed against the windshield, struggling to extricate ourselves from the cockpit. Although we were stunned and bruised, no one was hurt. Only Kipsoi seemed unfazed. Never having been in a plane before, he was probably under the impression that all landings terminated this way.

I was in a state of near shock, trying to absorb the magnitude of my miscalculation. After crawling out the window, I struggled to pull the tail of the plane down to a horizontal position—a desperate and futile act. Almost unnoticed, the sun slipped behind the western shore of the lake, beneath the Loriu Hills draped in purple shadows, ominous and eerie in the dying light of day.

We had crashed on a deserted island on a lake in one of the remotest parts of Africa. Krystyne, magnificently calm, immediately recognized that we were there for the night, without supplies or foreseeable means of rescue. I remained focused on the plane. Although I managed to right it, the propeller was badly bent, which meant there was a good chance the engine crankshaft was damaged. I wondered vaguely if I could straighten the propeller blades: a forlorn hope, since they were made of tempered steel and, at 2,700 revolutions per minute, would fly apart if they were less than perfectly symmetrical. Our situation was not encouraging.

I turned to the plane's HF long-distance radio. I knew that Wolfgang regularly switched on his radio at six in the evening to scroll through the African frequencies while waiting for nightfall. Shortwave reception, particularly from North America, is better at night because of less atmospheric interference. Besides, he liked to monitor the police frequency between 18:00 and 19:00 hours—a custom followed by most of the isolated settlements in the northern territories. Unexpectedly, I reached him, but he was barely readable. I informed him that we had crashed, that we were unharmed and required rescue. The transmission was short, our last communication (HF radio transmission should only be operated with the motor running) before the remaining power from the battery drained into the darkness that enveloped our small world like a thick blanket. We were on our own.

An hour later, at the north end of the beach, we saw a flicker of a light and soon a group of Turkana fishermen walked towards us. The sight of other human beings with a boat gave us encouraging thoughts of rescue. Kipsoi, though, panicked, quickly putting his arms around Krystyne, entreating her to save him from his enemies. He was terrified of the Turkana, for they detested the Samburu and he believed they were likely to harm him. The fishermen approach us laughing and gesticulating, which we interpreted as friendly. They were fascinated by the sight of our wounded *ndege*. Our predicament was just one more incomprehensible example of the white man's curious behaviour.

These fishermen were the outcasts of the Turkana tribe, which explained their presence on the island. In spite of the fact that Lake Turkana is filled with fish (Nile perch and tilapia), rich in protein, the Turkana remain a nomadic tribe, subsisting on a diet of blood and milk from cattle—they consider fish unclean. Cattle are the tribe's prized possessions, traded and stolen over vast tracts of semi-desert. The Turkana, the most warlike, independent tribe of the Northern Territories, pay no heed to authority, particularly that of Kenya's central government in Nairobi.

Despite his terror we had no alternative but to thrust Kipsoi forward as interpreter and he managed to communicate through a mixture of Samburu and Swahili. The Turkana fishermen were intrigued by our presence. They invited us to join their encampment at the far end of the beach. Sitting around their small fire we watched the younger men wade into the murky shallows, naked bodies glistening in the flickering light of the fire, as they tossed a large seine out into the water for fish.

Slowly, they drew their net to shore, hand over hand, in slow rhythm to a low guttural chant, interspersed with grunting, an evocative kind of panting. Kipsoi explained that it was an invocation to the lake to release its fish. The effort, however, produced only two small tilapia, one of which we bought for fifty Kenyan shillings (ten cents). Baked in a hot bed of sand piled against the rocks of the open fire, the fish—our Christmas dinner—though meagre and bony, tasted delicious. The older men ate nothing, content to sit around the fire talking and smoking foul-smelling cigarettes. In the meantime, three or four of the younger boys, to our amazement, sneaked back to the plane to sniff aviation fuel which they managed to suck out of our plane's tanks through the fuel vent.

Krystyne and I looked at each other in wonder at our predicament. The eerie strangeness of our surroundings drew us closer together. The night sky, a blizzard of stars, turned a royal blue, then black as soot. Gradually, a full moon rose from behind the dark lava ridge, flooding the beach in a luminous, buttery light. Soft, warm breezes drifted in from the water, over the sand, and up the escarpment.

Sitting on the beach, overlooking the still water, our anxiety over rescue faded into the beauty of the night. While we might not have chosen to be stranded on South Island, Christmas night, eight thousand miles from home, imprisoned on that remote and beautiful beach, together, alive and unhurt, we found much to wonder at and to be grateful for.

Later, when it was time to sleep, the fishermen invited us to share space with them under a small crescent sail they had spread over the sand, but the warmth of the evening, the magic of the star-filled sky, had us preferring to lie in the open, not under canvas. One by one the older fishermen crawled under the sail, grunting and shuffling for their allotted space. The younger ones, in due course, returned from the plane and sat around the fire talking and laughing in loud excited voices until they, too, crawled under the sail, filling the last of the space. Within an hour, the reason for this odd behaviour became clear to us. The wind rose without warning into a gale and whipped the beach into a volcanic sandstorm. We scrambled to seek protection under the sail amongst a tangle of arms and legs. Eleven Turkana fishermen, Kipsoi, Krystyne, and I huddled under a sail not much larger than a bedsheet. It made for a restless night.

———————————

The wind rattled all night over South Island, subsiding only slightly before the long-awaited arrival of dawn. The press of bodies eventually drove us out from under the sweat and stink of the sail into the early-morning light. The volcanic landscape had lost the shadows of the night and stood barren and stark in the first rays of sunlight. The windswept lake was far too rough to cross by boat to the mainland. The prospect of another night—and perhaps longer—on that desolate, burnt-out island slowly took root in our consciousness. Wolfgang's problematic rescue effort was little more than a pious hope. I remembered seeing nothing on the mainland larger than a canoe and a fibreglass dory with part of its side missing, neither of which stood a chance of remaining afloat in such a rough sea.

South Island is approximately ten miles across open water from the main shore. Winds in that part of the Rift often blew steadily at twenty-five to thirty knots for a week or longer without cessation. Wolfgang would never in a thousand years attempt the crossing himself, and who else was there to volunteer?

Our best hope, it seemed, was the Turkana fishermen. I proceeded to negotiate, using Kipsoi as an interpreter, but they were cunningly aware of our situation and drove a stiff bargain. Following an hour's argument, they agreed to paddle us the six or seven hours it would take to reach Loiengalani by open canoe—once the wind subsided. In the meantime, there was little alternative but to settle down and wait.

We were resigned to enduring another day of pounding heat; there was no shade anywhere on the island. By nine o'clock the sun forced us to seek shelter under the wing of the plane. As we huddled like refugees, the first pangs of hunger gnawed at us; aside from the one small tilapia, divided by three, we had not eaten for twenty-four hours. More importantly, we had finished our last bottle of water. There was only the lake water to drink, and that almost certainly would make us sick. Our situation, while not life-threatening, was turning more and more uncomfortable.

Suddenly, from far off, we heard a miraculous sound: the *thwop, thwop, thwop* of army helicopters approaching South Island. The noise grew louder and, within minutes, two army attack helicopters loaded with rockets and machine guns swooped in over the lava ridge towards the beach. The terrified Turkana scattered, abandoning their boats, fishing nets, and personal gear. The helicopters hovered, before settling onto the sand next to the plane. I confess that at that moment I felt a pang of guilt over my skepticism about Wolfgang's ability to mount a rescue effort.

The helicopters whipped up clouds of sand in the downdraught of their rotating blades. Emerging from the swirling mixture of wind and sand strode an African army major, dressed immaculately in khaki uniform, who informed us that he was here to transport the two of us back to Loiengalani.

"What about our Samburu?" asked Krystyne.

"No room," said the major, tersely. "We are here to pick up two *muzungus* (white people) only." Obviously comfortable giving orders, he fully expected them to be obeyed.

"I'm not leaving without the Samburu and that's final," Krystyne exclaimed, standing in front of the towering major in her bathing suit. She looked him straight in the eye without wavering. I thought she was taking her role as "mama" to Kipsoi a little too seriously, but she remained adamant. The major was in a quandary. He had taken a decision in front of his men. In the meantime, blowing sand and the noise of the helicopters lent urgency to the situation. Had Krystyne recognized the major's option was to simply leave without us? To his credit and my relief, the major turned to me and asked if we were really responsible for the Samburu's welfare. I nodded apologetically.

Two minutes later, the helicopters, packed with soldiers, Krystyne, Kipsoi, and me, hovered over the beach in a cloud of whirling sand. As we lurched out over the whitecaps of the lake I cast one final look at my plane, lying broken and sad on the beach. At that moment I made a solemn promise to myself to return and rescue her no matter the cost.

———————————

Back at Wolfgang's lodge, the major and his men joined us for a late breakfast. Our rescue was a big event for Loiengalani, especially for Wolfgang, who basked in well-deserved praise. He had managed to persuade the major to temporarily abandon his task of suppressing rebel factions of the Turkana tribe to fly the helicopters into South Island. The rescue was viewed as a positive diversion by the major and his men whose only task was the constant harassment of the Turkana. The Turkana's raids on other tribes, stealing cattle and creating unrest along the eastern shores of Lake Turkana, had long since become a way of life. The army's ill-judged and unprovoked attacks on the Turkana merely aggravated what was a volatile part of the country.

The major, a Kikuyu, was an educated man, well read, civilized, and socially sophisticated. He viewed the Turkana as essentially lawless, beyond the influence of Nairobi and the army; he thought it would be better to simply leave them alone. These people had managed to live on their own for hundreds of years without laws and regulations promulgated by the federal government. What discipline could the army possibly hope to impose on the Northern Frontier District? Still, he was a soldier, and it was his duty to follow orders, even though privately he questioned the wisdom of forcing modern society's laws on nomadic tribes. It inevitably led to misunderstandings and tragedy.

After breakfast, the major instructed his men to prepare the helicopters for departure. We exchanged addresses, arranging to meet him and his wife in Nairobi in ten days' time. There was much shaking of hands, even a smart salute from the major to Krystyne following an exchange of family photos, prior to their exit from the lodge. The major's refusal to accept payment for our rescue was refreshing and quite unusual for the Kenyan army.

Twelve minutes later Miglia came running into the lodge to inform us that the major's helicopter had been shot down by a rebel Turkana's automatic Kalashnikov 47. A bullet had hit the fuel tank, and the helicopter had exploded into a ball of flame. Everyone on board had been killed, including the major. We were stunned and silent with the shock of this news, which soon spread afar, creating panic amongst the Turkana. The tribesmen, anticipating harsh reprisals from Nairobi, began to scatter over the desert. Lake Turkana was immediately declared a war zone. No one was permitted to leave or enter the Loiengalani Lodge compound. Once again, we found ourselves prisoners of circumstances, though this time not of our own making.

Shock at the death of the major, the pilot, and his three men, and our confinement to Loiengalani, had me restless and fretting, incapable of action or decision. The desire to rescue my plane from South Island only added to my frustration and feelings of helplessness. The day following the downing of the helicopter, I managed to contact the Flying Doctors Service hangar at Wilson Airport using Wolfgang's HF radio, to have a conversation with the temperamental Colin Davies. He registered little surprise on hearing of my accident, as if such an event were not unexpected. He asked no questions as to why the hell I tried to land on South Island. His attention was focused on the extent of the damage and what parts— beyond a replacement propeller—were required from Nairobi. He said he could manage to fly up to Loiengalani with his friend and pilot Pat Neylan in two days' time.

"What was the security situation up there? Would it pose a problem?" Colin's voice over the HF radio was matter-of-fact more than concerned. The helicopter crash had already been reported in the Nairobi newspapers.

"Nothing going on at South Island," I joked, rather half-heartedly. "We'll ensure that the Loiengalani strip is open for your arrival." I was anxious to minimize any complications that might discourage him from coming as soon as possible. In fact, providing we all stayed within the Loiengalani compound or on South Island the security risk was negligible. But the prospect of even a two-day delay keeping us prisoners in Loiengalani seemed like an eternity.

Boredom made the hours crawl. We had nothing to occupy us except one shared paperback novel and a set of dreary meals served in stifling heat under a swarm of flies. The gates of the lodge were padlocked, guarded by soldiers: no passage was permitted beyond the pathetic wire fence without an armed escort. A young, good-looking African second lieutenant called Robert Obomo was in charge. He had commandeered Wolfgang's HF radio, depriving poor Wolfgang of his one distraction in life beyond that of drinking beer. The army also took possession of the lodge as its headquarters while it prepared an assault on the Turkana. They demanded that Wolfgang provision the soldiers without payment, and he had little choice.

The soldiers lolled about the main lodge, feet on the furniture, smoking, chatting, and ordering drinks from the bar. Streams of Turkana women, children, old men, and cattle moved slowly past the camp heading north up the eastern shore of the lake as a diversionary feint to mislead the army. Meanwhile, the Turkana men responsible for shooting down the helicopter escaped south into the mountains. For two days we witnessed this unending, weary procession passing within sight of the soldiers, who both feared and distrusted the Turkana. The soldiers grew increasingly restless, tired of waiting for instructions, sitting, cursing, swatting flies in the suffocating heat. Mainly Kikuyu, they were dressed in hot khaki uniforms, and sweated profusely, unaccustomed to the punishing heat of the desert. They longed to return to their farms in the cool, rich coffee and tea plantations of the highlands north of Nairobi.

It was demoralizing for Lieutenant Obomo to receive conflicting orders through a command structure directed by Nairobi, three hundred miles away and completely out of touch. The Kenyan army was no match for the Turkana, whose guerrilla instincts were vastly superior to Kenya's conscripted, badly trained young recruits. Day after day the families of the Turkana followed the few water holes buried beneath the desert sand, while the Turkana warriors waited patiently in the mountains for an attack everyone predicted would occur before the arrival of the new moon.

Colin Davies and Pat arrived two days later at Loiengalani in Pat's Cessna 180, an older version of my plane, which had flown into most of the landing strips of East Africa. The plane, with its baggage hold crammed with spare tools, a second-hand prop, and an extra supply of emergency fuel, was five hundred pounds over legal weight. Pat, an old hand at flying in Africa, had landed his plane once before on South Island, ten years before, but he was clearly nervous about flying in there again. However, Colin had talked him into leaving his flower farm in Naivasha to fly into South Island on the promise of payment of $200. He needed the money, yet his business could hardly afford his absence, so he was impatient, anxious to return as soon as possible.

Pat paced up and down the Loiengalani porch, while Colin grilled me over and over on the extent of the damage to my plane. It was important to determine exactly what spare parts and tools would be required on South Island. With me as a second passenger, the plane would be seriously overloaded. It was understood by everyone that Krystyne would have to wait for us in the lodge.

On the flight to South Island, I was in the back seat with the spare propeller across my legs, while the other two concentrated on navigation and the upcoming landing on the island. Pat circled South Island twice, flying low over a small plateau three-quarters of a mile from the beach. He was extremely tense as he trimmed the controls on his final approach onto a narrow ledge of windswept sand and rock, which appeared to me a most unlikely place to land a plane. I realized then I had much to learn about flying in Africa.

We settled down on the hardened surface and, with locked brakes, soon stopped short of a rock face that eliminated any chance of an overshoot. Rivers of sweat ran down the back of Pat's neck and inside his collar; he was too old for that kind of flying. We taxied across open ground to the edge of the escarpment, avoiding large boulders that lay scattered in the waving desert grass. My damaged plane lay broken just as I had left it, three hundred yards below on the beach. There was no sign of life anywhere. The fishermen had departed; only the wind whispering up the escarpment offered a forlorn greeting.

We lugged the forty-pound propeller and the bag of tools under the liquid blaze of noon down to the beach and began to work on disassembling the old propeller. The sun beat mercilessly on the black lava sand like a blast furnace, making it difficult to breathe. Colin did most of the work, saying hardly a word beyond his gruff instructions to pass a tool or to hold a part. The cowlings had to be removed and the seals broken on the damaged propeller. Critical measurements were required between the propeller and the back plate attached to the crankshaft to ensure proper alignment. Pat paced back and forth in the hot sand, impatient with Colin's methodical attention to detail.

Three hours passed. We exhausted our supply of drinking water, which only added to Pat's desire to complete the job and get off the island. Afternoon shadows lengthened over the beach; the day had run its course and night was approaching. The pressure on Colin to complete the job before the light failed threw him into a sullen and uncommunicative mood. Pat kept reminding him they needed time to fly back to Naivasha before dark. His landing strip at the flower farm had no lights.

The replacement propeller was installed, the cowlings refastened, and careful measurements had been checked and rechecked. I started up the engine and its low-throated roar, reassuringly familiar, gave no hint of crankshaft problems. How then to get the plane off the beach, since it was impossible to taxi the plane in the soft sand? Colin had reduced the amount of air in the tires to flatten their surface area. The combination of the plane's propeller pulling at full throttle and Colin and Pat pushing the wing struts managed to inch the plane over the sand to the western end of the beach; it was a time-consuming and exhausting business.

A debate then took place amongst us: was it or was it not safe to attempt a takeoff from the beach? It was a tough call. The longer we discussed it, the less certain the outcome and the more agitated Pat became about time. I speculated that, once the plane achieved any momentum, the lift from the wings would reduce the weight on the wheels, allowing the plane to gain acceleration over the soft sand. But the first fifty yards would be tricky. The beach was long enough to accommodate a prolonged takeoff roll, but whether the plane could reach the critical takeoff speed of fifty-three knots in such soft sand without nosing over was the unanswered question.

Ultimately, this kind of decision rests with the pilot; it was my plane and I was the pilot. Eyes turned to me, seeking a decision. Without a word I climbed into the cockpit, started up the motor again, went through the pre-takeoff checks, and indicated to the others that they were to commence pushing.

The plane wallowed in the sand, inching forward far more slowly than I expected, like a slow-motion film or one of those dreams where, regardless of effort, movement remains beyond reach. The wheels pushed rather than rolled through the sand as the engine raced under full throttle. The propeller blades whipped sand into my companion's faces as they pushed with everything they had on the wing struts. Slowly, the plane lumbered forward, gaining acceleration, though hardly enough to realize any appreciable lift from the wings.

Then, suddenly, the plane took a sickening veer down the slope of beach towards the water. Unable to correct for direction by stepping on the right brake, for fear the wheel would dig into the soft sand and flip the plane on its nose again, I had no choice but to let it take its own direction. Committed, I maintained acceleration, badly off course, heading straight towards the lake.

"Christ Almighty, I'm going to hit the water," I thought. My only hope was that I could gain enough speed to hydroplane on the surface of the water and then possibly maintain or increase speed and lift the plane into the air over a sandbank that stretched beyond the water directly ahead.

The plane hit the water, hydroplaned, increasing speed straight towards the low-lying sandbank. At the last second I yanked back on the stick, hoping to clear the sandbank, in what was almost one of the most spectacular air stunts of all time. Instead, the left wheel caught the sandbank, the undercarriage crumpled, and the plane nosed into a gigantic spray of mud, sand, and water that ended with a sickening thud. I was thrown against the shoulder straps and my head and neck snapped forward with such force I momentarily blacked out. The next thing I remember seeing was a soggy mixture of mud and sand sliding slowly down the Plexiglas windshield. In the darkness of the cabin I sat, immobile, stunned by my second serious miscalculation in less than a week.

I vaguely remember hearing the voices of Colin and Pat as they ran down the beach, worried that I was seriously injured. Since the door of the cockpit was partially jammed, I would have to extricate myself once again through the cockpit window. I could hardly comprehend this turn of events. How was it possible? I prided myself on being a competent pilot, on having good judgment.

Colin and Pat arrived, having walked around the small bay onto the sand spit, where the wrecked plane lay on its side. The aluminium cabin roof had a significant wrinkle along the left side; a bad sign, indicating the main spar of the port wing was at least bent or possibly broken. The undercarriage had been ripped away from the fuselage. Major repairs were necessary before this plane could ever hope to fly again. The three of us walked back up the escarpment to Pat's plane in silence. I was utterly mortified.

Colin and Pat dropped me off at Loiengalani before flying on to Naivasha. There was no room for Krystyne and me along with all the tools and spare parts. They left feeling badly, while I needed time alone to collect myself. I was facing the complete write-off of my plane and considerable loss of pride. Even Krystyne's sympathetic understanding caused additional agony.

All night the howling of the wind and the doum palm leaves whipping and slapping the sides of the *banda* kept me awake. Demons swept over me, again and again, as I tried to recover from my abortive takeoff. I twisted and turned in a sweat under the hot mosquito netting. The night pressed in, suffocating. Had the whole African adventure come to this? Could the malaria pills, Lariam, known to cause delusional side effects, have contributed to such lapses of judgment? Fifteen years of flying without an incident, and suddenly two crashes in a week. There had to be some rational explanation. Self-interrogation in the early-morning darkness tightened like the slow turn of a screw.

By the next morning the atmosphere at Loiengalani had become increasingly tense. A German tourist trying to reach the lodge in a convoy of Land Rovers had been shot dead by the Turkana. The German embassy was upset and was exerting pressure on the Kenyan government. The Kenyan authorities, anxious to avoid an international incident, were frantically instructing the army to evacuate remaining tourists from those areas exposed to the Turkana rebels. Hysterical communications from Nairobi streamed in over the HF radio, complicating Lieutenant Obomo's already impossible task of trying to control the rebels with inexperienced soldiers. Nairobi ordered reprisals against the Turkana, an inane instruction, since escalation was likely to throw the whole Northern Frontier District into civil war.

On our fourth day at Loiengalani, in the middle of mounting confusion, a French photographer driving a white Suzuki pulled up unannounced at the gates of the lodge. Unshaven and covered in dust, he seemed unaware of any crisis with the Turkana. He strode into the compound as if on a Western film set, ignoring the heavily armed soldiers who demanded to know who he was and where he had come from. His unexpected presence unnerved them, since they mistakenly thought the roads were blocked and no vehicle could pass without the army's knowledge or permission.

Serge Petillon, a tall, rugged-looking young man from Bretagne in the north of France, had just driven across the Chalbi Desert alone—a risky undertaking. He was on a three-month photographic assignment in Kenya for a travel organization. His three-week-old beard, puffy cheeks, and rather flat face gave him the look of a pugilist, a toughness that was strangely attractive. His large frame held the intensity of a coiled spring, one that could unleash surprising strength, and his independent demeanour could appear menacing, so people approached him with caution, if at all.

I watched with interest as he was immediately surrounded by soldiers, whose questions he found offensive. He drew himself up—he was a head taller than his interrogators—and volunteered little information, which only encouraged further suspicion.

"Where have you come from?" a young corporal asked.

"The desert," Serge replied, looking at him with contempt.

"The desert is large. Where in the desert? Who are you?"

"I am a photographer. French," he added, as if France might make a difference. An increasing number of soldiers gathered round him.

"Show me your passport," said the corporal.

"It's in the car," Serge replied, making no effort to get it.

"What are you doing here? Are you aware this is a war zone?" The corporal raised his voice in order to impress the others.

"So Kenya is at war with its people?" Serge asked.

"The Turkana are very bad, they steal cattle," volunteered a young soldier next to the corporal. "We must kill them."

"The Kenyan government is also bad; it steals from its people," said Serge. He appeared cynical, like most outsiders, about the state of affairs in Kenya. "Look," he went on, "I'm thirsty and tired of your questions." He pulled his soiled knapsack from the front seat of the car and swung it over his shoulder, turning his back on the soldiers before heading towards the lodge.

The corporal raised his rifle, pointed it at Serge's back, and barked, "Halt!"

Unconcerned, Serge nonchalantly crossed the open stretch of sand, past the army vehicles, up the stone steps, taking them two at a time, until he reached the lodge, where he strode onto the terrace, sat down at the bar, and ordered himself a beer. His casual disregard for authority was impressive. How had he managed to slip through the area north of Baragoi, officially designated a war zone and crawling with soldiers? Every track had a roadblock. When we questioned him, he merely shrugged his shoulders and smiled.

Krystyne speaks fluent French and we were the only other tourists in the lodge so it was not long before we engaged Serge in conversation. He had been on his own for over a month, photographing and writing in remote areas beyond those that might interest the normal tourist. Serge was a loner. If an area or tribe interested him, he pursued it, regardless of the obstacles in his way. Since the three of us were confined to quarters, before long we became co-conspirators and friends. We speculated as to how we might extricate ourselves from the army's incompetence and Wolfgang's outrageous charge of $130 per night for a rundown cabin and three meals of goat meat a day.

Eventually, we persuaded the lieutenant, Robert Obomo, to provide us with an armed escort over the Kibrot Pass, through to South Horr, and across the El Bartia Plains as far as Baragoi. Lieutenant Obomo had begun his career as a member of Richard Leakey's paramilitary force in the Kenya Wildlife Service during the 1980s. Richard Leakey, the son of Louis and Mary Leakey, the famous anthropologists, was director general, and had earned the reputation of having single-handedly saved the game parks from collapse.

Leakey had been determined to eradicate poaching and had built up a tough and highly effective force of game wardens. His men, intensely loyal and highly professional, were frequently sent to Israel for military training, and had been ordered to shoot to kill when they encountered poachers—no second chance. It was Leakey's idea to burn five tons of ivory tusks in a publicity stunt that won President Moi and Kenya international acclaim. However, Leakey had become so successful that the president began to fear him and had him removed from his post. With Leakey gone and much of his private army disbanded, the management of the game parks slowly reverted to incompetence, a decline that paralleled Kenya's deteriorating tourist industry and economy.

Lieutenant Obomo was a soldier born to command. Confident and alert, he had the wiry physique and coiled energy of a leopard. He was not going to take any chances with his charge of three tourists and twenty-five soldiers when we finally pulled out of Loiengalani under the soulful gaze of Wolfgang, who stood in his undershirt in the half-light of early morning. He gave strict instructions that there was to be no stopping en route to Baragoi. The convoy consisted of six army jeeps; Krystyne and I were jammed, shoulder to shoulder, in Lieutenant Obomo's jeep between soldiers who were mere boys, wide-eyed and frightened, armed with automatic guns and grenades. Serge drove his Suzuki, accompanied by three soldiers, an army vehicle in front and behind.

The jeeps bumped and lurched over the rock-strewn track cutting through the mountain passes, while loaded rifles swayed back and forth under our chins. Parts of the route, especially through the mountains, were no more than washed-out riverbeds. Our slow progress improved once we reached the silt-covered Horr Valley, where the rock bed turned into a mixture of sand and red murram. Clouds swirled up from the wheels of the convoy, enveloping us in a cocoon of dust so thick it darkened the blinding glare of the sun. We choked on dust. The jeeps had no suspension, and our efforts to brace ourselves against the sudden lurching and pitching of the vehicles were exhausting.

Lieutenant Obomo's jeep was in the lead. He maintained constant radio contact with the rest of the convoy, and his eyes were alert for ambush and snipers. He searched for the slightest sign of enemy movement on the plunging rock embankments alongside the road. Every turn or cut through the narrow passes held the potential of ambush. Overhanging cliffs and crevices offered perfect protection for snipers who could trap us in a crossfire of bullets. Yet, mile after mile, nothing stirred.

Hours of non-stop driving over rugged tracks of rock and sand, and there was still no sign of the Turkana. Passing through scattered villages we saw abandoned *matatus* and empty daub-and-wattle huts; the men, women, and children had vanished from the villages to wait in the hills for the feuding to die down, for life to return to normal. The Samburu and Rendille, long accustomed to warring raids, viewed the Turkana as not unlike the rainy season; they came in a flash and then disappeared—a phenomenon to be endured, a matter of survival.

At Baragoi, Robert Obomo informed us that we were out of the war zone, and it was now safe to proceed on our own. At the southern limit of his territory he could escort us no farther. We sensed his lingering reluctance to part. Duty called him and his men to return up north to the thankless, unproductive pursuit of the Turkana, but his heart was not in it. He snapped us a salute, turned, and barked out an order that turned the convoy back through the mountain passes into the Kasuit Desert.

We were left standing, three of us, on the main street of Baragoi, eyed by curious Samburu children, who maintained a respectful distance, content to stare at the strange appearance of *muzungus* clutching their plastic bottles of drinking water. Covered in dust, belongings at our feet, unable to communicate, we were aliens from a different planet.

Krystyne and I were now totally dependent on our new-found friend Serge and his Suzuki to get us to Maralal, located several hundred miles north of Nairobi. Though the track ahead was much improved, the soft sand made for a rough ride in a Suzuki, particularly with Serge at the wheel driving with manic impatience. Krystyne rode in the back seat, arms and legs stretched wide to brace herself, while the Suzuki rocked crazily from side to side, leaving behind a tornado of dust, as we crossed the El Barta Plain and then hurtled down a steep winding mountain track. Two hours later, we reached the small town of Maralal, perched on the northern edge of the Lakipia Plateau, where we were able to book ourselves into a civilized safari lodge and luxuriate in our first shower in eight days before proceeding the next morning back to Nairobi.

I continued to fret about my plane, abandoned on South Island. Serge was convinced we could rescue it by floating it across the lake on a raft of canoes and then trucking it down from Lake Turkana to Nairobi. I was skeptical of this idea, having experienced first-hand the high winds and waves of Lake Turkana. There was only one decent-sized canoe on the shore near Loiengalani, and the plane weighed over two thousand pounds. Even if we managed to float it to the mainland, transporting it by truck from Lake Turkana to Nairobi over the rock-strewn tracks we had just covered would probably destroy it. The problem of the plane's rescue became my obsession. Could it be rescued? I dreaded the humiliation of returning to Nairobi and the Flying Doctors Service hangar without it. Krystyne had a more balanced perspective on events: at least we were alive and a new plane could be purchased one day. That did little, however, to deflect my determination: somehow, I would retrieve my wrecked plane and expiate an ignoble loss of pride.

7

Repairs and Reconciliation

I SUPPOSE I now knew how Michel must have felt when he climbed the Flying Doctors Service hangar stairs to face the music after his flight into Sabarei. The news of my crash had preceded my arrival and was the subject of conversation in the pilots' common room. A waiting crowd was eager to hear the details of what had happened at Lake Turkana. There was a surfeit of sympathy, which was hard enough to bear from others, but much worse from the other pilots in the hangar, particularly Trevor Jones. He had narrowly escaped a crash only two weeks earlier and could see I was suffering from a loss of face.

"Scott, there isn't a pilot in Africa that hasn't crashed at some point in their flying career," he assured me. It was true. Every pilot in the hangar had come a cropper at some point; even Benoit had lost part of the undercarriage of a Cessna 402 two years before, although it was considered unwise to mention it. Trevor put his arm across my shoulders in a friendly gesture. It was generally agreed that I should just accept that recovery of the plane was impossible. I was advised to have the electronics stripped out of her and resign myself to buying another plane some day in Canada. This irrefutable logic only doubled my resolve. I had flown over two thousand hours in that plane and I was emotionally bound up in her fate. To leave her on South Island as a monument to my incompetence was simply unacceptable. Besides, a spectacular rescue, assuming it could be achieved, might lead to partial redemption.

The physical difficulty of rescuing a crashed airplane on an island in one of the most remote and hostile parts of Africa, while daunting, was only part of the problem. The Kenyan aviation authorities would need to investigate the accident. The Ministry of Transport bureaucracy was legendary for being obstructive and, depending on whom you dealt with, corrupt. So, my first task was to placate Ministry of Transport officials, located at Kenyatta Airport. Armed with what I hoped would be an acceptable story, I drove along the airport road with a heavy heart.

I reported: "A minor incident in Northern Frontier District with a foreign-registered plane that I intended to fly back to Nairobi, where it could be inspected more easily at Wilson Airport." Luckily, I encountered a reasonable official. This innocuous explanation, to my immense relief and surprise, was accepted at face value. Perhaps the logistical difficulties and expense of transporting a government inspector to the accident site was too daunting for a minor official. In any case, I escaped the clutches of the Ministry of Transport, who could have insisted I pay the costs of their investigation.

The next two weeks were divided between work at the Flying Doctors Service and investigations into my plane's rescue. Although I finished the final draft of the Flying Doctors Service business plan for the upcoming AMREF board meeting in February, my mind was focused on South Island. Colin Davies had lost interest in the fate of my plane, partly, I suspected, due to his conflict-of-interest issue with the Flying Doctors Service and his private airplane maintenance business. He had been forced to resign from the Flying Doctors Service. He needed the lost salary and I believed he attributed his misfortune to me; his feelings of resentment were palpable.

I approached Trackmark, a charter airline that flew relief supplies into the southern Sudan from Lokichokio, an NGO staging post just inside the Kenyan border. The vice-president of operations thought that my plane could be disassembled, loaded onto their Caribou cargo plane, and flown to Nairobi. The cost, though, would be horrendous. And what pilot would ever attempt to try and land a Caribou, a short-field cargo plane—approximately five times the weight and size of my plane, worth millions of dollars, and designed to land on a tarmac—on South Island?

I persuaded a couple of Trackmark pilots on their next run up to Lokichokio to fly over the island and assess the possibility of landing a Caribou where Pat had put down on South Island. Bush pilots flying out of Wilson prided themselves on gutsy flying, but these guys returned saying there was no way a Caribou could ever make it onto that island and live to tell the story. The idea was ridiculous.

What about a helicopter? There was only one in East Africa capable of lifting a plane: the Department of Defence helicopter owned and operated by the army under the direct responsibility of the president of Kenya. Permission from President Daniel arap Moi was unthinkable and the costs unimaginable. I was running out of ideas.

Five days later I received a lucky break. Denis, son of Pat Neylan, who worked for Colin Davies at his controversial private air-maintenance shop, came to see me. He roared into the Flying Doctors Service hangar on his Triumph motorcycle, cocky, young, and full of confidence, in typical "Kenyan cowboy" style.

"Scott, gimme a shot at rescuing your plane," he said, standing in front of me, thumbs hooked into his belt. He was twenty-three years old, and his tanned, boyish face and short haircut made him look like a college student. "I need $1,500 to get started," he said. It was clear from his tone that he felt this was a trifling sum. "I'll have to rent a plane and purchase camping supplies. I have two guys from Colin's shop prepared to help me. We'll camp on the island and work on her until she's ready for you to fly her to the mainland."

There was something endearing about Denis and his boyish confidence, in spite of the fact that he had no track record in rescuing crashed airplanes. But he was an Aircraft Master Engineer (AME), and his desire to prove himself within the Wilson Airport community was irresistible. I badly needed a partner in my obsession, particularly one who believed no job was impossible, so I readily agreed to let him take a crack at it. Recognizing his chance to make a reputation, he shook my hand, saying, "Scott, I won't let you down." I watched him take off on his bike in a cloud of dust, sensing that my acquiescence was an act of desperation verging on folly.

Denis plunged into the task with enthusiasm, collecting a thousand pounds of camping gear, food, and an assortment of tools and spare parts. Two days later, he and his companions were ready to fly to South Island in a rented Cessna 206. Assuming he managed to repair my plane, I agreed to go to Loiengalani myself, and from there he would fly me to South Island. We set predetermined times for daily communication over a portable HF radio, and I watched him and his two African helpers depart from Wilson Airport, as excited as boys leaving for summer camp. Colin Davies, resentful that I was no longer dependent on him, viewed the exercise as a total waste of time and money. I settled into an anxious three-day wait.

On the fourth day Denis's excited voice came over the HF with incredible news. He and his helpers had jury-rigged a temporary fix to the landing gear and enlisted the Turkana fishermen, who had returned to the island, to help push the plane up the escarpment to the landing spot. In Denis's opinion the plane could actually be flown off the island. It scarcely seemed possible.

I consulted with Jim and Colin whose experience rescuing planes all over Africa was invaluable. They were astounded. Colin, the best in the business, had of course seen the plane after my abortive take-off, and his assessment was that the plane had undergone serious structural damage. He was adamant that I not fly it before he had had a chance to inspect Denis's work.

It was clear that a second expedition to South Island was necessary. Colin became the unofficial leader, recharged with the idea and excitement of rescue. He supervised the collection of great quantities of angle iron, pop rivets, aluminum sheeting, and a portable gas-powered compressor for a rivet gun. There was no Flying Doctors Service pilot prepared to risk flying into South Island, but they would transport us at no cost to Loiengalani. Denis, following his father's lead, had mastered the challenge of landing on the escarpment overlooking the infamous beach. He would fly us into South Island, following our rendezvous at Loiengalani. Considerably chastened, I regained confidence and faith that I might be able to fly my plane again and soon be rid of that accursed island.

Colin and I hitched a ride in a Flying Doctors Service plane that was on a routine flight to Lodwar on the western side of Lake Turkana; it was not much of a diversion for the pilot to drop us off at Loiengalani. The three-hour flight passed without a word spoken. I felt awkward in Colin's presence, even though I had grown to like him. I knew he disapproved of my unbridled enthusiasm—there was something about his taciturn manner that brought it out in me. His short, square frame and pugnacious jaw, tense and uncompromising, spoke of his disappointment that it was Denis and not he who had won my gratitude. I sensed underneath his gruff exterior a warmth that was almost impossible to reach. It was as if the world had simply overlooked the full compass of his humanity—somehow, he disguised it. Krystyne saw it, though. "Here is a man," she said, "that would attract the maternal instincts of any woman." All I knew was that I was now totally dependent on his skill and judgment, no matter what he thought of me.

The streams of Turkana refugees had long since disappeared into the northern desert. The rebels were still hiding in the mountains safely beyond the range of the army, resigned to their miserable station at Loiengalani. Wolfgang, beer in hand, received us as if we were important dignitaries arriving from Nairobi. The South Island saga had become a financial boon for Wolfgang, as well as providing a sense of purpose to his lonely existence. Denis was standing by when we arrived, his Cessna 206 ready to transport us and a fresh load of equipment and supplies to the island.

My heart leapt as I caught sight of my plane on top of the escarpment as Denis banked onto his final approach. It looked ready to fly.

No less than a miracle could have resurrected the broken structure I had abandoned only ten days previously. We landed and walked over to where it sat. The landing gear had been fastened to the fuselage with sisal rope wound tightly in an intricate weave of complicated knots. It was ingenious and apparently solid. Colin circled the plane, inspecting the work without saying a word.

"Take it apart. We're starting over again," he said finally, wiping the back of his hand across his sweating forehead and then onto the seat of his short pants. This brutal assessment was accepted without complaint from Denis who knew his place next to Colin. Over the next two hours the plane was methodically reduced to its former status, broken and graceless, stricken once more to the ground.

Colin then took a pair of cutting shears to the area known as the saddle, and opened the belly of the plane (part of the fuselage that cradled the landing gear), creating a huge gaping wound. His unrelenting attack on the fuselage, excising suspect parts, was like a surgeon opening the chest of a patient riddled with cancer. Doubts only led to larger and deeper incisions. It was hard to watch. As he dismantled Denis's work, I wondered if Colin was secretly enjoying reducing my plane to its former state, incapable of flight. There was little we could do or say, however, for Colin's authority was absolute. His aviation experience and skill in repairing planes was indisputable. We had no choice but to follow his terse instructions and remain silent.

The afternoon wore on under the punishing heat of South Island, pounding us into submission. There was no sign of life anywhere. The shimmer of hot air reflecting off the black lava rock distorted the landscape. Occasionally a five-minute break was called and we had a drink of water under the shade of the wings; otherwise we worked in silence, or at most a monosyllabic exchange about some piece of equipment or the search for a tool. It was too hot to engage in conversation; repairs to the plane became our common focus. The African helpers had set up a tripod to carry the weight of the plane once the undercarriage had been removed. Finally, Colin stepped back to admire his work on the stripped fuselage, now hanging in its sling like a half-eaten carcass.

"There," he said with satisfaction. "Now we can put her back together." He wiped his hands again on the back of his shorts and called for the rivet gun. The work took on a different pace and rhythm; he measured every step of the reconstruction carefully, checking and rechecking joints, supports, and surfaces. It was a privilege to watch Colin work; his use of angle iron was original, far beyond the imagination or skill of a typical aircraft mechanic. His methodical attention to detail, combined with his understanding of the stresses placed on the structure, illustrated a streak of genius.

Over 90 per cent of an airplane's fuselage consists of lightweight materials designed to maintain the craft's shape rather than to support direct structural loads associated with the plane's undercarriage. Like Buckminster Fuller's famous geodesic dome, an aircraft's design is integrated and self-supporting, capable of absorbing unusual loads and stresses from the overall structure itself. Unlike most other constructions, it does not rely upon a foundation. In the case of an airplane the design itself *is* the foundation. Only the area directly connected to the undercarriage can support the total weight of the airplane, and this had been entirely ripped away.

Colin's challenge was therefore to design and install support for the landing gear that could take the full weight of the aircraft and yet not damage the fragile structure of the fuselage. It was like trying to affix a landing structure to an eggshell. He gave no hint as to how he proposed to accomplish the task. He merely set about it, instructing us to pass him a tool from amongst the accumulation of scattered equipment or to start up the gas generator or to cut a piece of angle iron or rivet a section of aluminum over an exposed part of the fuselage. He preferred to work in silence, ignoring us altogether.

We remained on the island for three days and the work routine hardly varied. Half an hour before sunset we packed up the tools, set them under a tarpaulin, and clambered down the escarpment to the beach for a swim. One of us remained posted on guard to watch for crocodiles, while the others ducked into the murky but blissfully refreshing water for a swim. I remembered that Peter Beard had a photograph of a man's leg taken from the stomach of a crocodile near Loiengalani. Swimming in Lake Turkana was not without risk.

There were more crocodiles breeding in Lake Turkana than any other place in Africa. A crocodile's stealthy approach, barely detectable, could suddenly erupt into an explosion of energy, turning the water into a boil as it clamped its jaws on an unsuspecting victim, dragging him under water until he drowned. To be eaten by a crocodile was a monstrous and revolting proposition, and yet the Turkana remained amazingly casual about the danger from these reptiles. This, in spite of the number of people killed or maimed by crocodiles each year in Lake Turkana, which over time had become legendary. As a result, we didn't remain in the water for long.

The lake water, non-potable, was nevertheless clean and acceptable for cooking. After our swim, we would fill a couple of plastic containers and transport them up onto the escarpment as the evening fell into night. Our African helpers, John and Joseph, made a campfire whose flames flicked shadows over the one lone acacia tree on the island, which shaded our encampment. Two large tarpaulins pegged onto the open ground served our needs: one for storing supplies of food, tools, and our HF radio; the other for sleeping. Our one meal a day consisted of baked beans and warm beer.

The evening's conversation often turned to the Flying Doctors Service, money, and political problems, and from there to the organization's personalities. Inevitably, talk drifted from the Flying Doctors Service to the political disintegration and endemic corruption that plagued the country. Kenya's political situation was in turmoil. An election was due and, while the opposition was divided, the ruling party under President Daniel arap Moi was not only corrupt but brutal in dealing with the slightest sign of opposition or unrest. As a result, there were countless incidents of bloodshed, including one that had police entering the Anglican cathedral in Nairobi and beating up refugees, even the archbishop. The general disintegration of the country was a subject that haunted the likes of Colin and Denis who had staked their careers on Kenya's questionable future. Denis, being young, remained optimistic that somehow things would work out, but Colin considered himself a victim of circumstance and he chafed at the realization.

Voices slowed as we lay on our backs gazing up at the sky. I wondered about my life after Africa. Although we had only been in Kenya five months the possibility of returning to a business career in Toronto seemed increasingly remote. Yet it would remain a preoccupation that returned regularly over the next two years. Eyelids grew heavier as one by one we fell silent and thoughts of the future drifted into sleep.

Colin worked virtually non-stop, sunrise to sunset, and on the fourth day the plane was off the sling and ready to fly. Though badly scarred, my plane resembled its former self, in shape at least. But was it airworthy? It was my plane and I was the pilot. Once again the decision rested with me.

Colin had serious reservations about the condition of the port wing. He had discovered a half-inch discrepancy in the measurement of the distance between the port and starboard wing tips and the tail of the aircraft. This suggested the port-side wing spar was bent, cracked, or broken, but it was impossible to determine the exact amount of damage without completely dismantling the wing. That was a job requiring replacement parts from North America.

Colin paced back and forth, his eyes tracing the surface of the port wing, looking for the slightest hint of interior damage. He rocked the wing up and down and, using a dentist's mirror, peered inside the inspection ports looking for cracks or bent metal. The consequences of misjudgment this time would almost certainly be fatal. It would not be possible to recover from a collapsed wing in flight. The plane would simply spin out of the sky. Colin, a registered senior aircraft mechanic, had his professional reputation on the line. If the plane suffered a structural failure following his authorization to fly, his career was finished. The consequences for me as pilot were not worth contemplating. It was Russian roulette.

While the plane had been lying on its side, the Turkana fishermen had drained the fuel out of the tanks, save that which was unreachable through the drain cock. We calculated that the fuel remaining, including a small amount in a jerry can from the gas generator, would be enough for twenty to twenty-five minutes of flying time at most. The flight from South Island to Loiengalani was approximately sixteen minutes, which left little room for error.

Finally, the terrain for takeoff was not level. The first four hundred feet was straight and level, but then the ground sloped down into a depression that extended six or seven hundred feet before rising steeply against the side of the hill. In order to avoid the hill I would have to execute a sharp right turn the moment the plane was airborne, at which point the plane would fly over a steep cliff that fell a hundred feet into the lake below.

This time there was no pressure to get airborne before dark. I paced out the distance carefully, studying every inch of the terrain. My plan was to try and rotate the wheels off the ground before reaching the depression. This would give me additional time and altitude to allow for a gradual right turn out over the water. To become airborne within four hundred feet would require a jump-start with full power and no flaps. Immediately prior to reaching the brow of the downward slope, I would pull on twenty degrees of flaps and ease back the stick.

I climbed into the cockpit, suddenly aware that my legs had gone wobbly. For the first time since I started flying I found myself genuinely frightened at the prospect of takeoff. I remember thinking, "Stay calm, you know exactly what has to be done. Concentrate. This time there can be no mistake."

I started the engine and proceeded meticulously with the pretakeoff checks: the mags, trim, gauges, switches, and flight controls— all gauges in the green. I checked them a second time, just to be sure, gaining more time, my adrenaline pumping. Taxiing close to the edge of the escarpment, I turned the plane, ready for takeoff. Manoeuvring a Cessna 180 on the ground is difficult, because the small wheel at the rear causes the nose of the aircraft to ride high in the air, blocking the pilot's frontal view. I strained to see the direction over the nose and received a thumbs-up from Colin. I was conscious of the others, their eyes glued on me, waiting for the aircraft to start its roll. I had never felt more on my own. Nothing else of importance existed at that moment, nothing besides the execution of a successful takeoff from South Island.

I applied full throttle, maintaining maximum pressure on the brakes, holding the plane stationary. The engine screamed, revs climbing to 3,100 per minute. The plane shook and vibrated as the propeller pulled against the brakes, like a racehorse at the starting gate straining for release. I shot a last look out the side window to Colin as he stepped back from the swirl of dirt raised by the racing propeller. Releasing pressure from the brakes, hunched over the controls, my heart pounding, I leaned forward on the throttle and committed to the takeoff.

I was shocked to find the first twenty feet of the plane's roll slower than anticipated. The prospect of another failure flashed before me as the plane slowly began to accelerate. I leaned down, grabbed the flap handle, and pulled it into the twenty-degree position just as I hit the brow of the slope. I eased the stick back. The timing was perfect. The plane soared like a bird on the wing of a thermal. I had ample time to bank over the water in a gentle right turn, across the blinding sun into shadow, north towards Loiengalani. Below, I sighted the Lilliputian figures of my comrades, standing, hands shielding their eyes against the sun, as they followed my trajectory over the Jade Sea.

The next fifteen minutes disappeared in a blur of relief at being airborne again. Recovery of the plane somehow reaffirmed my personal sense of purpose in Africa. The plane crash, now relegated to a mere setback, was proof that I was human enough to make an error but determined enough to recover. And yes, lessons had been learned. Flying was a serious business requiring uninterrupted concentration. There was no room for hubris.

I touched down at Loiengalani, landing as gently as possible, content to sit in the sweltering heat of the cockpit and wait for the others to arrive. I had a moment to reflect on my escape from South Island and, more importantly, on the support and confidence I had received from Krystyne, who had remained a beacon of good sense throughout my three-week private nightmare. Sitting there immobile, I experienced a rush of well-being unlike anything I had ever experienced in the past.

The drone of the other plane arriving heralded a celebration at Wolfgang's bar, before we refuelled the planes and departed for Nairobi. A small hand pump pulled Wolfgang's emergency fuel supply from two-hundred-litre drums, half each into the planes, enough for the return flight to Wilson Airport. A final farewell to Wolfgang and we took off in tandem, climbing to twelve thousand feet in search of calm air. In the sun's blistering heat of early afternoon, I wondered if this would be my last view of South Island as it slipped, dark and sinister, past the underside of the starboard wing.

———————

It would take four and half months to repair the plane in the Flying Doctors Service hangar. When the port wing was disassembled it was discovered that the rear spar was, in fact, broken, and only the aluminium outside skin had held that part of the wing together. One good jolt from turbulence could have broken the main spar, and the wing would have separated from the fuselage in mid flight. In addition, the engine crankshaft was found to have a hairline crack, which could have resulted in a catastrophic engine failure. These sobering facts were best not dwelt upon.

The famous spear purchased from Kipsoi was mounted over the door of the pilot's common room for the remainder of our time in Africa. The final cost of repairs to the plane far exceeded Kipsoi's asking price of a mere thousand Kenyan shillings—and a plane ride.

8

Life in Nairobi

FOLLOWING OUR RETURN from Lake Turkana, the routine of our life in Nairobi was interspersed with excursions into different parts of the country as our African sojourn swiftly ran from weeks into months. Newspapers wrote of President Bill Clinton's refusal to put United States troops into Bosnia, but for us, time in Africa was measured by the rainy seasons, which came and went, like fall, winter, spring, and summer in northern climes.

My work at the Flying Doctors Service absorbed a five-day work-week. Krystyne, arriving in Nairobi with few introductions, however, wanted a project of her own; one relevant to Africa, a project that would capture her imagination, and it was not long before she found one. She became fascinated by African beads, which soon became her obsession.

Over many centuries, millions of beads found their way into Africa in exchange for slaves, spices, and ivory. They passed through the ancient trade routes of Arabia, from Portugal, from Venice, from the Indian subcontinent, from as far away as China. Africans have long traded beads and worn them as adornment, stringing them into earrings, bracelets, necklaces, headdresses, and into the fabric of their clothing. Some beads can be traced back to centuries before Christ, steeped in the history of migrations criss-crossing the Continent.

Beads are the footprints of religion: Islamic prayer beads, for example, followed the path of Islam from Arabia right across North Africa.

The English word *bead* originated from the Anglo-Saxon *bede*, meaning prayer. In Africa, historically, most women were denied personal possessions aside from their beads, but these they traded with great astuteness, creating what amounted to a form of currency that financed trading in the souks of North Africa. The cowry shell became the financial instrument of the slave trade; at its peak, a prize slave could be bought for several kilos of cowry shells. Their ubiquitous spread permeated the African continent, adorning the secular and religious possessions of tribes deep in the jungles of central Africa.

Krystyne was particularly interested in Islamic prayer beads, called *yussr* beads. These are carved black coral and studded with silver nails in intricate designs. Black coral obtained from the Red Sea, now depleted, has increased in value. Traders transport what can be found across the Red Sea in dhows from Yemen to Djibouti, where the beads make their way south to Nairobi. Krystyne found them in burlap sacks piled in the back rooms of the Asian *dukas* (shops) in the Biashara, the market of downtown Nairobi. Gradually, she became more knowledgeable about their origin and value. She designed a collection of necklaces using the Islamic prayer beads as well as antique silver beads, crafted by Jewish silversmiths in Yemen over a century ago. Some of these silver beads, the *Yahudi* beads, can be traced to 400 BC.

Every morning she set out on foot from the Nairobi Club, in spite of protests from friends who thought it dangerous. Tall, silver-haired, carrying no handbag, wearing no jewellery, she strode amongst throngs of Africans bustling along the crowded N'gong Road down the hill to the centre of town.

She became part of the morning routine for those she met along the way: striding past the outdoor barber whose chair and mirror were propped against the large gum tree in the park, stopping for coffee at the stand-up Maasai Café, the bright orange corrugated-tin shack that served roasted corncobs and fried bananas for breakfast; chatting with the Indian shopkeepers at the Regency Hotel, strolling along Banda Street, behind the mosque, past the garbage and beggars next to the Nairobi city market, until she reached Biashara Street. Here, in the Asian market, filled with *dukas* tightly jammed together, the trading was more serious than in the African sections of Nairobi, the businesses more sophisticated, the competition more cutthroat.

She got to know the owners, gained their confidence, and began to trade in earnest. She spent hours huddled in the back rooms of their shops, picking through beads, sipping sweet tea. She listened patiently to their complaints about the government's unfair treatment of Asians, the increased levels of legislation, higher taxes, and the lack of tourists.

Krystyne's open, engaging nature won the Asian owners over, increased their loyalty along with the flow of precious black coral beads. She enlisted their staff to clean, polish, and string her necklaces into designs that subsequently were sold in Toronto and New York. The search for new supplies of black coral eventually led her to the source, Yemen, which we later visited several times. By the end of our stay Krystyne had earned a reputation in Nairobi and then later in New York for her original designs and rare pieces. Following our return to North America, she exhibited and sold her collection through Bergdorf Goodman on Fifth Avenue, New York.

Krystyne's interest in beads also drew us into the Asian community, a close-knit society that is insular and defensive, under permanent siege in Kenya. Asians, or "coloureds," a euphemism for Indians, have long represented the merchant class of East Africa. The British brought them to Africa from India four and five generations ago, as labour for the building of the railway from Mombasa to Kampala in the 1850s. Their residency has remained tenuous ever since and in the case of Uganda they were forcibly expelled from the country, losing their homes and businesses during the outrageous reign of terror of Idi Amin.

The Asians, mercantilists by tradition, quickly established themselves, with the departure of the British, as the merchants of Nairobi.

Historically, they regarded themselves as superior to the Africans, treating their African employees badly. Once the Africans gained political power they took revenge against the Asians, seizing every opportunity to make their lives as difficult as possible. Racial hatred between the two far exceeded that between the blacks and whites, which seemed to have become no more than a residue of memory from colonial times.

We got to know several Asian families and were invited into their homes. Confidences led to friendship and an understanding of their fears at being a minority in an unsettled environment. Two Asians we knew, one in the construction business and another who owned a hotel, carried loaded pistols on them at all times.

———————

Krystyne and I felt at home in Nairobi. Those serving us in the Nairobi Club, colleagues at the Flying Doctors, the Asian *duka* owners in Biashara, even the expatriate officers of aid agencies, all gained increasing importance in our lives. We acquired friends, acquaintances, a social life, and a perspective on Nairobi that went well beyond that of the passing tourist. More important, our lives allowed us time to engage the manservant in conversation when he delivered tea early in the morning, to talk with the ramp attendants at the hangar, the men who polished beads for Krystyne's necklaces, and the waiters at the restaurants we frequented. Their genuine interest in our welfare was both flattering and endearing—a startling difference from Toronto where such interchanges seemed more focused on the transaction than the participants. Ours had become a slower, gentler world, one that drew us closer to each other and imperceptibly nearer to the human soul of Africa, one that combined eternal beauty and heart-rending sadness.

———————

Plane crash on South Island, Lake Turkana.

Christmas dinner, South Island, Lake Turkana.

Beach landing in Lamu, Kenya.

Zebras on the Serengeti.

Scott and Krystyne, Lake Malawi.

Landing on the Salt Pan, Shaba, Kenya.

Sand dunes—Namib Desert.

Flying over the Kalahari Desert.

Teleki's crater, Lake Turkana.

Low flight up the Skeleton Coast.

Himba girls with CF-WMJ.

Flight along the Luala River Delta.

Dunes of Sössusvlei.

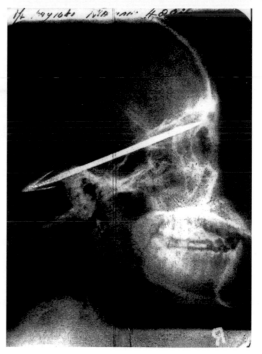

(left) Himba girl running to meet Serge.
(right) Flying Doctors patient who walked into the outreach clinic with an arrow embedded in his skull above the eye. The patient and his eye were saved.

Camels at the edge of the Chalbi Desert

Dwelling near Marsabit.

Rendille family in front of their home.

There was a certain satisfaction at living in Nairobi, learning to adjust to the challenges of being independent and reliant upon our own resources. Krystyne's regular morning excursions to Biashara, her Tuesday visits to the Maasai market, and my quotidian trek to the Flying Doctors Service at Wilson Airport became regular features of our lives, simple and full of harmony. Canada seemed so far away. Letters from home were infrequent; we longed for news from our daughter who was only nineteen, an art student in Montreal, and something of a rebel. Her personal code of ethics frowned on communication, particularly with her parents. We bore this with good grace, but it left a gap in what otherwise was perfect contentment with our lives in Africa.

My attempt to reorganize the Flying Doctors Service was not a large assignment, well within my business experience and capabilities, but in some respects it was more satisfying than running a larger company in Toronto. The staff was passionate about their mission, with a vocation that went beyond making money for themselves or shareholders. Their attitude had an effect on me over the course of our two years in Kenya and, as a result, I underwent a transformation, a re-ordering of my personal goals. I formed insights on the subject of aid for underdeveloped countries, how it should be administered, and by whom. It was very different from the business world with which I was familiar.

And yet I could not shake off my business instincts entirely. I was still keen to measure results, to distinguish the difference between success and failure, to take corrective action. This was an alien concept within the Flying Doctors Service, where responsibilities and accountability—especially financial accountability—tended to be confused. One of my earliest efforts was to rationalize the control of funds between the Service, which incurred all the expense of a medical evacuation service, and the Society, which controlled all the revenues. But the Society remained stubbornly independent, even though their organization was constitutionally mandated to support the Service, which made my goal of financial independence for the Flying Doctors Service virtually impossible.

The AMREF board meeting at which I was to present my recommendations was held in February 1997. The rains had come and gone and the three-or-four-month-long dry season was well entrenched. Even the lush flower beds of Karen, the well-to-do suburb of Nairobi, lay dried and yellow. Lawn sprinklers fought valiantly, but were no match for the tropical sun that burned the grass mercilessly day after day. The city's water levels had fallen dangerously low as the Masinga Reservoir lay exhausted, a giant scab on the northern plateau. Frequent power outages in Nairobi—as many as six or seven a day— placed a premium on gasoline-operated generators. Restlessness had spread across the country, as the drought dug its claws deeper and deeper into the land. Kenya was parched and suffering.

Yellow-billed storks circled high above the N'gong Hills. Vultures sat on dead branches in rows, like hooded monks silent in prayer. Dust and flies swirled indiscriminately. Every morning the nation's eyes looked skyward, searching for early signs of rain. There seemed to be no end to the dry season and the waiting.

The board meeting was a near disaster. I had suggested to Mike Gerber that my plan to amalgamate the Society and the Flying Doctors Service should be distributed to the directors in advance of the meeting. But Mike decided to withhold its distribution, hoping to avoid a political storm; the Society was certain to fight the plan to the death.

My heart sank as I watched the board meeting gradually spin out of control. Emotional arguments turned vitriolic. Chairman Bethuel Kiplagat, a sophisticated African and a born diplomat, struggled vainly for a compromise. The issue turned on the Society's potential loss of independence; they would not allow their long history to be set aside so easily. Kiplagat proposed a committee be struck to find a solution, following which the plan could be resubmitted at the next board meeting in six months' time. It was a reasonable suggestion, although there was little chance of agreement and I could not hang around inactive, waiting for six months. I despaired at the board's indecision.

I suggested the board approve the plan in principle, subject to a working arrangement with the Society, and to my surprise this was accepted. The Society didn't object, since they retained an effective veto over amalgamation. And so the board approved a proposal that was at best unclear; for me, though, a conditional agreement was better than outright rejection or a six-month delay, either of which could only have meant my immediate and premature departure from Africa. I could only hope that sheer momentum would drive the amalgamation through before the next board meeting.

Armed with the board's conditional approval, I set about reorganizing the Flying Doctors Service. Jim was instructed to sell two surplus planes that had been written off on the books. He managed to get $300,000, including a large down payment, which provided enough funds to construct a new Flying Doctors Service Centre to house the nurses, radios, pilots, administration offices, and ambulance facilities at the back of the hangar. Jim opened a separate bank account, organized the Flying Doctors Service as a separate cost centre, and started the process of selecting an architect and contractor for the construction of the medical evacuation centre.

Jim had the old hangar thoroughly cleaned and painted, white with dark green trim. Truckloads of old junk were removed, and within weeks the place was barely recognizable, transformed into a new facility. We optimistically reserved space for the Society in the engineering drawings, confident that at some point they would see the light and join the Flying Doctors Service. The staff was excited, and even Colin Davies, although no longer an employee, had to admit that the improvements were impressive. Within a month, the foundation for the new medical centre at the back of the hangar was poured. The speed with which all this took place was a real achievement; progress of this sort was rarely seen in Africa.

My days were fully occupied with arrangements involving the architect and the contractor, supervising the accountant Stephen Mugungo's new activities, and keeping Jim and Mike Gerber fully informed of developments. Mike's agreement that Jim should control his own banking had put an end to the acrimony between Jim and AMREF's director of finance. There was a general feeling of optimism. At last, the Flying Doctors Service was under control and one day, with the Society's anticipated amalgamation, it would cease to be a financial drag on the AMREF organization.

———————

Over the months of living in Nairobi we befriended many Africans in various stations of society. They were always warm and friendly, and almost without exception they were strongly patriotic and held a belief in the ultimate renaissance of the African continent. This was true of the most sophisticated as well as the simplest, least educated African. We were especially impressed with the Nairobi Club's staff, who over time drew us into the emotional tumble of their lives.

The night clerk, Elijah, who lived behind the reception desk, was the first to break the ice with us. Eager to chat, he would regale us with the latest scandal concerning a member of the club or the political intrigues of the administration. Constantly sweating from repeated attacks of malaria, he was forever rearranging his ill-fitting, soiled clothes that hung from his enormous girth like wash on the line. He had no money, one wife, and seven children who lived "up country." A devout Seventh-day Adventist, he spent hours reading the Bible, believing that God would one day resolve his financial worries. We brought him small presents for his children, and while he was always grateful his reaction remained subdued. Once, unable to stand it any longer, he inquired if we had anything for *him*. I immediately presented him with my cheap pair of sunglasses. His eyes shone with gratitude, convinced this was the beginning of a long and profitable relationship. The thought of him fathering seven children, while barely able to fend for himself, was alarming; however, he was sweet and gentle, and never stopped talking about his children, though he said not a word about his wife.

Living in the Nairobi Club was fine, except for the dining room.

Not only did one have to dress for dinner, but the food was inedible. The club had inherited English turn-of-the-last-century cooking, grey overcooked meat soaked in thick, floury gravy and soggy vegetables. The huge kitchens, originally designed to serve hundreds of meals, smelt of coal, sour milk, and stale grease. The African cook, complete with white chef's hat and surly staff, produced no more than half a dozen meals a day. The cavernous dining room, frequented by only one or two regulars, was dreary and funereal. We soon got into the habit of eating our evening meal at one of the half-dozen acceptable restaurants in Nairobi. While the prospect of dining out every evening initially seemed tiresome, we turned it into an event marking the end of day.

We had to be careful. Nairobi by night was essentially lawless, seedy, and dangerous. The downtown area was wide open, inviting crime. Empty, unlit streets remained the province of stray dogs, the homeless, and prostitutes calling "Darling, darling" to the few cars that circled the back streets like vultures picking through an old kill. Only the disadvantaged walked the downtown streets at night.

A few so-called first-class hotels claimed the central area of town; isolated oases of neon lights, high atriums, and marble entrances, they struggled to maintain the myth that Nairobi was still an international city. Doormen concealed their weapons and carefully unloaded tourists out of taxis, guarding them from the unseen dangers of the African night. Inside, bellhops rushed to and fro, and restaurants catered to a scattering of guests, while mezzanine bars served cocktails to businessmen eyeing prostitutes dressed to kill.

Nairobi's discos, by contrast, were alive with a distinctive African beat that hammered long into the night. Crowded with young people, they pulsated with sexual energy; the African women particularly loved to dance. Occasionally, young white "Kenyan cowboys," intent on a good time, braved the unwelcoming stares of the black clientele. Their sudden appearance, bringing the prospect of money, stirred the prostitutes to abandon the dreams and boasts of black companions, and this could provoke bloody skirmishes that ended at the Nairobi Hospital or the Milimani police station.

The New Florida, a disco built over the Texaco service station at the corner of Loinange and Banda Streets and locally termed the "Mad House," was the most popular, featuring a midnight floor show of bare-breasted dancers in a swirl of feathers that simulated the Folies Bergères. The show was considered a cultural event.

After dinner, Krystyne and I habitually drove to the downtown 680 Hotel Bar for a Baileys Irish Cream before returning to the sepulchral atmosphere of the Nairobi Club. Downtown bars were considered dangerous and mostly deserted. Inevitably, we found ourselves alone except for two or three prostitutes seated round the bar. Lucy, a prostitute, regularly frequented the 680 Bar; approaching middle age, she was not particularly pretty. She befriended us, taking a particular interest in Krystyne, whom she considered to be "a sophisticated lady." She complained regularly that business was hard, what with the lack of tourists and the police increasingly dangerous. The cops waited until the girls got out of a client's car and then beat them up until they handed over their money.

Once I asked Lucy which of her clients she favoured most—that is, which nationality? She looked at me with a raised eyebrow and took a long swig from her quart-sized bottle of warm Tusker. Crossing her legs and pulling at her short red skirt, she leaned forward a few inches from my face.

"The English are terrrrrible lovers . . ." she said, "but, you get dinner and, more important, you get paid." She leaned back on the stool with a big grin on her face, looking across at the others, seeking confirmation. They stared back at her vacantly, bored. "Then there's the Asians. You get no dinner, but it's fast. You fight like hell for the money, but in the end you get paid." Lucy wiped a loose strand of her wig back behind her ear and took a deep breath. "Africans, they're the worst. No dinner. Never stop, all night. Early in the morning you get jabbed in the ribs, 'Hey,' the guy says. 'No sleepin' on the job!' Most times you don't get paid."

At one point Krystyne returned to Canada for three weeks; her mother was not well and a year had passed since she had seen our youngest daughter. I remained in Nairobi. Walking across the street to the restaurant, La Trattoria, for dinner with friends, I heard my name called. It was Lucy.

"Hi, Scott. Where's Krystyne?" she asked, swinging her purse back and forth as she approached.

"Hi, Lucy," I said. "Krystyne is in Canada. She returns Monday. Are you going up to the 680 Bar?" She ignored the question. Standing with one hand on her hip, she made her intentions perfectly clear.

"Scott, you want a good time together, yes?" It was not an issue of disloyalty for her, merely a business opportunity to be seized upon—particularly at a time when so few existed. I smiled.

"I'm on my way to dinner, Lucy."

"No problem, I wait for you," she replied. My refusal left her without a hint of rancour. The next week, obviously pleased to see us, she greeted us like old friends—especially Krystyne.

———————

Krystyne and I explored areas of Nairobi that were beyond the purlieu of the normal tourist; some places were considered too dangerous to wander in on foot, especially alone. River Road was one, with a reputation for violent crime that went well beyond petty theft; even the police stayed clear of River Road. A Japanese female tourist, having wandered there alone in error, was robbed and stripped of all her clothing in broad daylight. As she lay naked in a state of shock on the side of the road, an African woman covered her with a *kikoi*, a shawl. The authorities never even responded to calls for assistance.

The notorious East End Hotel on Dubois Street near River Road was an establishment we visited where unregulated trading took place. West Africans came from Ghana, Ivory Coast, and Senegal, loaded with giant sacks of merchandise for sale. Young men packed into small airless rooms for weeks, slept and ate amongst carvings, beads, and textiles for wholesale distribution. Entry was through a grille guarded by a senescent, toothless woman, suspicious and watchful.

We spent many a Sunday afternoon burrowing through the jumble of goods stacked high to the ceiling, an Ali Baba world of artifacts, beads, masks, strange medicines, and circumcision knives, pursued by unsavoury vendors whose prices dropped as we strayed from room to room in search of black coral. Heated arguments, with pushing and shoving, usually signalled that it was time to leave.

In Eastleigh, another area off limits to the prudent tourist, was a large Somali market seething with humanity, vibrant and colourful, filled with merchandise smuggled through Wilson Airport, next to the Flying Doctors hangar. Krystyne's buying reputation in Biashara earned us a special escort through a labyrinth of back alleys, between kiosks selling live chickens, goats, spices, nuts, and jellied mounds of sticky, sweet desserts that wobbled and shook on boards covered in a rime of powdered sugar. Confident, Krystyne pushed through a sea of flowing blue and white djellabas, past stacks of haberdashery, the tumble of hardware and construction materials: all of it was enveloped in the choking smoke of cooking fires that swept over the market like storm clouds, obscuring the illegal trade in stolen goods.

We stood at a tiny door, which opened a crack, revealing a pair of almond eyes, deeper than dreams, inviting us into another world. We were ushered past multicoloured swaths of flowing silk and cotton hanging from doorways, into a courtyard where dozens of seated, veiled Muslim women raised their black-gloved hands, thin wrists adorned with gold bracelets, fingers stacked with the golden glitter of rings for sale. Waving hands, mellifluous calls in Swahili, all bid for eye contact. It became impossible to avoid negotiation; hesitation only provoked frenetic appeals and unrelenting supplication, which gradually wore away our resistance until we succumbed to the unwanted purchase.

————————————

On Monday evenings I became a regular player at the Nairobi Club squash courts where there was an active and competitive mix of

Indian and African players. David Huntington, my friend from the United Nations, would sometimes join me, but he was more a spectator than a player. Mondays were known as "mix-in," at which I met all the players and gradually gained acceptance. The Indians took the game more seriously than the Africans; pride and social position were at stake. Inevitably, the week's evening would come down to the same playoff game: the best African, Peter Kyrennie, against the top Asian, Sanjit Ryad.

Ryad's superior skill allowed him to toy with Kyrennie, driving him from one side of the court to the other in an exhausting dash to retrieve a winning shot. An intense rivalry hung over the sharp crack of the squash ball; raised voices of support divided along classic racial lines. Kyrennie's superb physical condition kept him in the game, leaving Ryad frustrated at his inability to score against the African. Ryad usually won, but only the conviction that next week's outcome would be different blurred the strong feelings of players and fans—which faded with the quaffing of Tuskers following the match.

The conversation during the after-game drinks often included some venting of the frustrations of the African players, who all belonged to the emerging black middle class; heated political arguments would follow. Most of the African players were from the Kikuyu tribe, the largest in Kenya, and strongly critical of the government of Daniel arap Moi, who was a Kalenjin. The Kikuyus, the most industrious and commercially oriented of the Kenyan tribes, were depressed and angry about their lack of political representation in the government; at the same time, they were fiercely patriotic and hopeful about the country's economic potential. Convinced that a change in government was the only cure for Kenya's deteriorating economic performance, they railed against the power, privilege, and corruption of Moi's government. Although it was their argument, not mine or David's, we could sympathize with them, and that created a bond. The evenings would end with friendly banter and the slam of car doors. More often than not, it was left to me to switch off the lights.

I remember those evenings so clearly, walking back across the cricket pitch to our room on the second floor of the club's residence, comfortably tired from play. The cool evening breezes rustling through the tall gum trees on the east side of the field gave pleasant relief from the heat of day. Overhead, the southern stars lit the African sky like a tapestry of diamonds. I could see the lights of our room spilling into the night and Krystyne at the window, reading or busy with some detail of our living quarters. I felt an enormous surge of contentment, reflecting on how our time in Africa had drawn us closer together, imperceptibly, like the stellar pull of a new constellation.

Month after month drifted seamlessly into a year, marked only by the coming and going of the rainy seasons and the increasing number of people we knew in Nairobi. David Huntington remained one of my closest friends, and I remember my rendezvous with him the last Thursday in November 1998. Patches of blue sky signalled the end of the short rains. Nairobi was in full bloom, jacarandas, nandi flame trees, and bougainvillea splashed a torrent of colour over the public gardens next to the Nairobi University grounds. The Norfolk Hotel, adjacent to the university, was surrounded with students coming and going, animated and youthful. The warm equatorial sun filtered through the giant canopy of the chestnut trees planted at the turn of the century by Lord Delamere in front of the Tudor-style hotel. It was an immensely civilized day.

I parked my car and ran up the front steps onto the veranda of the hotel, a renowned and popular place to meet for a drink after work. David Huntington was sitting at the far end of a row of tables, scribbling in one of his canvas-covered diaries. He always chose the same table for our Thursday-afternoon meetings.

His short-sightedness had him bent over his book. A shock of wavy blond hair covered his face, masking a shyness that had dogged him most of his life. He looked up as I approached, and quickly closed his diary.

"Ah, late again. Unreliable, you Canadians." He offered his hand, in deference to my North American habit, and launched into his latest story of United Nations incompetence. Hardly listening, I waved the waiter over to our table and ordered a cold Tusker, momentarily interrupting him.

"How are you, David? No, don't tell me," I said with a smile.

David and I made a point of swapping stories on African-aid projects gone wrong; the subject was close to inexhaustible. It was a harmless and amusing activity, but as the stories accumulated it had a tendency to become depressing. After all, we could hardly escape the fact that we too were participants in the "aid industry." Aid appeared to be either a sinecure for those administering it or a source of corruption for those trying to gain control of its distribution. What we naively interpreted as innocent screw-ups by well-intentioned aid givers often blew up into the next public scandal.

The international press corps based in Nairobi was totally cynical, feigning interest and co-operation with NGOs in return for good copy. This had reached a fever pitch over the disasters of Rwanda and Somalia, where it was difficult to determine who was more hypocritical, the press in their attempt to create sensational stories, or the aid agencies scrambling to feature in them.

One of the more incompetent aid disasters related to me by David was the Italian attempt in 1982 to construct a huge, refrigerated fish-processing plant on the west shore of Lake Turkana at a place called Ferguson's Gulf, complete with a wharf and motorized fishing boats. Lake Turkana is full of Nile perch, the largest on record weighing 298 pounds, high in protein. The plan was to feed the Turkana and to truck the surplus fish to Nairobi for sale packed in dry ice. The only problem was that the Turkana were meat eaters, with little taste for fish and, more important, the lake's shoreline was receding approximately eight hundred feet a year from evaporation under the hot desert sun.

Lake Turkana's only source of water is the Omo River, which springs from the mountains of Ethiopia. Normally, the runoff drains into Lake Tana, which falls into the Blue Nile and travels north into the Sudan and Egypt. Approximately once a decade there is an unusual deluge from the Ethiopian highlands, which overflows south into the Omo, dramatically restoring the size of Lake Turkana.

Krystyne and I had flown over Ferguson's Gulf and were amazed to see the massive hulk of a rusting plant whose wharf extended a mile over drifting sand in a desperate bid to reach the lake—a monument to the incompetence of Western aid.

"Italian incompetence yes, but at least it was not as cynical as the GTZ (a German development service)," David added. "It poured millions into an agricultural project designed to teach the Rendille how to grow vegetables." The GTZ selected the location of their training centre near Marsabit after carefully researched soil tests. The Rendille, a nomadic tribe, showed up, attended the courses, collected a nominal fee for completing the course, planted their vegetables, and then moved on in search of fresh grazing for their cattle. The unharvested vegetables were left to rot.

Petra, the wife of Peter Allmendinger, the gliding instructor at Mweiga, was a member of the GTZ and I was under the impression she actually ran the program. I made a mental note to ask her the next time I flew up there.

When I later questioned her, she talked openly about the failure. Unbelievably, the Germans were going to make a second attempt at convincing the Rendille to farm. When I queried the logic of training nomadic tribes to grow vegetables, she merely shrugged her shoulders, saying, "Look, we send reports back to Germany indicating this is stupid, but headquarters remains unconvinced, sends us money, and frankly it supports our lifestyle here. Without GTZ support we could never make it on the revenue Peter gets from the gliding club. We would have to return to Germany and leave everything we have built here behind."

David's greatest criticism though was reserved for the missionaries in Africa. He could see no redeeming value in their presence. Particularly distasteful, he thought, were the newly arrived American evangelicals—Baptists, Jehovah's Witnesses, Pentecostals—many of whom were using Africa's plight as a means to raise funds in the

United States. Trying to offer some perspective, I suggested he consider the extraordinary efforts of individual priests and nuns still working in the Northern Frontier District of Kenya. Many of these individuals were truly outstanding people, dedicated and hard-working, living under incredibly difficult and lonely conditions.

"Scott, it's the squalid competition between religious sects, the scramble for converts, in this day and age, that is totally unacceptable," he said, becoming more agitated. It was true they bribed Africans with offers of food and second-hand clothing to attend church services and schools. These handouts slowly created dependency on the mission. The tribe's cattle, their only source of independence and wealth, gradually diminished as the available grazing surrounding the mission was exhausted. I had seen it first-hand. These settlements had become human garbage dumps.

And yet there were exceptions: I mentioned one to David. "What about the nuns at Wamba? They take in girls from different tribes all over Kenya and train them to be excellent nurses." Graduates from Wamba were the backbone of the medical infrastructure in Kenya. Several worked with the Flying Doctors Service, and they were as competent as doctors—if not more so. The Flying Doctors Service could not have survived without them.

Krystyne and I had flown into the missionary convent at Wamba the previous weekend with a young Pokot girl we had met who was anxious to train there as a nurse, and the place had left a real impression on us. The Consolata nuns were a Catholic order living entirely on their own in northern Kenya, devoted to God and their earthly vocation of nursing. These "brides of Christ" had built a small community in the middle of harsh terrain, remote and inhospitable, miles from the nearest African village. They had drilled for water, constructed their convent, chapel, and hospital, planted their gardens, and operated financially independent of both the state and their founding order in Rome.

When we flew in the first thing we saw was the landing strip, an extension of the dirt road leading up to the convent. The moment we came to a stop a group of African children pressed up against the windows of the plane. At the convent's gate we pressed the button of an old-fashioned bell, and waited as the Mother Superior's assistant, her nun's habit flowing like the wings of a crested crane, made her way down the manicured path.

Inside the convent courtyard, the carefully groomed flower beds were filled with blooming azaleas and roses, exquisitely arranged in geometric patterns, resembling an Italian villa. Nuns swished along the garden paths, seemingly oblivious to the fact that the convent was sitting in the middle of a rock-strewn desert, miles from civilization.

We had introduced ourselves and the sixteen-year-old Pokot girl to the Mother Superior, an Italian nun, quiet-spoken and dignified. She had spent most of her life in Africa, arriving in Kenya at the age of twenty, thirty-five years before. The Consolata Order granted her two weeks' holiday, once every five years, to visit her family in Italy. This year's holiday was an exception, as her mother was dying of cancer.

The Mother Superior reviewed our candidate's school certificate, slowly shaking her head. The marks were not good enough. The girl must repeat her final school year if she wanted to be admitted into Wamba. I explained that she could not afford another year's school fees, and that perhaps an exception could be made based on the girl's character and her fierce determination to become a nurse.

The Mother Superior remained adamant. There was little point my taking on the moral authority of the Church on her own ground. She pulled me aside and, speaking firmly, said that, if the girl was as determined as I maintained, she would find a way to return next year—properly qualified. We left with the Pokot girl downcast and me somewhat chastened by the iron-willed Mother Superior.

The sun shone down on our table as I told David about our visit to Wamba. We wanted another beer, and tried to gain the waiter's attention, with little success.

"One waiter for this place is absurd." David said. His negative frame of mind cast a pall over our meeting. We fell silent. The crowd grew more animated as the place began to fill. A pair of Haidada ibises flew low over the veranda croaking their prehistoric "harrar, harrar, harrar"—eternal sounds of late afternoon in Nairobi.

"Scott, it's the self-serving attitudes in so many of the aid organizations that bothers me. It's worse than providing no aid at all." David leaned forward and gripped the table as if to reinforce his point. "I'm more and more convinced that only Africans can solve their own problems. Aid initiatives by non-Africans are rarely successful."

The lone waiter, sweating profusely, was trying his best to keep pace with the crush of new customers, but the more he tried, the more he fell behind. It looked as if we were in for a long thirsty wait.

"Your example of Wamba is an exception, and of course the Flying Doctors Service," he said with a smile. "Even that service has political problems, and yet they remain one of the most respected NGOs in Nairobi, perhaps because 90 per cent of the staff is African."

"True," I replied. "But the funding is foreign, and that can be a problem for NGOs trying to maintain independence from governments. They are totally dependent on public and private fundraising at home to finance their operations."

Fundraising produces its own set of horrors, which often take precedence over the aid projects themselves. Shockingly, NGOs remain accountable to no one. Enormous annual expenditures are made on self-serving advertising programs in order to raise money. Fundraising becomes an end in itself, so competitive it leads NGOs to distort the truth about their activities in the field. The lack of independent audits and accountability means that some NGOs perpetrate fraud, misappropriate funds, and exaggerate the value of their activities.

David was still complaining. "Don't forget, African governments are also culpable, threatening NGOs with expulsion from the country, effectively blackmailing NGOs who have built up resources and a reputation in a country based on funds raised in the West. And of course many NGO aid programs are being directed through spurious African companies, and well-connected individuals are benefiting personally." He stopped and then added, "God, how did we get into this business?"

The problem goes beyond determining the amount of aid required for Africa. The type of aid, the problems of implementation, how it should be dispensed, over what period of time, and under what conditions: these are the really difficult issues. Their resolution will demand a real commitment on the part of the West: a knowledge and understanding of Africans, their history, tribal matrices, traditions, and cultures. Refusal to take the time to really understand Africa, to pay more than lip service to the Continent and its problems, is where the West has gone wrong. The emotional commitment required is too great; the West's vital interests are simply not at stake.

I was slowly formulating my own views on the subject of aid to Africa. It started from the premise that the West has a moral obligation to help Africa, a responsibility that goes beyond geopolitics, economics, or the problems of immigration; it is a deeper, more profound responsibility, one that reaches to the roots of our humanity, a spiritual imperative to share in mankind's universal burdens and redemption. For these deep psychological and spiritual reasons the West cannot afford to ignore the plight of Africa.

I told David I considered myself lucky to have come to Africa not as a career aid giver, but with the romantic belief that my help might make a difference. He said this was noble but naïve, and that I had much to learn about the corrupting influences of aid in Africa. He was probably correct but, thankfully, I had not yet become cynical. In fact, I remained hopeful, even optimistic, that aid could not only make a difference, but that the West had the moral obligation to ensure its success. Both David and I had developed a love of Africa, but David's deeper understanding of its problems was rooted in despair, something I had thus far managed to avoid.

We finally caught the waiter's eye, waved him over, and ordered two more beers. It was then I noticed David's signet ring glinting in the last rays of the sun. His small hands and long hair made him look more like a poet than a United Nations bureaucrat. Sensitive and vulnerable, he demanded impossibly high standards of himself—

standards he couldn't possibly hope to meet. His career was a disappointment and his marriage troubled; he cared terribly about his need to be useful, and he wanted desperately to remain in Africa.

The beers arrived. David stretched his long gangly legs full length under the table, more relaxed now that cool Tuskers were within reach. The veranda was overflowing with a mix of students and newly arrived tourists. A couple of prostitutes had positioned themselves strategically across from our table; they made half-hearted attempts to gain our attention.

"So what's the alternative, David?" I asked, leaning back on my chair. "Do we simply pack up and leave Africa to drown in its problems?"

"Yeah, maybe," he said, wistfully. "It might be less complicated for those living here."

"You can't be serious," I replied, impatiently.

We were into old arguments, ones without resolution. Africa, seen from the West's perspective, is a basket case—a depressing, unavoidable fact. From my own experience, wherever one looked, it seemed the fabric of African society was unravelling. Corruption and lawlessness had become permanent features of the political and institutional landscape. What could the West do? Constructive help more often than not was seen as interference. Providing aid had become a devilishly tricky business.

David looked at his watch and immediately rose from his chair. "Look, I'm sorry. I've got to be on my way," he exclaimed. He beckoned the waiter over, while tucking the back of his shirt into his trousers. "God, I'm late. Amanda has invited some United Nation types over this evening, and I said I would help with dinner. She's a frightful cook, really," he added, almost as an afterthought. He picked up the tab and looked directly at me with his light blue eyes, smiling. "Next week's on you, Scott."

He waved, a parting gesture as he made his way through the tightly packed crowd waiting to find a table. By now the Norfolk was rocking with the laughter of a hard-drinking crowd. Empty beer bottles lined the tabletops, thick as soldiers on parade. I watched him cross the street, brushing the fall of hair off his forehead. He turned one last time and waved before disappearing. I never saw him again. He was killed that weekend in a head-on car crash, driving alone on his way back to Nairobi on the Naivasha highway. Amanda left for England eight days later and never returned to Africa.

9

Weekend Safaris

ALMOST EVERY WEEKEND we took to the sky in our repaired plane, Charlie Foxtrot Whisky Mike Juliet; flying to all parts of the country, particularly northern Kenya. On the way north we made a habit of stopping at a small grass strip near Mweiga where the sixteen-member gliding club was run by Peter Allmendinger, the husband of Petra who was a member of the German aid agency GTZ. There, we would watch the gliders launched like swans from a cable pulled the length of the field by an old Ford truck, their long thin wings soaring high above us into the cerulean blue of the Aberdare sky. Camping vans lined the edge of the field, with children playing tag while mothers cast their eyes skyward, seeking reassurance that their husbands were still aloft.

On our second visit, I went up in a glider for the first time and was surprised by how sensitive it was to the slightest movement of air—a significant difference from my plane. Later that afternoon, Peter picked us up in his rusted Volkswagen and drove us to the luxurious Aberdare Country Club. We registered as guests and he joined us for a beer before returning to his home outside Mweiga.

The clubhouse was a rambling old grey stone building struggling to maintain the aristocratic grandeur of its former colonial club members. Now, however, it was filled with prosperous Indian families on holiday, mothers fussing at the tables on the open-air porch while their men gathered in twos and threes to conduct quiet business conversations about where to invest money.

Children in party dress ran riot over the lush green lawns, manicured by a permanent staff of eight gardeners. Cascading bushes of trumpet lilies and flowering bougainvillea in sunset reds, oranges, and magentas framed the aging elegance of the English-style garden. Bee-eaters and mouse birds flitted in and out of the hedgerows, while down the long, sloping lawn, golfers strode past the skittish trotting of wild warthogs and the bold advances of curious baboons.

A sudden late-afternoon thundercloud massed over Mount Kenya, whipping the land with spindles of rain. Guests scurried for cover beneath the stone-pillared porch, where tea and scones were served in the finest English tradition. White tablecloths fluttered nervously in the sharp gusts that blew up the steep rise from the savannah below. Then, just as suddenly, the clouds swept past the Aberdares and all of the Highlands fell into a flaming sunset that stretched across a mackerel sky.

An evening chill crept over the ground. At an altitude of seventy-five hundred feet, the night air cooled rapidly, even though the Aberdare Country Club was within one degree of the equator. Inside the main building, wood fires crackled in the large stone fireplaces. Guests gathered for drinks before dinner, talking in excited voices, happy to be on holiday, having left their worries behind in Nairobi. It was warm and comfortable—almost Canadian, had there been snow.

Over the course of our first year in Africa, Krystyne and I had flown into virtually all of the national parks in Kenya: the rain forest of Kakamega, the desert mountain of Marsabit, the Amboseli plain, the vast Masa Mara, and the coast of the Indian Ocean. We had visited every corner of the country and had had many flying adventures and a few close calls.

On Easter weekend, 1998, we flew into Shaba National Park on the southern edge of the Lakipia Plateau. The plane's wheels touched down on a dirt strip that looked to be frequently washed out by rain, as loose stones and mud were thrown up against the underside of the wings. The sound was unnerving, but we landed safely, stopping near the riverbank.

I had gained confidence in my ability to handle African bush flying since our crash on South Island; I had grown used to the sudden unexpected downdraughts, the landings on dirt roads, the need to fly without navigational aids, guided by GPS and geographical features on the ground. My Cessna 180, a tail dragger, was the ideal bush plane for Africa, having lots of power, low stalling speeds, rugged construction, balloon front tires, and a small tail wheel that bounced lightly over the roughest terrain.

Within minutes of our landing a Land Rover arrived at the strip, and two Africans, immaculately dressed in khaki uniforms, escorted us to the Shaba Camp. It was surrounded by semi-desert, four thousand feet lower than the Aberdare Country Club, and the air was hot. But it was still a far cry from the desert conditions we had encountered in previous safaris up in the Northern Frontier District.

Later that afternoon we left the campgrounds for a walk along the Larisoro River, a tributary of the larger Ewaso N'giro, which drained the dry savannah of the Lakipia Plateau. Herds of antelope, unconcerned by our presence, drifted through the dried scrub lining the banks of the river. Shaba, while not officially designated a game park, was administered as one and protected from poachers by private guides. Guests were instructed to remain within the camp limits unless accompanied by an official guide in a vehicle.

Krystyne and I walked out to the camp gate. Seeing no guard, we proceeded cautiously along the upper bank of the river, with a clear view of the muddy water below and the flat plain extending to the mountains of Maralal. Crocodiles, somnolent, half-covered in mud, lined the shore waiting for unsuspecting prey. A flock of cattle egrets flapped upstream and settled in the dried clumps of elephant grass waving in the afternoon breeze.

Peering through binoculars, I sighted an exquisite vermilion malachite kingfisher sitting on the dead branch of an umbrella tree overhanging the river. I carefully brought it into focus. Suddenly, without warning, a large bull elephant lumbered out of the acacia thicket directly ahead of us and moved towards us. Krystyne gripped my arm and, white as a sheet, utterly speechless, she froze. Then, as if charged with electricity, she turned and ran faster than I thought possible.

I remained motionless, not moving a muscle, recognizing that we were downwind and had not yet been detected, in spite of Krystyne's panicked departure. The old bull was scarred, one ear badly torn, obviously no longer part of a herd. He appeared enormous at close range, advancing as he fed, still unaware of my presence. His massive frame toppled trees as if they were mere twigs. I waited, struck by his pungent smell and noisy feeding.

A Samburu man on the other side of the river, thinking I was unaware of the danger, frantically waved his arms in warning. Surreptitiously, I backed away, unnoticed. I found Krystyne inside the park gate, out of breath, determined to remain within the safety of the camp, regardless of armed guides and vehicles promised for the next day's early-morning safari.

During Krystyne's one trip back to Canada to see her mother and our daughter studying at Concordia in Montreal, I received a call from Chris Field, an eccentric friend living in Nanyuki, north of Mount Kenya. Chris was a zoologist, whose first assignment after graduating from Cambridge, aged twenty-two, was the study of rats in Birmingham. Before long he ended up in Uganda, doing research on army ants, and two years after that he embarked on a sixteen-year project to introduce camels into southern Kenya. He had married a beautiful Somali girl whom he met in a town called Wajir in the northeastern desert of Kenya, and Krystyne became the godmother to their eldest daughter. He called me suggesting I join him on a thirteen-day camel safari over the Chalbi Desert and up the notorious El Kajarta Gorge that cut through the eastern face of Mount

Kulal. We would sleep in the open, surrounded by bats, vipers, scorpions, and the ancient bones of elephants. I liked Chris Field enormously. I understood his romantic attachment to Africa; in that sense we were kindred spirits. The invitation was irresistible, and I accepted immediately.

Our safari was to include Father Sean, an Irish priest who was working with the Pokot tribe in northeastern Kenya, and Gunter Schramm, a German aid worker who was also working with the Pokot. I had met Gunter at Peter Allmendinger's gliding club in Mweiga. Chris Field knew both of them well, since he had convinced them that introducing camels to the Pokot would help the tribe in times of drought. The Pokot dependence on cattle rather than camels made for subsistence living sometimes verging on disaster.

As it turned out, Father Sean was unable to get away from his mission post because his replacement failed to show up. I was disappointed, since he was known to be an entertaining character. Then Gunter too failed to show in Nairobi at a pre-arranged rendezvous—no phone call and no message.

I waited twenty-four hours and finally set off in my Nissan for Nanyuki with Miglia, the driver from Loiengalani, who had taken us to visit the Il Molo tribe at Lake Turkana the previous Christmas. Poor Miglia was beside himself, as Wolfgang owed him three months' salary and had told him to come to Nairobi if he wanted to get his money. By the time Miglia arrived, however, Wolfgang had disappeared to the coast, and Miglia had not a shilling to his name and no way to get back home. I gave Miglia some money and offered to drive him as far north as Nanyuki if he would help me purchase supplies and pack up the vehicle. He was desperate to get to Marsabit before the new moon—he was going to be married and Rendille weddings can only be held when the moon is new.

Gunter's disappearance was also awkward for me, since he was to provide the four-wheel-drive vehicle to get us from Chris Field's house in Nanyuki to Nogorinit, south of Baragoi, to meet up with the camel drivers. Such a vehicle was absolutely essential north of

Isiolo, as the roads were otherwise impassable following the rains.

Later that evening, Chris and I learned that Gunter had tried to phone me at the Nairobi Club, but the message never got through; apparently he had just missed us. His young son had contracted amoebic dysentery, and was bleeding badly; he had to be hospitalized. Gunter was desperately trying to make arrangements to fly him back to Germany, which meant Gunter was out and the safari was down to Chris and me.

We debated at length how we might reach the camels and their drivers, with whom we had no means of communication. There seemed nothing for it but to spend money neither of us had to get Jamie Roberts, who owned the small air charter in Nanyuki, to fly us up to Nogorinit on the chance that the camels and their owners would still be there. By now we were two days overdue. Our original instructions had been sent by word of mouth via foot messenger—our cook—ten days earlier, but they had never been confirmed.

When we arrived the camels and their drivers were there, unconcerned, patiently waiting. Following a wet night we set off on our thirteen-day walk through the Ndoto Mountains towards Mount Nigiro, and then across the semi-desert to the east side of Mount Kulal. It was a relief to be on our way.

Chris was convinced that a trip through the mountains would be more interesting than simply trudging directly across the Chalbi Desert. What clinched it for me was the possibility of reaching the El Kajarta Gorge, a natural wonder, straight out of H. Rider Haggard. Cliffs rose a thousand feet from a stream that alternated between a raging torrent in the rainy season and a dry creek bed with rock pools of brackish water near its source in times of drought. These pools were the only source of water within a hundred miles of the desert in the dry season.

The Chalbi Desert lies to the north and east, while the Kaisut Desert is directly south of Mount Kulal. Every living thing must compete to get up that gorge for water in times of drought, including every kind of wild animal, prey and predator alike, and cattle and goats owned by the Rendille, but alas, no longer any elephants. The passage is long and treacherous, as evidenced by the bones scattered everywhere from animals that have died of thirst and exhaustion. The gorge is so steep and narrow that enemies have to confront one another in order to pass, and it is filled with vipers, cobras, bats, and baboons, all hiding in a thick, dark, gloomy tangle of fecund vegetation.

Chris's description was enough for me. We had to get there.

We walked alongside the camels, which were carrying our gear for eight to ten hours a day—a fair amount of walking. Chris had lived in Africa for twenty-two years, so I had much to learn from him. He was in good shape, enthusiastic, and totally unworried about personal safety.

We passed through insecure areas where the army and bandits were constantly fighting (three people were killed in a small village just hours before our arrival). As a security measure, we took a young Samburu warrior with us who carried a Czech semi-automatic rifle he had bought for 30,000 Kenyan shillings ($15) from a Somali. We heard shots at night, but we were careful to extinguish all lights and no untoward incident dragged us into action.

The mountains of Ndoto were spectacular, much like those near Maralal where Krystyne, Serge, and I had spent the night on our escape from Lake Turkana. Walking all day with the same landmarks in sight was a strange sensation for us, in the fast-moving twentieth century. We crossed many dried-up *luggas*, or streams, that spilled out of the mountains to the desert's edge. These could be dangerous because they flooded without warning from rain that gathered in the mountains. Suddenly, a strange roar would signal the arrival of a virtual tidal wave of water, carrying rocks, trees, and silt with a ferociousness that was frightening. Just as abruptly the water would stop and the *lugga* would dry up again.

On the whole, we were lucky with the weather. The rainy season had only just ended, but there was considerable moisture in the clouds. We had showers just about every night, but they were generally light. Only two nights did it really pour. I was pleased that, at the last minute, I had remembered to bring my tent, which afforded me some protection, although in the heavy rains nothing worked since the water just came up through the floor.

The desert after the rains was beautiful. A profusion of flowers of every conceivable colour and type—glorioso superba, the desert lily, tribulus, and cleome in sherbet yellows, mauves, and whites—arose in splendid array from the desert sand overnight. It was as if life had been transformed by the rain; every living thing burst into frenetic growth, compressing a full life cycle into three weeks before the return of the dry season. The rains marked only a brief respite before the punishing heat of the sun resumed the relentless cycle of birth, death, rebirth, and death.

The tension of the desert was strangely attractive; everything existed on edge, precariously balanced.

Over the brief thirteen days of our safari, days slipped into nights and back into days and our routine slowly became a way of life. The nights were memorable, as they always seem to be in Africa. Somehow, as we sat around our fire out there in the desert, the sky sprinkled with stars, with the camels snuffling in the background, there was an aura of magic.

We talked late into the night, recounting our pasts, our dreams for the future, and, of course, our wives, who took on the qualities of romantic divinity they seem to acquire when men are on their own, in close companionship.

The Southern Cross had marked our departure from Nogorinit, and the Dipper pointed towards the North Star, which was unable to pull itself into view over the horizon. The Hale-Bopp comet made a spectacular early-evening appearance from the west, and the moon shone large until midnight, a little slimmer every night until it quartered into a scimitar.

I realized on that safari, more than any other time during our stay, just how important our time in Africa had been for both Krystyne and me. How stuck we had become in Toronto, how empty the relentless pursuit of a career had become for us. Thank God we had made the break.

Life has so much to offer. All one ever needs is the imagination and energy to chase down one's dreams. Something I swore I would never lose sight of, no matter the cost. Of course, I wondered about our future: where we might live, what careers to pursue. Imponderable thoughts, unresolved. Somehow, out there in the desert these questions seemed less pressing and I was content to leave them unanswered, to let them drift. I was confident that the future would unfold as divine providence saw fit.

Inevitably, my thoughts turned to Krystyne, while crossing so much varied terrain and gazing through so many starry nights. I repeated over and over to myself just how lucky I was to have her as a companion and a wife. She was in a sense my polar star.

PART THREE

10

Captive in Tanzania

U NDER PRESSURE, I would have to admit I knew our position before we landed. A satellite GPS navigating instrument is accurate to within one hundred feet; so it would be hard to argue that I was unaware we were just inside Tanzanian airspace. Krystyne and I were flying over the Masa Mara on a Saturday morning, with not a cloud in the sky and herds of wildebeests roaming the vast savannah below. It was a day's excursion only, since we were invited to dinner that evening in Nairobi to meet officials from CIDA (Canada International Development Agency).

We circled a field of open grass on the edge of the Mara River, which formed the border between Tanzania and Kenya. It was lunchtime. No one was in sight. It was a perfect spot to land—irresistible! With the flaps extended, we glided into the Serengeti Game Park, unnoticed.

Parting the tall saw grass, eyes alert for Cape buffalo, we made our way over to the fast-moving water of the Mara River, a hundred yards from our plane. A small herd of Grant's gazelles skirted our path, stopped to stare at us, hind feet stamping, tails flicking, before they disappeared into a thicket of acacia trees near the bend of the river. The sun beat hard on the red soil, still damp from the morning's rain. Clouds of white butterflies rose from the grass, their incandescent wings floating on the gentle currents of midday air.

We spread our lunch on the warm rocks at the river's edge. The water, at a seasonal high level, was a muddy chocolate brown, swirling and eddying past us, shafts of sunlight deflecting off its rippling surface. On the far shore a woolly-necked stork sat immobile in the branches of a bean tree; its beady unblinking eyes stared imperiously at our unexpected presence. Farther up the river we could hear the snorts and grunts of hippos feeding on water lilies. The afternoon was ours alone.

Suddenly, there was movement in the tall grass. We had company. Four uniformed men armed with AK-47 automatic rifles approached us and the day took on a different hue. Tanzanian wildlife rangers, armed and suspicious, wanted to know where we had come from. What were we doing in this restricted part of the Serengeti?

"Good afternoon." I volunteered, as they circled us cautiously. "What a beautiful day." I tried again, but there was no reply. Eventually, the closest ranger spoke, while holding his rifle in both hands at the ready.

"What are you doing here?" he asked.

"Oh, we are having a picnic beside the river," I said, trying to maintain an air of unperturbed amiability.

Our efforts to remain nonchalant, and friendly—even offering to share our food—did not mollify them. Their questions grew more persistent. The interrogation veered inexorably into complications beyond the scope of their rules and regulations. We had no passports, no landing clearance, no overflight clearance, no game-park pass, no exit clearance from Kenya, and no flight plan. What were Canadians, resident in Kenya, doing in Tanzania? How did a foreign-registered plane, temporarily based in Kenya, get into Tanzania without a clearance? We were obviously not a threat, but our illegal entry called for the attention of an authority higher than local wildlife rangers. We were instructed to accompany them to the Lamai Fort, a two-mile walk from the river.

The Lamai Fort consisted of four concrete buildings and a half-dozen daub-and-wattle huts enclosed by a fourteen-foot-high cement wall topped with barbed wire and broken glass. The main entrance had a set of double steel doors wide enough to accommodate a vehicle, which were kept locked, and a smaller door large enough for an adult, which remained open but could be quickly closed in the event of attack. The fort was impenetrable from the outside and closely guarded by armed soldiers inside.

We were ushered into a windowless cement room, where we were detained and questioned for several hours. The senior park warden then decided to review our situation with his captain, who was based in a small town called Negoti, reachable only by HF radio. All eyes turned to an antique HF radio set operated by an old man in civilian clothes, whose raddled face and shapeless mouth resembled India rubber. His incoherent mumbling and limited capacity to grasp our story gave rise to repetition and further confusion. The prospect of early release slowly receded as the day drifted lazily into the afternoon.

The air hung heavy and humid. Cluster flies buzzed around us, sticking to our hands and faces in the torpid heat. Soldiers snoozed under the lone acacia tree in the middle of the small yard. Several dirty, unkempt children—belonging to soldiers' families—appeared from behind the radio hut, barefoot and gawking. They stood at a safe distance, their ragged clothes hanging from their skinny, malnourished bodies. We tried to engage them in conversation, but they didn't speak English and remained quiet, unmoved by friendly gestures. We had little else to do, aside from waiting.

The Negoti captain had trouble assessing our situation over the radio. The Lamai Fort came under his jurisdiction, and yet it was in a remote and inaccessible part of the Serengeti, not normally given to problems requiring his intervention. Typically, he prevaricated before stating that we should be transferred to the Tanzanian police. So where were the police? The local police chief was in Ikoma, sixty miles away. Armed guards would escort us there; however, there was no vehicle at the fort and no one could say how long it might take for a truck to come from Ikoma to pick us up.

This was too much. We needed to regain the initiative. I informed our captors that sending us to Ikoma was unreasonable, and that it was our intention to return to the plane. I instructed Krystyne in an undertone to follow as I strode resolutely towards the main gate. Before we had taken a dozen steps, orders were barked out in Swahili to the sleeping soldiers in the square to quickly padlock the gate. Our futile attempt at a dignified departure had landed us under lock and key.

My immediate concern was our dinner engagement in Nairobi with Mike Gerber and the Canadian director of CIDA. The dinner had been arranged at my request. It was important to find a way to inform Mike of our predicament. Our social obligations were of little interest to the Tanzanian rangers, who viewed us with increased suspicion. Nevertheless, I persuaded them to permit me to use their HF radio. To my dismay, I discovered the radio crystal was locked onto a single frequency reserved for Tanzanian wildlife rangers only—presumably, a safeguard against possible rebel activity.

The heat reduced us to listlessness. The park warden, having lost interest, disappeared, leaving his rangers to stand guard over us. The day had slowed to a crawl; only the flies were active. In Africa, one spends an inordinate amount of time whisking absent-mindedly at the goddamn flies. They buzz in tight concentric circles, alighting on exposed parts of one's body, clinging for an instant, then taking off on a mindless flight, only to return.

We were anxious about a situation that was clearly beyond our control. Obviously, our dinner engagement was a non-starter, and the prospect of incarceration overnight loomed closer. I tried requesting permission to use the HF radio in my plane.

"I'll leave my wife here, and you can escort me under armed guard and monitor my transmission," I said. The reasonableness of the request went unheeded by the rangers, rooted in stubbornness. I appealed to the park warden, who had mysteriously reappeared in the radio hut. He hesitated, uncertain of our status; we might be important. After all, we owned a private plane. He nervously relented and instructed two of his rangers to accompany me.

I managed to reach Judy, the Flying Doctors nurse, although the communication was brief. A plane's HF radio rapidly drains the battery without the motor running, and I had been refused permission to start the engine. Starting the plane's motor was seen as an invitation to escape, regardless of Krystyne's presence back at the fort. Judy was quick to understand that Mike Gerber would have to entertain our guests without us.

The late-afternoon shadows soon slipped into dusk. I re-entered the fort to find Krystyne sitting on the concrete steps of the radio hut reading a Tanzanian guidebook that she had stuffed into her bag before leaving Nairobi. There was still no sign of the truck from Ikoma. We were obviously prisoners of Lamai for the night. There was no possibility of escape. The cement walls around the fort and the locked steel doors were guarded by soldiers slumped over their rifles.

The first indications of evening chill crept over the yard as the sun dropped below the west wall. We were dressed in shorts and T-shirts and the prospect of a cool night ahead had us regretting our casual approach to clothing.

The park warden reappeared and led us to another cement building, our dwelling for the night. A single cot in the corner of a dark cell, barely visible in the half-light, was the only furniture. Windrows of dead flies carpeted the floor. The ceiling was thick with bats; susurrating squeaks signalled a great coming and going through the cracks of the roof. The toxic smell of their droppings was overpowering, mitigated only by their ability to devour hordes of malarial mosquitoes. A tree hyrax screamed beyond the walls of the fort as our small world closed in and the dark equatorial night took hold.

A young woman, lantern in hand, appeared with a basket on her head containing a bowl of fried *manioc* (plantains) and a pot of hot tea. She placed the food at our feet and, without speaking, picked up her lantern and disappeared, plunging us back into pitch darkness. We sat alone without light on the outside step of our cell, eating the sticky *manioc* with our fingers. The night noises of the bush, loud and close, competed with the distant voices of the rangers gathered around a campfire at the far end of the fort.

"So, now what shall we do?" Krystyne asked.

"I think we should befriend the park warden," I replied. "He's intelligent and clearly wishes to avoid confrontation. Possibly, he will tell us what to expect in Ikoma." I was hopeful, remembering his leniency over the use of the high-frequency radio.

"Scott, how is it we always seem to get into these situations?" Krystyne asked, a little plaintively.

"Sweetheart, let's just concentrate on getting out of here, okay?" What else could I say? I was hoping that, once we were back home, the question might seem less relevant, and after all we had flown into some pretty amazing places in Africa over the past year, mostly without incident.

We finished our *manioc* and set off to find the park warden. We had been left unguarded for the night, since there was no possibility of escape. Free to move within the fort, we felt our way in the darkness, hands extended, along the rough cement walls of the buildings until we came to a small window through which we saw the park warden reading by the light of a paraffin lamp. Startled by our knock on the door, he rose and immediately invited us in and offered us tea. His living quarters were extremely modest, but neat and clean, reflecting a disciplined character, unusual for someone stuck in a forlorn posting in the middle of the bush with no wife or servants.

"I hope that we are not disturbing you," I said.

"No, not at all," he replied, hastily stuffing papers into a dog-eared file folder. "I was just preparing my monthly report, but there is no urgency since I have no way to send it to headquarters." I noticed that there were five or six reports sitting in the file all written in a neat, meticulous script. He quickly added, "My name is Robert Mugali."

We introduced ourselves formally to him, and before long he was recounting his life story and his loneliness in the fort—over three years without a break. He and his fiancée planned to marry in

September, but the marriage had been postponed twice now by extended periods of duty. He longed to return home to Arusha, marry, and raise a family. He worried about his fiancée as she had not written to him for over two months. Shy, gentle, and well educated, he was more professor than range warden. He held his command uneasily, preferring not to mix with his men, agonizing over the smallest decision. His evasiveness over our situation and his refusal to speculate on what might befall us under the jurisdiction of the Tanzanian police was not reassuring.

We were still talking at eleven o'clock when we heard the Ikoma vehicle come to transport us to the police, arriving amid the shouts and confusion of the soldiers, who ran in every direction in search of the keys to unlock the gate. The truck's headlights stabbed the night as the wheels laboured over the earthen track leading into the fort and up to the park warden's house. A driver and two young soldiers, still in their teens, knocked on the wooden door. Robert stiffened, nervous about his role and our presence in his private quarters, in spite of the soldiers' junior rank. He served them tea. Local gossip was exchanged in the singsong tones of Swahili.

We bade Robert and the men good night and slipped back into the darkness of our small room. There, we lay on a grass-filled mattress, silent in each other's arms, surrounded by bats and mosquitoes and the noises of the bush. We stayed awake a long time, through much of the night, speaking of our predicament and how we might find a solution that would see us free and allow our captors to save face. Sleep eventually came as the jungle went quiet and the distant sound of the men's voices faded into the early-morning hours.

————————

Our truck lumbered out of the fort as the first rays of sunlight peeked over the concrete wall and the flies descended on the night's accretions of bat droppings. Krystyne sat in the front seat between the driver and a soldier, while I stood in the back, overlooking the cab, soldiers with loaded rifles flanking me left and right. The early-morning air was refreshingly cool.

Bucking and slewing over black cotton soil, the truck crawled along the banks of the Mara River. Occasionally the track, ribbed with roots and fissures of washed-out soil, simply ended without trace, and we were forced to bushwhack over open terrain. The moist earth, steaming in the morning sun, smelt of molasses and wet grass. It was not yet eight o'clock.

The noise of our vehicle raised masses of wild game. Impalas bounded over the tall grass; zebras, their startled heads raised, eyes alert, shifted nervously, ready to bolt at a given signal. Vervet monkeys looped from branch to branch through the cotton trees that towered above the banks of the Mara. Wild game in this remote northwestern area of the Serengeti was rarely disturbed. Our sudden intrusion spread alarm: dik-diks, Grant's and Thomson's gazelles, and duikers panicked and scattered for cover. The trumpeting of elephants heralded our progress along the richly varied terrain of savannah, scrub, and forest. Our Tanzanian captors unknowingly provided us with a private safari through a unique and unspoiled part of Africa that would normally have cost the tourist a fortune to see.

Once out of the Serengeti, we turned south along a dusty track towards Ikoma, forty miles distant. The rutted track wound through undulating country, sparsely covered in dried grass, thorn, and acacia. We saw no other vehicles and only a few signs of habitation, the occasional *manyatta* (small settlement) of mud huts with conical grass roofs, enclosed by a *boma* (thorn fence), filled with cattle and goats tended by half-naked children. Their heads turned as we passed, and looking back I could see them still standing and staring as ribbons of dust settled over the scrubland.

Two hours later we entered the outskirts of a town called Mugumu and our escorts apparently decided on a change of plan. Instead of passing through the town, the truck suddenly wheeled left, past the frightened squawk of chickens and the curiosity of old men standing immobile by the roadside, and we drove through a gate into the dirt square of the Mugumu police station. We dismounted, hot and dusty, only to learn that this was not an unscheduled stop: protocol required us to meet with the police chief of Mugumu before proceeding to Ikoma. However, the police chief was not at the station, so we clambered back into the truck and drove to the chief's residence, a mud hut, sitting resplendent on the bank of a small river on the outskirts of town.

The police chief was a large man with an enormous belly wrapped in a cloth the size of a curtain. He invited us to sit on an old, broken-down sofa while he listened to the soldiers recount in Swahili the story of our sudden and unexpected flight into Tanzania. Voices grew louder as the soldiers contradicted each other's versions and a heated debate arose over details. Abruptly, and without explanation, we were instructed to get back in the truck, return to the police station, and wait for the police chief's official arrival—following his breakfast.

An hour dragged by as we sat and waited on the outside steps of the police station, our patience wearing thin at the inactivity and lack of communication.

"What do you think is going on?" Krystyne asked.

"I don't know, but it's driving me crazy waiting around like this," I replied, leaping up to pace back and forth.

I worried that my plane, left unguarded in a field forty miles away, might be vandalized, and at this rate, I could see us spending another night in Tanzania under guard. The longer we stayed in Tanzania the more complicated our situation would become, each step leading us deeper into a bureaucratic quagmire.

"Somehow we must convince them we are innocent," I said. "We have to show them it's in their interest to simply let us fly back to Kenya." I knew as I spoke it was not that simple. "Isn't it ironic," I mused. "Police in less developed countries have more difficulty dealing with innocence than guilt. If one's guilty, you get thrown into prison, and that justifies a powerful police force. If one's innocent, on the other hand, it renders the police force impotent. And so, there is a determined search for evidence of guilt even if it has to be manufactured. Let's hope that's not what is going on here."

Krystyne let slip a wry grin. "Why don't we simply plead guilty to some crime and help them out of their dilemma? After all, we did land illegally. We could pay a fine and then fly away." Before I had time to reply, the police chief drove into the station yard dressed in uniform and riding a yellow Suzuki motor scooter. Ignoring our presence, he walked past us into the police station. Immediately, the place snapped to attention.

Within minutes Krystyne and I were summoned to the police chief's office, which was stacked high with brown file folders and yellow papers in wire trays. The chief's official demeanour was stiff, in contrast to his familiar and casual attitude of an hour earlier. His assistant stood ramrod straight behind us, as if he alone was supporting the ceiling. The chief gave us a brief lecture on the size and nature of his jurisdiction, and then ordered us into separate rooms for interrogation. A junior policeman, who spoke very little English, recorded both questions and answers in Swahili. Sworn statements required our signatures on all four margins of each page of testimony.

Luckily, I had had the foresight to clear with Krystyne an agreed-upon story justifying our unexpected landing in Tanzania. I was reasonably confident our separate statements would withstand scrutiny.

"A sudden rise in the manifold temperature gauge necessitated an emergency landing to check the oil . . ." I vaguely wondered whether Krystyne would remember the term "manifold temperature," since I knew she had no idea what the engine manifold was. The interrogation was polite but thorough; the persistent questioning lasted almost two hours. The laborious recording of facts onto a soiled pad of paper, with four carbon copies carefully inserted, slowly ate away the afternoon.

We were well into our second day of captivity, and it was apparent that no one had a clue what should be done with us. Whose jurisdiction did we fall under: the wildlife rangers, the police, immigration, or the army? The police chief urgently needed guidance from his superior by telephone, but the lines were dead. These *muzungus* dropped into Tanzania, without warning, without invitation, and without documentation, and had now become a considerable headache. He was desperate to speak to a higher authority; apologetic, he informed us we would simply have to wait.

The idea of joining the shiftless, unkempt collection of recidivists who were waiting in the corridor outside the chief's office was unappealing. The place reeked of hopelessness. We decided to try to win over the police chief with friendly conversation. Soon we were on a first-name basis, sympathizing with his problem of supporting a wife and eight children on a pitiful salary, paid intermittently. His name was Israel. Every few minutes, he distractedly lifted the receiver of his old-fashioned telephone, only to confirm the line was still dead. Eventually, he realized that communication by telephone was out of the question. He announced that he would accompany us to Tarime—a distance of one hundred and twenty miles—to meet his boss in person.

There was no fuel remaining in the truck and no money to purchase gas. The problems of our incarceration were compounding. I volunteered to pay for the fuel if Kenyan shillings were acceptable, and Israel and the driver took off to commandeer the reluctant Asian proprietor of a gas station to sell them gas in return for useless Kenyan shillings, exchangeable into Tanzanian shillings only in Dar es Salaam, eight hundred miles away.

Finally, the truck returned full of fuel, and we piled on board. This time Israel squeezed into the front alongside Krystyne, his large frame forcing the driver to sit sideways, shoulders sticking half out the window. Krystyne gave up any pretence of decorum, her legs on either side of the gear stick. I resumed my standing position at the back of the truck, overlooking the front cab, armed soldiers on either side as before. We lumbered out of Mugumu in a cloud of dust.

Tarime is near Lake Victoria. It was here that Israel hoped to find his boss, the Tarime district police inspector. I fretted as we drove farther and farther into the interior of Tanzania. The likelihood of us being shipped back to Kenya without the plane increased with every kilometre that separated us from our landing spot. If we were taken out of the country, I knew I would never see the plane again. I was determined to resist such an outcome, but I knew the civility accorded us thus far would quickly evaporate if there was a confrontation.

The red laterite road to Tarime was washboard, full of ruts and potholes that slowed our progress to a crawl. In places the road was reduced to a track, where temporary repairs of logs and second-hand lumber strained to bear the weight of our truck as it lurched over makeshift crossings. Pedestrians crowded the narrow cut road, sidestepping muddy streams of water that poured over the red-clay soil. The closer we approached the shores of Lake Victoria, the thicker the lush vegetation that crept out from the jungle onto either side of the road. Overburdened oxen with maize heaped in burlap sacks plodded apathetically alongside an unending stream of people on their way to market.

Women, talking and laughing, clothed in colourful print *kikois* (sarongs), *totos* (babies) on their backs, lined the road. They carried personal belongings effortlessly on their heads, including large stalks of bananas, fish, and even furniture. Statuesque, they slowly turned as we passed, bemused looks breaking into wide grins, revealing perfectly white teeth.

I could see Krystyne through the rear window of the cab talking non-stop to Israel, who was practically on her lap. She was explaining that we were important Canadian citizens deserving special treatment. Her husband held an important position with the Flying Doctors Service—Israel was familiar with the Flying Doctors Service, as were most officials in East Africa—and that we were close personal friends of Canada's ambassador for Tanzania and Kenya, Bernard Dussault. Israel listened, intrigued, at the same time holding stubbornly to his responsibility, unmoved by the bona fides of his captives.

Four interminable hours passed without a stop. The truck's rusted suspension bounced and jolted it over potholes and ruts, leaving us fatigued, desperate to arrive in Tarime. We drove through numberless small settlements, passing thatched roofs, small cooking fires, and the domestic business of everyday living.

Small children, wide-eyed and quick with excitement, ran alongside our truck, yelling, "How are you?" and "Everyone stand up!" (English phrases learned at school). Their spindly legs and bare feet slipping and sliding on the greasy soil, nimble as goats, they kept pace for as long as possible. We waved to them, dispensing smiles and goodwill as we progressed along our route. And so it continued, until the red ribbon of road wound through the green hills that overlooked the bustling town of Tarime.

Tarime's central market surrounded a chaotic bus terminal that teemed with people from the country eager to buy and sell. Aside from the self-aggrandizing collection of government buildings and a small collection of stores and noisy bars, Tarime was little more than a slum of mud huts, lacking proper sanitation or electricity. Large diesel trucks whined and roared down the main street, sending clouds of choking dust and exhaust into a crowd of faces. Tarime was in the middle of the North Mara district, coffee-growing country that catered to truckers who brought commerce and disease to the area.

The district police inspector was nowhere to be found. We were hungry, not having eaten for almost twenty-four hours, and we persuaded Israel to stop at the local hotel for a meal, for which I would pay with my remaining Kenyan shillings. He agreed. Krystyne had cultivated enough friendship and trust to allow us to participate in decision-making on almost everything, short of our release.

We sat around a table on the patio of the Paradise Regained Hotel. Israel and his men drank beer, discussing Nigeria's chances in the upcoming World Cup soccer games. Krystyne and I ordered chicken with rice and Coca-Cola. We could see the chef in a filthy apron at the back of the restaurant slaughter the chicken less than twenty feet from our table. With one foot on the chicken, the chef delivered a blow to its head, spraying a geyser of blood over his arms and apron, leaving our dinner headless and fluttering. No one paid him the slightest notice.

It was Sunday and we were told that the district police inspector was out of town, gone with his family to the country. Reached by radio telephone, he refused to meet us and instructed Israel to transfer us to the Tanzanian Ministry of Immigration. This we viewed as a setback, since an immigration officer would have the power to deport us, and then we would never get back to retrieve the plane.

After lunch we climbed back into the truck and set out in search of the immigration officer. I prayed that, it being Sunday, he too would be unavailable. Remaining under Israel's charge was our best bet, since he had neither the authority to ship us out of the country nor the means to look after us; his only solution short of transferring us to someone else was to let us go free.

The immigration office was closed tight as a tin box with no sign of an official, but Israel had the immigration officer's name and, desperate to find him, decided to search Tarime's local bars. By the time we had traipsed through the last of these smoke-filled dens, reeking of stale beer, it became obvious that there was no one to whom he might transfer us. Israel was downcast and defeated.

The sun plunged over the Mungani Hills surrounding the western outskirts of Tarime. Large crowds stood milling around the main square waiting for *matatus* to transport them home from the market. Thick, choking dust swirled over their heads as they stood in endless queues, arms loaded with pink plastic bags of produce. A few *matatus*, overflowing with passengers, streaked by the bus stop at breakneck speed, dispersing a mixture of diesel fumes and dust. Small boys ran barefoot through the traffic, pushing miniature replicas of motorcycles and cars at the ends of sticks—ingenious fabrications of wire and tin. The ground was strewn with rotting fruit and plastic bags, detritus of the marketplace. Vendors tried to hawk end-of-day wares to stragglers departing on their long trek home—a familiar scene over much of Africa.

Israel faced a number of pressing questions. Where to stay overnight? How to feed us? We were a long way away from Mugumu; his driver and soldiers were hungry, anxious to return to their families. He was on the edge of panic. The moment was at hand; it was time to seize the initiative. I took him aside.

I put my arm around his shoulders and suggested we think out the next move together. He was unlikely to find the immigration officer before nightfall, that much seemed clear. There was no more money and no lodging for us or his men. More important, he had no authority in the district of Tarime. The only sensible solution was to return immediately to the plane. He could inspect the plane, satisfy himself there were no weapons or illegal contraband aboard, declare our landing an emergency, and permit us to leave for Kenya. He and his men would then be free to return to Mugumu.

I would mention his name to the Canadian ambassador, who would see to it that the Tanzanian authorities were informed of our fine treatment and his good "management" of a difficult situation. He was wavering, partially convinced, when Krystyne interjected an inspired suggestion that tipped the balance.

"We'll take pictures of you, Israel, inspecting the plane, pictures for your file," she said with enthusiasm. That decided it. Did Israel imagine pictures of himself and the captured plane on the wall of his office? He was certainly curious to see our plane. He nodded his head thoughtfully. His tentative decision had the desired effect on his men, who immediately climbed back into the truck, eager for home.

We were bone-weary. Our driver had been driving for more than nine hours with hardly a break. Another three hours over difficult terrain lay ahead, with the last half-hour in darkness. Still, the decision taken gave us a renewed sense of energy; only Israel was left entertaining second thoughts. As we headed for freedom, the trick now would be to avoid the unexpected.

The next three hours were a race against time. Could we reach the plane before it was too dark to take off? Another night in Lamai

Fort or the police station in Mugumu would almost certainly invite a change of instructions from senior Tanzanian officials. Our driver, sensing the urgency, drove like a man possessed, hunched over the wheel, swerving at the last minute to avoid potholes, any one of which could have disabled the vehicle and prevented our escape. We roared through village after village as the light began to fade.

Our headlights, at first only a faint glow on the rutted track, gradually jerked and plunged through the encroaching darkness as we closed in on the Lamai Fort. We passed it by and headed straight for the plane, bushwhacking through scrub and the shining dew-laden grass.

Evening shadows spread like a blanket over the Serengeti. We pulled alongside the plane, which rested exactly where we had left it two days ago. A crescent moon rose, casting a faint opaque light over the woods at the far end of the field. Ghostly shadows of wild game, barely discernible, drifted through the tall grass on their way to the river to drink—or was it our eyes playing tricks in the semi-darkness? It was too dark to take off safely from such a short field without lights, and yet another night in the hands of our captors was unthinkable.

I asked Israel to drive down the field and park the truck, headlights angled across the final third of our takeoff path. I needed a marker to judge the point of liftoff to ensure safe clearance over the trees at the south end of the field. There was little room for error and no time for niceties.

We gave a quick wave to Israel and his soldiers after I hand-propped the propeller to start the engine. A quick survey of the instruments showed them registered in the green. The truck proceeded halfway down the field and then unexpectedly made a U-turn and raced back towards us. Israel leapt out of the cab and ran towards the plane, passing within inches of the whirling propeller. I had visions of him cleaved in two like a ripe mango and us lingering in a Tanzanian jail for years. I yelled a warning to him and struggled to cut the fuel supply to the engine. Israel reached the cockpit window and breathlessly yelled, "What about the photographs?"

"Oh God, the photographs," Krystyne exclaimed.

"We don't have time," I said, exasperated.

"We have to, Scott. We promised."

Out we scrambled, taking pictures of Israel beside the plane, seated in the cockpit with a headset, and studiously inspecting the plane's documentation. We promised to send them to him, which we did, two weeks later, from Nairobi. Satisfied, Israel returned to the truck as we prepared a second attempt for a tricky short-field takeoff in the dark.

The truck rumbled down the field again, while we waited in silence for them to get into position. Then, with the throttle pushed full forward and the brakes set, the engine roared into life and ten seconds later our wheels rolled forward, the blades of the propeller threshing the long grass. Blinded by cut grass whirling out of the darkness, we peered through the windshield, on the lookout for game. The plane bounced over the rough ground, slowly gaining speed in the angled lights of the truck. I pulled back the stick early, hoping to reduce the plane's drag through "ground effect," a partial lift induced by the downward wash of air from the wings. The stall-warning horn bleated like a goat about to be butchered, indicating an impending stall, but as we passed the truck's lights, the plane slowly, miraculously, took flight, passing a few feet over the gum trees before soaring into the night sky.

Our sense of exhilaration was irrepressible as we banked over the river; the truck's lights slid beneath the greenish glow of the starboard wing. I looked over at Krystyne. No words were necessary. We were lucky, really lucky—perhaps undeservedly so.

Nightfall had blanketed the great continent of Africa. The sky, studded with stars, carried a new moon across the heavens. The plane seemed suspended in the night as if floating; weight, lift, drag, and thrust—the essential forces for flight—were in perfect balance. The land below was without light, sleeping. We flew in silence, lost in separate worlds of thought. Together in the cockpit, that evening, I treasured Krystyne's proximity, her physical warmth next to me, more than at any other time I can remember.

11

Wings of Sunlight

BY MARCH 1998 the construction of the Flying Doctors Service's new building was almost completed, and morale was high. Mike Gerber telephoned me at the hangar to ask if I could meet him at his office. I had no idea what was up. His board was scheduled to meet later that month in the recently opened AMREF South African offices. Mike had not seen them, and wondered if I would go there, check the premises, and discuss the arrangements with the new manager. Since I wanted to fly to South Africa and I knew that Krystyne would be enthusiastic, I accepted with alacrity. Mike had presumed that I would fly commercial, but registered no objection to my flying Charlie Foxtrot Whisky Mike Juliet.

Our plan was to fly down the east coast of Tanzania and Mozambique to South Africa, where we hoped to meet up with Serge Pétillon, our photographer friend. He would travel with us through Namibia and Botswana, then Krystyne and I would fly across central Africa to Zimbabwe and Malawi, and from there back north through Tanzania to Kenya.

I immediately set about requesting overflight and landing clearances for eight different African countries. A week later I had had only one response. African bureaucracy reacts slowly, if at all, through normal channels. We debated whether or not to go without the necessary permissions. Petty officials wield immense power in Africa; lack of proper documentation at the border invites unexpected difficulties—as we had discovered—and often provides windfall profits for corrupt immigration officials. Four more days of follow-up faxes and telephone calls produced only one additional overflight clearance. There was nothing for it but to go and take our chances.

Monday morning we taxied the plane, fully loaded with emergency supplies of food, water, and personal gear, onto Runway 14. Minutes later we were skimming over the wide expanse of the Athi Plain, heading for Tanzania.

The land was still in the grip of drought. Far off on the horizon massive thunderheads wrapped the Aberdares in thick, grey wool, full of moisture. Nervous gusts whipped the dry savannah anxious for rain. Slowly, we climbed over the Machakos mountains bordering northern Tanzania. It was exhilarating to be airborne, away from the dust and dirt of Nairobi, just the two of us, together.

At thirteen thousand feet we banked through towering peaks of white cumulus clouds. We lost all visibility as we crossed the corrugated sides north of the Machakos range; however, once over the southern slopes, we broke out into clear skies to see the Amboseli Plain stretching, flat as a plate, all the way to the Indian Ocean.

Behind us, wreathed in mist, loomed Mount Kilimanjaro, Africa's tallest mountain, rising from sea level to an altitude of 19,340 feet. Eddies of wind careened over the lee side of the mountain, causing powerful downdraughts—tricky flying conditions for a small plane.

Krystyne had never seen Mount Kilimanjaro, in spite of the fact that on three separate occasions we had flown through cloud within fifteen miles of its peak. We had never even sighted the foothills nearby. Was this snow-capped mountain, only two degrees from the equator, a sorcerer's fantasy? Krystyne was not the first to question its existence: a Christian missionary, the first white man to sight Kilimanjaro in 1849, faced the incredulity of the Royal Geographic Society in London, which refused to acknowledge its existence. It was not until forty years later, when Hans Meyer climbed Uhuru (freedom) peak, that Mount Kilimanjaro made its way onto the map of Africa.

We trimmed the controls for a descent from thirteen thousand feet to sea level to enter the clammy sweat of Dar es Salaam. The humidity was 98 per cent; the airport buildings were spotted with mildew. The monsoon had driven tropical storms over the Indian Ocean, drowning the city streets in rivers of red mud. The smell of accumulated mould and rotting garbage hung in the air, suffocating and claustrophobic. Dar es Salaam had the decay and weariness of a city battered by the tropics.

Still, the evening held a certain magic. The sunset fell over the Indian Ocean, more beautiful than a Monet canvas. We walked in silence along the waterfront, stopping by an open-air fish market to watch it closing down for the night. Wooden boxes lay piled alongside makeshift stalls, stinking of dead fish, busy with flies. The last few buyers wandered aimlessly past the counters, oblivious to the mud and garbage clinging to their feet. Vendors poked their wares, hoping for a last-minute sale.

We stood on a sandbank overlooking the water as the desultory light faded into evening. A soft mist drifted in from the angry sweep of cloud. The fishermen gathered up the last of their gear, shared a final cigarette, and trudged up the embankment before heading home. We stayed for what seemed a long time, resisting the oncoming rush of darkness, speaking of home and family and what might lie ahead on our return to Canada—for we had slowly come to realize that we had surrendered much of our hearts to Africa and that having done so, it would always tear at us, like no other place in the world.

The next day, we flew down the coast of Mozambique at less than 150 feet altitude over miles and miles of bone-white beaches, landing four hours later at Pemba in front of a small whitewashed building. It housed a sleepy guard who announced that ours was the first plane to arrive in three weeks—and there were no hotels or taxis within miles. He volunteered to speed off on his Chinese bicycle to commandeer his brother's truck, while we sat comfortably under the shade of a tall palm tree and waited.

Soon his truck clattered up the steep hill loaded with mangoes and curious African friends eager to meet the newly arrived *muzungus*. We drove twelve miles down the coast to a beach hotel that was still under construction and were shown a room, still smelling of wet cement with no lock on the door and a nest of unconnected wires dangling from the ceiling.

"In Africa, expect the unexpected, remember?" I said to Krystyne, whose face registered mild disapproval at our surroundings.

"Is there no other hotel nearby?" she asked, still resisting our only refuge available for miles.

"Nothing that I saw along the road," I said. "But don't let it bother you. Let's go down to the beach before we lose the afternoon."

"Where's the beach?" Krystyne replied, still inspecting our room. "Oh my God, there's no water!" she exclaimed, standing in front of a sink with unconnected faucets. At that moment, there was a knock on the screen door. A young girl stood outside with a plastic pail of milky water.

"Room service," I laughed. "Accept it, we're here for the night."

The afternoon sun threw a golden sheen over the palm trees, whose swaying fronds shadowed the white-ribboned beach. A lone fisherman stood in a dugout that dipped and bobbed on the turquoise sea. Children played along the shore, beyond supervision. Four African girls in their early teens approached us warily, eager to sell seashells. Dancing and giggling, they imitated adults with their erotic movements of legs, hips, and behinds. Flirtatious looks and screams of laughter erupted with each sale until we became half-buried in shells. Krystyne produced pens, lipstick, eyeliner, and other treasures buried in her purse. Friendship, at first tentative, turned possessive—the girls clustered around us like flies, unrelenting, until that evening at the restaurant they were shooed away by self-important waiters who viewed their antics as irritating and competitive.

————————

Approximately two hundred miles south we landed near the Ilha de Moçambique, an island fortress built by the Portuguese in the seventeenth century. The Portuguese were the first Europeans to arrive on the East African coast early in the fifteenth century. Prior to their arrival, Arabs and Indians had traded spices, beads, and cowry shells along the Indian Ocean coast for several millennia in return for white gold (ivory) and black slaves.

The Portuguese had built their settlement on the Ilha de Moçambique by cutting and transporting thick blocks of limestone from the mainland to construct houses, but these buildings had fallen into a sorry state of repair, and were now solely occupied by Africans. Occasionally, a roof would collapse, often with fatal results, which triggered an island debate as to the wisdom of living in stone houses. Panic would spread through the town and a general evacuation of these houses would occur lasting several months—until, gradually, superstition wore away and habitation resumed.

At midday the town slid into drowsiness from the overwhelming heat. Adults snoozed behind closed shutters, framed by Portuguese wrought-iron railings of exquisite design. Only the children continued their play behind the thick stone walls of the houses fronting the cobblestoned streets.

In spite of the heat I had a sudden urge to get some exercise.

"Would it bother you if I go for a run and a swim?" I said to Krystyne. I was restless from hours of flying.

"No, darling, go ahead," she insisted. "I'll wait for you here." So I left her with a book, on a stone bench under a large sycamore fig tree whose enormous branches threw islands of shade over the miniature square.

I ran along the western beach, over mounds of broken shells pounded into the pink sand. A stiff breeze lifted the waves into horses' tails. Wooden dugouts lay in rows along the water's edge, like olive pits carefully aligned on the side of a plate. The salt air was deliciously cool.

At the north end of the island I came upon the stone parapet of an ancient Portuguese fortress. At the apogee of Portuguese power, a self-contained community of over five hundred souls had lived within its walls, nine thousand miles from home. The fortress, built in 1740, was classically laid out, with ten-foot-thick outer and inner ramparts of quarried stone and a series of connecting towers. The fort had withstood repeated sieges during the Portuguese occupation, having an elaborate network of aqueducts to collect rainwater for two enormous underground cisterns.

These ancient cisterns still remained the island's principal source of fresh water. Every morning women and children gathered there to do their washing and fetch drinking water. A human convoy, the women carrying large plastic buckets on their heads, snaked its way to and from town. I sat watching as the children splashed in and out of the water, their black skins glistening wet in the sunlight, sleek limbs perfectly sculpted.

The rest of the fortress was utterly deserted. The original layout was still discernible through the weeds and vines that had grown between the crenellated parapets. The foundations of two chapels were still evident—one for the officers, another for the men—separate hospitals, even a blacksmith's shop where drop-forged cannonballs lay abandoned amid the scattered heaps of rubble; tools and weaponry, rusted and broken, remained untouched since the day the Portuguese had departed following three centuries of occupation.

Several years previous to our arrival, a small contingent of Portuguese soldiers had returned from Portugal to build a small commemorative chapel on the promontory at the north end of the fortress. Perched on a rock ledge, with the sea pounding its northern wall, the empty chapel remains a haunting reminder of Portugal's presence in Africa.

We stayed in a small guest house on Ilha de Moçambique, owned by a Japanese entrepreneur called Hiromi, whose wife and indeterminate number of children spent the whole day screaming insults at one another. Hiromi had his hand in every private and public enterprise on the island, including politics. He had grandiose plans to run for president of the country's political party, Renamo.

Hiromi became our guide, friend, and advisor, introducing us to the island's few eccentric white residents: the Danish curator of the local museum and his Japanese wife, an earnest French couple studying anthropology, and an old man with a Hemingway beard, known as "the Doctor." The Doctor was permanently ensconced on a bar stool regaling the unsuspecting with lascivious tales in return for a beer. The island had a curious mix of Africans, Portuguese, and whites from various parts of the world, all of whom seemed to live in harmony.

But we soon tired of Hiromi and were anxious to be on our way. He insisted on driving us to the plane, but first he had to show us his latest business venture: sea slugs. They were farmed and dried locally, and he intended to ship them by container to China, where they were to be sold—at immense profit—as an aphrodisiac. He was, however, short of working capital; I was invited to become his fifty-fifty partner. My owning a private plane was all he required in the way of credentials. I was to put up the money, he would provide the sea slugs. I admired his enthusiasm but declared that my venture capital days were over and that he would have to seek a partner elsewhere.

It was our seventh day in the plane. We flew beneath a race of cumulus cloud that swept in low from the Indian Ocean onto the deserted Mozambique coast. White breakers scalloped the beaches of fine-grained sand that lined the shore. Trade winds, driven by the monsoon, known as the *kazakazi*, push dhows laden with cargo down this African coast as far south as Kilwa every April to November, and then like clockwork, the weather swings round and the *kuzi* drives them back northeast, hurling blasts of angry weather at their quartered sails, all the way to Arabia.

We were midway down the coast of Mozambique. An enormous, fertile delta stretched inland, unbroken to the horizon. The land was devoid of human beings and livestock. The land was completely deserted, wasted by the tsetse fly.

John Reader writes in his book *Africa*: "The tsetse fly is a blood-feeding carrier of microscopic parasites called trypanosomes that transfer to the host's bloodstream. Once inside, these parasites breach the immune system by constantly changing their antigenic character through massive reproduction which causes 'sleeping sickness' in humans and domestic cattle. This small fly and the anopheles malarial mosquito between them have determined the demographics of the African continent."

The plane's satellite-guided GPS instrument indicated our latitude at fifteen degrees south, a point where the coastline backed suddenly towards the southeast. We decided to head west, inland across the delta to the small agricultural town of Quelimane which sat forty miles from the coast on the banks of the Luala River. The plane skimmed low over a mix of water and thick green vegetation. Shafts of sunlight reflecting off the swamp water stabbed the windscreen with refracted light until, gradually, the city of Quelimane emerged on the skyline, shimmering in an opaque light.

Quelimane was depressing beyond measure. The city reeked of dust. Plastic bags and papers whirled and floated in the air above the empty streets, which were littered with garbage. Poverty seeped into the heart of the city as if the place were cursed by the plague. Downtown, grim leftovers of Mozambique's endorsement of a socialist system lined the city square: store windows half-empty, pathetic displays of cheap running shoes, gaudy bathroom fixtures and synthetic clothing haphazardly displayed. Broken concrete drains filled with mud and garbage lay clogged and unserviceable. Potholes left many of the streets deserted. Police authority had abandoned the city centre, leaving it to function outside the rule of law. We'd never encountered anything so derelict.

The best hotel charged $275 per night for a room with a noisy air-conditioning unit that dribbled rust-coloured water onto a brown-stained carpet smelling of rot. Mismatched tiles had lifted from the rank bathroom floor; there was no hot water and plugs were missing from the bathtub and sink. There was no point in complaining; the absentee owner lived in Maputo and paid scant attention to his investment, beyond the regular weekly collection of cash receipts.

We wandered the streets of Quelimane, stopping at a small dingy café for a Coca-Cola. Only a few shuffling pedestrians passed and the occasional truck rattled down the main street, belching black diesel fumes into the humid air. Suddenly, the dismal commerce of the café was interrupted by the arrival of two expensive Land Cruisers, United Nations logos emblazoned on the cab doors. The young drivers, sunglasses cocked on the upper half of their foreheads, strode through the door as if they owned the place. These "Aid Givers of Africa," highly paid, living in lavish quarters in the south end of town, removed from the squalor of the slums, were loud and arrogant—a depressingly familiar sight.

I had an irresistible urge to confront them, to challenge their uncultured behaviour in public, as they discussed the value and price of things beyond the imagination of the Africans sitting next to us. Insensitive to their surroundings, these men behaved as if Africa was an unfortunate tour of duty, something to endure without respect or understanding.

Ironically, though, the Africans considered the kind of privilege they enjoyed as simply the result of good fortune—nothing to do with racial discrimination, assumed superiority, or education. Whites had simply got to the source of money first; it was fate or bad luck that had landed Africans in an economic backwater. This was one of the causes of the African tendency to embrace the "big daddy" syndrome, which idolized the big man whose luck it was to have money and power. It was an attitude that supported the reign of dictators and blatant corruption.

We spent only one night in Quelimane. The next morning we followed the Luala River back to the coast as it meandered through the delta like a large python, sliding through grasses, around diversionary inlets. A few inhabitants, fishermen in dugouts, waved as we passed overhead. Flocks of white egrets, startled by the sound, lifted from the marshland and circled before dropping into their nests; otherwise, the land appeared empty from the air.

Turning south at the coast, we flew non-stop over the port of Beira and along the barren shoreline until we reached the island of Bazaruto, the favourite island resort of wealthy South Africans.

Krystyne had underlined Bazaruto on the map with a yellow marker, indicating interest.

"Okay, let's go for one night," I said.

"Can we afford it?" she replied, smiling disingenuously.

"No," I answered as we circled to land.

Bazaruto was no more than a shifting sandbar covered with palm trees and gorse, but it was spectacularly beautiful and very expensive. In the middle of this aquamarine paradise the Bazaruto Island Resort catered lavishly to an "in crowd" from South Africa.

At the southern end of the island was a landing strip of sand interspersed with patches of dry grass where we sighted two Islander planes with oversized balloon tires. Circling low overhead to assess the characteristics of what appeared to be suspiciously soft sand, I could see pilots on the ground below watching with keen interest. Haunting visions of South Island on Lake Turkana flashed to mind. One of the pilots gave a thumbs-up, so we banked into a final descent and touched down without difficulty.

Bazaruto lived up to its reputation as a playground for the privileged. Pink-fleshed businessmen with svelte, bronzed girlfriends lay around the pool, lazily soaking in the sun and sipping exotic drinks served by black waiters dressed in absurd uniforms. South African politics, viewed from the white man's perspective, was the topic of conversation, laced with prejudice and bitterness. Servile and patient, the African staff served guests without envy or resentment, grateful for the jobs that allowed them to raise their families in the garbage-strewn community just south of the resort. Protected by razor wire and dogs, the self-indulgent Bazaruto Island Resort guests could afford to remain indifferent to African sensibilities.

Krystyne and I soon tired of the scene and left the resort for a late-afternoon walk along the untracked beaches that stretched for miles up the north shore of the island. The sand, fine as icing sugar, bleached and runnelled by the wash of waves, lay like felt under our bare feet. Thousands of crabs raced back and forth in a slow dance before the foam advancing over the beach.

Krystyne looked radiant in the soft sea light. She took my hand. There was a moment of tenderness, suspended, like the sea mist at tide's change. Gulls pitched and wheeled against the shadows of dusk. A parade of white clouds raced along the horizon, over the sombre sea. We walked in silence until the sea breeze died before we turned back into the approaching darkness.

High on the hill above us, a lighthouse stabbed the night with flashes of light. We climbed the hill, up the wooden steps, through a tangle of sand and gorse to the stone tower where the giant Fresno lens turned silently above us, shooting its angled beam across the water.

We rested there, sitting with our backs against the stone wall, watching the first stars penetrate the night sky. Below, we could see the two sides of Africa: the cooking fires of the African village flickering and the electric lights of the Bazaruto Island Resort, side by side, each with its human cargo of dreams, each untouched by the other's humanity. What was it about Africa that was so human, so utterly beautiful, but so capable of breaking one's heart?

The morning sky broke without cloud. Bazaruto's Land Rover, the side doors removed, swayed and swerved as it made its way over the sandy track to the airstrip. The young driver unceremoniously dumped us and the bags beside our plane. Our luxurious overnight stay was over.

In the distance, we heard a small single-engine plane approach the island from across the water. It was a Piper Cub, its engine leaking oil over the cowlings and a torn bit of canvas flapping on the outer edge of the starboard wing. It circled the strip once and landed on the sand, light and springy as a baby carriage. A wild-eyed white South African dressed in torn khaki drill and a floppy hat stepped down from the cockpit.

"Would you happen to have any engine oil?" he inquired, before I had a chance to say hello.

"Yes," I replied, hoping he wouldn't ask for more than a litre. Oil would be hard to find before reaching Johannesburg. "How much do you need? By the way my name is Scott, and this is my wife, Krystyne." We shook hands.

"Paul Dutton. Nice to meet you," he replied. "Two litres would do nicely, if you can spare it," he said. "This baby burns more oil than gas. The rings are shot, can't afford to replace them."

"So why Bazaruto?" I asked, thinking that one night here would pay for a new set of rings. I passed him the two litres from my diminishing supply.

"Oh, I'm doing a census count of dugongs along the coast." He took the oil and reached for his wallet to pay.

"Forget it," I said. "Happy to help out." He looked embarrassed momentarily, but accepted my offer. "What's a dugong?"

"Dugongs are sea mammals, and they're damn near extinction around here," he added, pouring the oil into his engine. "Something has to be done or they'll disappear." The dugong's survival had become Paul Dutton's life obsession. Whatever money he was able to save he spent on dugong research—and he was close to financial extinction himself.

Paul had just flown 350 miles up the coast from Durban, South Africa. Flying over long stretches of open water, out of sight of land, in a plane leaking oil, was of minor concern to him. He had sighted only three of the seven dugongs that were supposed to be breeding along that part of the coast.

"You're not heading south to Durban by any chance?" he asked, hoping to enlist us in his census-taking.

"No we're flying direct to Johannesburg from Maputo," I said, "and from there back to Durban. We'll be inland both ways." He insisted we look him up in Durban. We did so later, and spent a delightful evening with him and his wife, whom he had employed to help him run his struggling environmental consulting business. Several months later, back in Nairobi, I heard that Paul Dutton had crashed his plane but, undeterred, he was still conducting dugong research from the deck of a freighter plying up and down the Mozambique coast.

Leaving Bazaruto we flew down the coast to Maputo, formally, Lourenço Marques, the capital of Mozambique, poor and abandoned by its Portuguese founders. It was a delightful, though somewhat forlorn, city. With its wide boulevards lined with trees and outdoor cafés, it retained the grace of an old European city. Maputo, also known as Delagoa Bay, Mozambique's largest and most important seaport, although busy with trade, had back streets filled with unskilled drifters and begging children—truer indicators of her sad decline. We stayed only one night. Our departure the next day was the last contact we had with East Africa and the Indian Ocean coast. Our plane rose from the airport, turned westward, and slipped into the afternoon sun as we climbed over the eastern foothills of the Drakensberg Mountains of South Africa.

12

South Africa

OUTH AFRICA was a culture shock. We had arranged to stay with friends, a couple living in Johannesburg; however, there was no answer on the phone the evening of our arrival. Since we had confirmed arrangements only days earlier, the lack of response seemed strange. Not knowing what else to do, we took a cab to the nearest Holiday Inn.

Next morning we learned that our hostess, stopping at a red light on her way home, had been pulled out of her car by two black youths, robbed, and shot in the chest. Abandoned at the side of the road and bleeding badly, she managed to crawl unassisted to a nearby phone booth, where she called the police—only to receive a recorded message. Three white men passing in a car picked her up and drove her to the police station where they left her outside refusing to get further involved. Her husband, beside himself and in no shape for our visit, was encamped in the hospital. We could offer little else beyond sympathy and moral support. She eventually recovered, but for us it was a shocking introduction to Johannesburg.

In spite of dire warnings from the hotel doorman, we opted to walk over to a pseudo-Tudor-style English pub in the nearby shopping mall for beer and sausages. A gang of aging Hells Angels from Germany were at the bar, ogling a waitress who seemed pleased by the attention—which encouraged further lewd behaviour from her admirers. Middle-aged men in leather, the mugging of our hostess, and the garish materialism of the shopping mall had us reeling. Where was the Africa we thought we knew? This modern, hard-edged Johannesburg seemed at odds with the eternal beauty of East Africa.

————————

Our spirits lifted the next day on meeting the editor of the *Sunday Independent* newspaper. John Battersby, whose name had been given to us by a mutual friend, greeted us at the door of his house dressed in a pair of rumpled trousers and a plaid shirt. His broad generous face was blotchy from the previous night's drink and too little sleep. A limp strand of hair hung over his forehead, half covering intelligent eyes, beneath salt-and-pepper eyebrows.

He shook hands with us warmly, and his friendly demeanour immediately put us at ease. His house was a conventional low-slung bungalow, typical of white suburban Johannesburg, split-level floors designed to break the monotony of single rooms leading off a narrow corridor. It was a pleasant change for us to be in a real residence with comfortable chairs, magazines, and paintings. We readily accepted his invitation to spend the day with him touring Johannesburg and Pretoria.

John provided intelligent and interesting perspectives on South Africa. The country was a powder keg, and only the continuing miracle of Nelson Mandela prevented it from exploding. The Truth and Reconciliation Commission hearings were currently taking place under Mandela's leadership, and they had not degenerated into the feared witch hunt prophesied by white hardline opinion. The dignity of those hearings had stunned and impressed the world, and even the most rabid supporters of apartheid. Still, South Africa was a boiling cauldron of frustration. Generations of blacks had been forcibly restricted to the townships, and when these restrictions were removed the immediate result was massive unemployment.

Crime was a huge problem. John predicted it would become even worse. South Africa's history was a brutal one, where the application of force under apartheid had managed to contain recidivism within the townships, but now it was spreading into the white communities where it was visible and contagious. South Africa was undergoing the tricky transformation initiated by de Klerk from the previous white minority's iron-fisted control to the blacks' accession to power and a more open society under Nelson Mandela. Time was needed to manage and meet the unrealistic expectations of a new generation released from the gross injustices of the townships—it had all the elements of a social revolution.

Midway through our conversation a blond, barefoot girl in her early twenties, dressed in torn jeans and a skimpy tank top, sidled into the living room and plunked herself saucily on John's lap. Tossing her hair to one side she asked him if he wanted a cappuccino. A young prima donna, self-consciously aware of her sexuality and thoroughly spoilt, she seemed oblivious to our presence. Embarrassed, John introduced her as Katrina, the Norwegian daughter of his wife's best friend. She and her companion, Elizabeth, were staying with John, whose wife was in Cape Town. Although the girls had been in Johannesburg for three days, they had yet to leave his house.

Katrina and her girlfriend wanted to see more of South Africa, and we sensed that John was eager to see them under someone else's care. He suggested that we might consider taking them with us to Cape Town. It was an awkward request to refuse. We warned the girls it would be a tight fit in the plane, and that we planned to take four or five days to reach the Cape via Durban and the South African "Wild Coast."

Their enthusiasm was infectious however, and two days later, having relieved John of his charges, we took off, the plane crammed with our new passengers and their gear. The weather was unsettled, brooding and restless. A bank of pewter-tinted cloud far to the east of Johannesburg threatened rain, so the flight controller directed us south over the rolling hills of the Eastern Transvaal. The emerald quilted fields below resembled southern Ireland. Farms were interspersed with light-manufacturing plants and small country villages, prosperous and well maintained, the prosperity derived from rich land and cheap labour. For whites with money, life in South Africa appeared to be largely unchanged. Only the future threatened.

The prospects of bad weather ahead had Krystyne preparing, in advance of the approaching storm clouds, the IFR route charts and approach plates that contained specific information for the runways at Durban.

As we flew towards the Drakensberg Mountains the weather rapidly deteriorated into poor flying conditions. Visibility was reduced to zero. I requested and received an instrument clearance from the Durban air controller, and I was told to prepare for an instrument landing at Durban where the cloud levels were only just above the runway. The buffeting from turbulence had turned uncomfortable. The thrill of small-plane flying had evaporated for the girls; they sat immobile in the back seat, silent and grim, complexions pale green.

Durban approach had us flying out beyond the coast, past the outer beacon, to execute a procedure turn and line up with Runway 23. Flying without visibility, I rechecked the approach plate to confirm the landing data: minimum levels of descent, time and distance from the beacon to threshold, and the missed approach procedures. The rain drummed onto the windscreen and the plane jerked and bucked through the unpredictable gusts that blew in raw over the coast. This was "dirty flying," in the lingua franca of pilots, where cloud cover was down to "minimums," which for Durban was 225 feet above the ground. Our rate of descent of 500 feet per minute would give me twenty-two seconds to sight the runway, and then execute a landing once we broke through cloud.

The altimeter passed two thousand feet above sea level as we crossed the non-directional beacon inbound, and the needle swung 180 degrees onto the tail of the aircraft. I pressed the stopwatch and the sweep hand started its count to the runway threshold. Approaching at 100 knots we had a minute and forty-five seconds to go before touchdown. At 800 feet above the ground with still no visibility, knowing the city's buildings were on either side of our descent path, my hands began to sweat. I had not flown an instrument approach to "minimums" for almost a year. I felt terribly out of practice.

"Tell me when you see the ground," I snapped at Krystyne, who was peering out the window.

"I see nothing," she said nervously, "nothing." The altimeter slid past 650 feet, drawing us closer and closer to the ground. I found it difficult to hold the plane steady in the sudden violent gusts of rain pelting the fuselage. I was fully occupied flying the plane, balancing the approach plate on my knee, rechecking calculations, scanning the flight instruments and the stopwatch, working the radio.

"See anything now?" I shot out at Krystyne again.

"Nothing, no nothing . . ." Krystyne's voice trailed off weakly.

"You're sure? We're close. . . ." We slid through 450 feet above ground. Another few seconds and I would have to abort the landing and overshoot to a safe holding point. "Keep reporting, even if there's nothing," I insisted. We were running out of altitude.

"Yes . . . Okay, I see it . . . the ground," she exclaimed. "Right below us. I see it now."

"Jesus, we're high," I exclaimed, pulling back on the throttle.

The runway was two hundred feet below us. I was on target, but a hundred feet high, with barely enough time to flare the airplane in preparation for a touchdown before running out of runway. I pulled on the last ten degrees of flap, cut the throttle and let the plane sink onto the remaining four hundred feet of runway. The wheels touched the pavement and we stopped fifty feet short of the airport fence. It was not an elegant landing, but we were on the ground.

We taxied slowly onto the ramp and disembarked into weather that whipped and tore at us as we hurried across the tarmac. Huddled together for what seemed an absurdly long time in a cramped mobile trailer, we waited for the airport authorities and the promised transport to take us into the centre of the city.

Durban, out of season, was as damp, cold, and blustery as any sea-port on the south coast of England in winter. The rain sheeted the city. The wind howled through the overhead electric wires, dancing and tugging at their fixtures like rigging in a storm. Rolling banks of cloud swept down from the cape under the full force of a gale raging out of the southern ocean.

We checked into the Balmoral Hotel, a modern multi-storeyed building with a lobby, cavernous and garishly decorated with islands of fake art deco furniture. Less than a dozen people wandered about like lost souls in an empty train station; hotel staff outnumbered guests two to one. The same band of Hells Angels we had encountered three days previously in Johannesburg entered the lobby to register alongside us.

Later that afternoon the rain subsided to a drizzle. We wandered through the downtown area, into the local museum, around the central square, and finally into the Indian outdoor market. Large sheets of canvas, bellied with rainwater, hung over the food stalls and dripped onto sodden vegetables heaped high on wooden crates. Vendors were packing up their wares, tired and dispirited, eager to go home. As it turned out, Durban in the winter had little to offer beyond the delightful prospect of dinner with our new-found friend Paul Dutton, the dugong zoologist, and his wife. The Norwegian girls were considerably more enthusiastic about Durban, dancing through most of the night at one of the city's many discos. They staggered into the hotel in the early hours of the morning convinced that Durban was one of the most exciting cities in Africa.

———————

The weather cleared the next morning for our flight south along the coast. The girls had had little sleep the night before, and were in no shape to fly. Their heads soon rag-dolled onto each other's shoulders, where they remained until we reached Port St. John, at the mouth of the Umngazi River.

The source of the Umngazi is high in the Drakensberg Moun-

tains, and the water wends its way through a narrow gorge two thousand feet above the Indian Ocean. The village of Port St. John is
precariously perched on a narrow strip of silt at the mouth of the
river that defines the northern extremity of the South African "Wild
Coast," a remote rocky coastline inaccessible by road or boat.

The only landing place for a plane is a plateau two thousand feet
above the town; one end faces the Umngazi Gorge, the other termi-
nates at a cliff overlooking the Indian Ocean. Local flight conditions
include sudden unpredictable updraughts that turn a perfectly normal landing into a roller-coaster ride.

John Castello, our contact, sat in a Land Rover watching us approach with enough interest to be able to recount the details in the
event of a crash. We taxied over to his Land Rover and I swung out
of the pilot's seat and impulsively offered him the bottle of cheap
brandy that had been rolling around in the back of the plane since
our departure from Nairobi. He was stunned by this unexpected
act of generosity—and by the sight of Katrina, whose scantily clad
emergence from the plane was calculated to gain attention.

John's wife operated the only hotel in town, where we were provided cabins that were clean and attractive. The Norwegian girls
headed straight for the beach to swim, in spite of the freezing water
caused by the Antarctic current, which extends as far north as Port
St. John. Their white limbs, like porcelain china figures, appeared
fragile and stark against the incoming tide. Krystyne and I sat on the
hotel porch chatting to John and his wife. John's thinly disguised
interest in Katrina focused on her pale white form prancing back
and forth, skittish as a colt, against the breaking sea.

John was a thoroughly likeable man, a world-renowned ocean fly
fisherman, whose gregarious nature made him the town's friend and
confidant. His days were consumed by minor errands. He was the
only person within a hundred miles who owned a cell phone, which
he wore on his belt like a pistol.

The next morning he and I were in his Land Rover when his cell
phone rang. A reporter from Durban was inquiring about a ship
that had gone aground twenty miles down the coast from Port St.

John. Could John provide details? Perplexed, he could tell them nothing. Since the roads south of Port St. John led inland, making the coastline inaccessible, I suggested we fly there. He enthusiastically agreed and we roared up the winding switchback road in his Land Rover to the airstrip. As we drove, two more calls came in, one from the Johannesburg *Sunday Times*, offering money if we could provide pictures, another from a salvage crew seeking to hire us and the plane for two days.

Within fifteen minutes we were circling a twelve-thousand-ton cargo freighter that had rammed straight into the coast. The bow was crumpled onto a small rock shelf projecting out from the cliff twenty feet above the water. The freighter must have ploughed into the cliff face at full speed. The crew had walked from the bow of the ship onto the ledge and were huddled there, stranded, unable to pass beyond either side of the ledge, while the surf pounded and crashed below them. We flew within twenty-five feet of the freighter's deck through a series of tight figure-eight turns in high winds, while John managed to take pictures through the open window of the cockpit.

The ship rocked up and down in a swell that was slowly grinding the bottom out of her. Although no lives were lost it would eventually take fifteen hours and a helicopter to remove the men from the ledge. On the flight back, John managed to negotiate the sale of his photographs over his mobile to the Johannesburg *Sunday Times*, a transaction that contributed greatly to our friendship.

Later that evening, John, flush from his success as a press photographer, launched into his plans for an international fly-fishing tournament. His idea grew more grandiose with every draught of cheap brandy. By midnight, he and I were the only ones at the bar. Krystyne and the girls had retired to their cabins, leaving me half-heartedly listening to John's dreams of fly-fishing tournaments. The evening breeze had settled into a soft current of air that left the ocean undulating under an imperfect moon. Most of Port St. John lay sleeping on the narrow slip of shoreline with the dark loom of Africa ghosting behind it.

The brandy finished, I rose, bid John good night, and headed to my cabin through the back garden. Unexpectedly, I caught sight of Katrina through the window of her cabin, kneeling naked on her bed. The overhead light from the room illuminated her slender form as she brushed her hair before a small mirror hanging above the headboard of her bed. Had she left the window and the curtains wide open on purpose? My first thought, ridiculously enough, was sympathy for John for not being there.

John had suggested we fly inland across the Transkei to Somerset East, a small town nestled in the foothills of the Sneeuberg Mountains. He had arranged for us to stay as paying guests with his friend Bill Brown, who owned a farm there. We had seen little of the interior of South Africa, so we readily agreed. Somerset East had a local disused airfield and John was convinced we could land on it, although, after a few phone calls, he was unable to obtain reliable information. We decided to go and chance it.

The field lay unkempt, without markings, runway, or windsock. Long, uncut grass had grown so high our plane almost disappeared once the wheels touched the ground. We rolled two hundred feet down the field, unable to see more than a few feet in front of us, the propeller acting as a giant threshing machine, sending grass and seed in all directions to the amazement of a group of Africans standing nearby.

I instructed Katrina to walk ahead and guide us to the edge of the field, keeping an eye out for large boulders or holes that might damage the plane's undercarriage. Katrina was a comical sight, with her blond hair and miniskirt, strutting in front of the plane with a closed umbrella held high above her head. She led us to the fence, where the tall grass had been nibbled short by a tethered goat. The Africans stared, mouths agape, the younger ones shouting with glee at the prospect of our arrival.

We disembarked, locked the plane, and left it in charge of a man in tribal dress, who accepted responsibility for guarding the plane on the promise of payment. Then we walked over to the side of the road, trailed by a ragtag group of African children, to ask the driver of a parked truck where we might find Bill Brown.

"Well, I'm yer mun," he said in a curious accent, part Scottish, part South African. "I'm pleased ta meech yah. Are yah the Griffins that's com'n to stah with us?" A tight grin broke across his weathered face. The coincidence of his arrival just as we landed was a mystifying occurrence, one that seemed to happen often during our time in Africa.

Bill Brown was a seventh-generation Scottish South African, whose farm was situated five miles outside Somerset East. It was the best-kept farm I had ever seen: fences taut, gates painted silver, flowering gardens, hired hands in blue overalls, servants' quarters built with brick, the whole place clean and bright. Bill and his brother, Alastair, had adjoining farms that covered the floor of a wide valley ringed by the Sneeuberg foothills. Their great-grandfather, Robert Brown, had designed an irrigation system that collected runoff for a reservoir at the head of the valley. A giant paddlewheel fed a network of sluiceways that irrigated the entire valley, an engineer's delight. Both farms, as a result, were emerald green, rich in crops and sheep, a Garden of Eden by comparison to the sparse landholdings of their African neighbours.

But Bill Brown was a worried man. He feared the expropriation of his farm by the local authorities—and with good reason. Current trends in South Africa's politics indicated that before long his farm would be legally or illegally expropriated. Why should such valuable land remain in the hands of two white men, when literally hundreds around him lived in poverty? The fact that he and his family had, over generations, chosen the land, designed the irrigation system, and worked the farm was irrelevant. The whites always seemed to get the good land and the blacks, impoverished, were left to farm a dust bowl.

The thought of losing his sole inheritance preyed on Bill Brown, marring his sleep, etching deep lines across his brow. His blue eyes carried the angst of a man haunted by the knowledge that time was running out. No matter how hard he tried to bury his demons beneath the punishing routine of farm chores, the spectre of his land being parcelled up into uneconomic lots drove him mad. He desperately clung to the forlorn hope that fate would somehow allow him to pass his farm on to his son.

We sat at the family oak table transported to Africa from Scotland by Bill's ancestors. Heaping platters of hot food, fresh from the farm, the product of hard work by these God-fearing people, sat steaming on the sideboard. I was asked to say grace and managed to resurrect something in Latin—the residuum of a boarding school education.

Bill recounted how his great-grandfather in 1850 had commissioned the gigantic paddlewheel of the irrigation system from a firm in Manchester, England. It was sent to Africa by ship, disassembled, and transported by oxen 150 miles from Port Elizabeth over the Sneeuberg Mountains, the same inhospitable mountain range we had flown over that day.

Bill had a lifelong fascination with planes, an interest he had wanted to pursue since boyhood. I offered to fly him over his farm, and he was ecstatic at the prospect. He took particular pleasure at our swooping low over the guests at his wife's annual flower party, clearing the gum trees around the house by less than fifteen feet. He was like a boy released from school, thrilled by the sensation of speed over the ground. We roared up and down the sides of his ancestral valley, carving figure-eight turns, twisting through ladders of sunlight in acrobatic flight.

His enthusiasm over the mechanics of flight, his natural ability at the controls, and his interest in the navigational equipment wrested him from his worries, so that during those couple of hours he suddenly appeared younger than his years. Never having taken a holiday in his life, he was a man in harness, struggling to stave off an ominous future, one destined to deprive him and his family of everything they had ever owned or cared for.

A sense of doom permeated the air. Despite Bill's superhuman efforts to remain faithful to his oath of loyalty to his ancestral inheritance, it was slipping from his grasp. A new Africa was emerging, fast displacing the one he understood. The impending expropriation of his farm was already the talk of Somerset East. The first migrants from the town had moved into the southwest field, adjacent to the entrance gate of his barn. He swore he would resist to the bitter end, but, if he lost it all, then he would simply walk away, taking nothing with him except a broken heart.

After tea, I wandered down the path that led behind the barn to a small knoll. There, amongst the whisper of pines, I came upon the family graveyard. Granite tombstones recorded the lifespan of Browns, Stricklands, and Turners. At the bottom of the hill a small trout stream meandered quietly through a field of ferns and disappeared into a grove of willows. On the far bank, a flock of sheep inched their way up the hillside of his brother's farm, bells tinkling soft and distant across the valley. The place was utterly at peace in the slanting shadows of the late afternoon, undisturbed, as it had been for generations.

In Africa, life and loyalty have always been transitory. To forget this was to court disaster. Time was clearly running out for Bill Brown, and he knew it. His personal tragedy lay waiting beneath the whispering pines while nightfall crept stealthily through the valley, anxious for morning.

————————

The remaining flights to Cape Town took two days, with a stopover at Plettenburg Bay, and they were uneventful until we ran into bad weather north of the Swartberg Mountains. Thick banks of ocean fog rolled in over the warm land and up the mountainsides, rapidly cooling the moist air and creating ideal icing conditions. Almost immediately a thin coating of rime began to accumulate on the leading edges of the propeller and the wings. I requested a lower altitude to warmer temperatures from the controller. It was dangerous to continue flying loaded with ice and no visibility over mountainous terrain. The controller refused my request. Any lower would take us below the authorized MEA (minimum en-route altitude).

The back-seat passengers awoke with a start, suddenly aware their well-being was in jeopardy. Flying below the MEA was strictly against instrument flight rules, and yet we urgently needed the warmer temperatures at lower altitudes. The outside temperature was close to freezing. I needed to go only five to eight hundred feet lower. But the rule was ironclad.

The plane became heavier as we accumulated more ice. I adjusted the aircraft's pitch to compensate, raising the aircraft's nose, increasing the "angle of attack," which ultimately leads to a stall and then into a spin.

It was time to break the rules. The authorized MEA contains a margin of safety of one thousand feet above the highest obstacle. I eased the stick forward, dropped eight hundred feet, and gained two degrees centigrade, enough to start the melting of ice.

Ice began to fly off the propeller, striking the fuselage; within ten minutes the plane had regained its normal angle of attack, permitting me to return to the authorized eight-thousand-foot altitude. Slowly ice began to re-form, forcing us back down within four or five minutes into the warmer air. We continued this nerve-racking roller-coaster ride, alternating between serious icing and flying eight hundred feet below the authorized MEA with no visibility.

I knew the landing procedures at the Cape Town airport would be tricky. South African controllers have long had a reputation for being difficult, particularly with non-professional pilots. I prepared the plane for an instrument approach. It was then that I noticed a warning flag on my glide slope instrument, indicating that it was defective. The glide slope is part of the ILS (instrument landing system); it provides key information via a set of crosshairs to guide the plane's rate of descent and direction down the final flight path to the runway threshold. I had never experienced an ILS instrument failure before; this time the approach and landing would have to be executed with a "partial panel" of instruments. Tension rose in the back of my neck.

The loss of an ILS instrument is not, in itself, a disaster; it merely increases the workload for the pilot. Krystyne, alert to the situation, warned the girls to remain quiet, and I informed the controller that my ILS was defective and at eight thousand feet I was accumulating ice. A laconic reply came back over the radio.

"Charlie Foxtrot Whisky Mike Juliet, what are your intentions? Are you declaring an emergency?"

"Negative," I replied. It was not an emergency; I merely wished to alert the controller that I had my hands full and was hoping for assistance. Normally, under such circumstances, a controller might vector or provide compass headings to help align the aircraft with the runway. No such luck. Admittedly, there was traffic in the area; too much, perhaps, to warrant individual treatment?

"Charlie Foxtrot Whisky Mike Juliet is cleared to the Star Greyton Two Alpha approach for Runway 01. Inform Cape Town passing Delta Twenty, Romeo India Victor." This was a clearance for a full-instrument approach, no special consideration. As a pilot I was on my own. Either it was an emergency or I was expected to fly the same approach as other commercial aircraft with full crew, backup instruments, and the latest computer equipment. I read back the instruction, trimmed the aircraft, and commenced the descent.

The non-directional bearing needle swung 180 degrees to the aircraft's tail announcing the crossing of the Delta beacon inbound. My precise position was clearly established, even though there was zero visibility. There was no point fuming about the controller's attitude; I needed to concentrate and fly the approach using the instruments that still functioned. Wiping my hands on my trouser legs, hunched over the controls, I gripped the yoke and scanned the instrument panel, holding the plane on course.

Suddenly, the white strobe lights of Runway 01 flashed in short explosive bursts through the parting cloud. We were on target as the runway came into view, and seconds later we were on the ground.

Taxiing off the runway, we passed alongside the enormous wings of a Boeing 747 waiting for us to exit the ramp, its lights flashing through gusts of driving rain. It was my second instrument approach to minimums within a week.

The next morning Krystyne and I sat alone at the breakfast table and overheard two pilots in uniform chatting to each other.

"Did you hear that Canadian yesterday on the radio in a Cessna 180 flying into Cape Town?" The junior captain was talking to his senior officer as they sat drinking coffee. "The controller made it as difficult as he could for the poor bastard. He'd lost his ILS and the controller refused to vector him in unless he declared an emergency. Talk about brutal. Typical of those guys."

The older man remained silent as if thinking about something else, before replying, almost absent-mindedly, "I guess you have to wonder what the hell he was doing up there in that kind of weather." Pretending not to hear the last comment, I shrugged my shoulders and let slip the merest hint of a smile in Krystyne's direction, but she never revealed her thoughts to me.

13

Diamonds and Blood

C
APE TOWN was as beautiful as we imagined—remarkably similar to Vancouver in many respects, prosperous, clean, and surrounded by spectacular physical scenery. We took a cab directly to the AMREF offices on the outskirts of town in order to report back to Mike Gerber their suitability for his board meeting. The place was simple, nicely decorated, with posters of nurses ministering to the sick, Africans helping Africans—digging wells for clean water, installing mosquito nets, and warning about AIDS. The meeting room was small but I was confident the directors would leave with a good impression. The staff had plans to serve African food, including goat and *ugali*, a ubiquitous maize-like porridge popular with Africans. I called Gerber and recommended that he proceed with his plan to hold his board meeting there. It would be fine.

We abandoned the Norwegian girls in Cape Town. Forlorn at the prospect of being left with their elderly, retired relations, they expressed eagerness to continue with us, but we had grown impatient with their narcissistic behaviour and were anxious to be on our own. Looking back through the rear window as they drove away, Katrina blew a kiss in our direction, both hands extended in a theatrical pose. We never saw or heard from either of them again, in spite of the exchange of addresses and fervent promises to stay in touch.

We entered our third week away from Nairobi. We had flown a total of three thousand miles down the east coast of Africa. Our plan now was to head north from Cape Town up the Atlantic side of South Africa to Namibia's border, along the Diamond Coast and the Skeleton Coast bordering the Kalahari Desert, to Angola. We planned to spend ten days in Namibia.

Namibia, once a part of South Africa, is a region of remote deserts, desolate coastline, and igneous rock formations formed over three billion years ago. It has been an independent country since 1990, after years of occupation, first by the Portuguese, later by the Germans up until the First World War, then by the white South African government. It has been exploited for its rich minerals—zinc, uranium, copper, lead—and it remains one of the world's foremost sources of alluvial diamonds. As such, it has been a prize possession of outsiders who have consistently swept aside the interests of the San or "Bushmen," the Khoisan, and the Bantu, in the indecent scramble of colonial and multinational exploitation of the country's wealth. The interests of indigenous tribes have long been ignored; the bulk of Namibia's limited viable farmland was divided into six thousand farms, all of which were given to white settlers under mandate by South Africa's apartheid government.

Historically, the blacks were confined to "reserves," forced to provide scarce labour for the mining industry through a combination of pass laws and taxation. Injustices, driven by unrivalled greed, reached a level hardly imaginable today, sowing the seeds of eventual rebellion by those with nothing to lose. Resistance movements developed, such as the South West Africa People's Organization (SWAPO) and the Democratic Turnhalle Alliance (DTA), formed with Marxist-oriented support from places like Angola and Cuba. Local organizations were manipulated by the United Nations, the United States, and the Soviet Union into a struggle that eventually led to protracted negotiations and finally Namibia's independence.

But in spite of independence Namibia remains in the grip of exploitation of multinationals for its minerals, especially its diamonds. The country is one of the richest sources of diamonds in the world. Diamonds, the Western symbol of love and caring, have ruthlessly cut a bloody swath through the country's history, one filled with greed and human misery.

We flew up the Atlantic coast to Alexander Bay, the port of entry into Namibia, situated at the mouth of the Orange River. The sun's glare blasting off the desert sand had washed the sky into a milky haze. Construction trailers surrounded the narrow airstrip that lay half submerged under drifting sand. Sand swirled and sifted into the smallest crevice, around sheets of flapping plastic covering the windows, under the doors of makeshift offices, into the office files bulging with yellow paper. The air was thick with the dust of blowing sand. Only the gnarled cacti, it seemed, worn ragged by the desert wind, survived the sand's relentless blast.

Inside the reception hallway of the airport, heavily armed soldiers, their boots crunching the linoleum floor, strolled past us, bored and unfriendly. Immigration officials viewed our sudden arrival with suspicion. What were we doing in a small plane in this private part of the country? Thirsty and hot, we inquired whether we might purchase bottled water. There was none for sale and little sympathy for our lack of foresight.

Unshaven, tough-looking white foremen oversaw gangs of black workers with downcast eyes and slow gaits—men too long in harness. The atmosphere was tense; security was tight. We cleared customs in the main building while a dozen construction workers filed into an adjoining trailer, where they were stripped and searched—standard end-of-shift routine.

Alexander Bay, one of the most prolific areas for diamonds in the world, is the De Beers company's territory, a private state within a country. Diamonds are the principal reason for the white man's presence here: it has been that way for almost 150 years, fuelling some of the worst of human behaviour.

Diamonds travel almost eight hundred miles under water, buried in the thick effluent of the Orange River, from Kimberley to the Atlantic, where they eventually wash up on the Diamond Coast. Uncut diamonds surface on the beach, where they lie untouched, there for the taking: except that they belong to De Beers. De Beers owns everything, reigning supreme over the land, controlling the inland waters, operating the mines, supervising the workers, running management and law enforcement agencies. Patrolling the beaches, De Beers guards have orders to shoot trespassers on sight. Stories are legion of half-crazed renegades, ex-employees, and adventurers, risking everything to infiltrate the company's defences in search of fortune. Heavily armed motor cruisers, complete with frogmen, patrol the waters off the coast, eager to administer justice on the spot.

John Reader relates how the rush for diamonds began near Hope Town in March 1869, when a native herdsman found a large diamond weighing eighty-three carats. It later became known as the "Star of Africa." This discovery set off a feverish search for diamonds that centred on Kimberley, once a quiet place where many tributaries, including the Vaal, all feed into the Orange River. Thus was unleashed unparalleled greed and untold depredation upon the indigenous African pastoralists and nomads who had lived there peacefully for centuries before the arrival of the white man. South Africa's most famous diamond mines now occupy their homeland.

Reader explains that "diamonds are formed under cratons, massive slabs of rock that exert heat and pressure on carbon, producing diamonds, which are carried to the surface through volcanic pipes in the craton. The Kaapvaal craton, which covers a considerable part of southwestern Africa, was formed over three billion years ago and is one of the world's largest, more than 160 kilometres deep. Its content of diamonds has been unequalled. As a result the Kimberley area has been and continues to be—along with the gold deposits of Witwatersrand—one of the two richest mining sites in the world."

Inevitably, the lure of untold riches pitted Boers against the British, who imposed separate and conflicting laws concerning property and mineral rights on land arbitrarily confiscated from Africans.

"The Boers and later the British South Africans needed labour to operate the mines and black male Africans were not only deprived of their land and separated from their families but were indentured into slavery. They were forced into heavily guarded compounds that held as many as thirty thousand workers, paid as little as ten shillings a week, and supervised by a brutal police force operating under the Diamond Trade Act of 1882, passed in order to facilitate the mine operators' needs, and specifically those of Cecil Rhodes.

The use of convict labour allowed even lower wages and longer hours of work, and so the slightest infraction led to arbitrary justice, subject to initiation and manipulation by De Beers, which produced a surplus of convicts." The De Beers convicts, Reader goes on to say, "were made to strip in the search houses and were sent naked to their cells, where blankets were the only available coverings. At the end of his sentence, each man was confined to his cell for five days, naked and with unwieldy leather gloves locked on his hands. This practice was designed to flush out any diamonds he might have swallowed, in the hope of selling them once he was free."

We informed the authorities in Alexander Bay, employees of De Beers, that we intended to fly north, up the coast of Namibia, and we were instructed to fly higher than fifteen hundred feet above the ground or be shot down. There would be no second chances. With this admonition still reverberating in our minds, we took flight heading north over the grey Atlantic coastline.

Far below, we could see the De Beers bulldozers clawing back and forth over the empty beaches, pushing mountains of sand, like giant crabs working the beach between the movements of the tide. Huge screens for sifting sand rotated slowly beside the water's edge, like the extended wings of prehistoric birds. Gunboats bristling with small-calibre machine guns plied the waters of the Atlantic in search of intruders. We peered down at this activity as we inched our way up the Diamond Coast to the small seaport of Lüderitz, shining golden in the setting sun.

When we landed, a blast of wind-driven sand threatened to scour the paint off the fuselage of my plane. I approached the De Beers guard who sat crouched inside the door of the company hangar, offering him a tip if he allowed me to put my plane inside overnight. His face slid into a grin indicating anything was possible. Together, we hand-pushed the plane, against what seemed like a gale-force mixture of wind and sand, into the cavernous old hangar, which rattled and banged as if a huge caged beast were trying to break out through the walls.

Lüderitz is a surreal relic of the German colonial era perched on the edge of a rock promontory with the cold Atlantic on one side and wind and sand blowing in from the Kalahari Desert on the other. Street names like Bismarck, Goering, Wilhelm, and Lepplin add to the bizarre make-believe atmosphere of the place—the Hollywood Durango of Africa.

The townsfolk spend their time battling the desert. Sand sifts into every corner of the town. No matter the defences, dunes inch in stealthily overnight, like banks of drifting snow, sweeping down the streets, nuzzling up against the wooden-framed houses. The sand is so fine in texture it floats like dust; airborne particulates seep into the nostrils, eyes, and hair, rendering people half crazed in appearance and attitude. What holds the inhabitants in this strange place? Conspiracies connected to diamonds? Are they the descendants of escapees from the First World War? What possible explanation can account for this small German community with its Lutheran churches, rich delicatessens, and noisy alehouses?

Within twenty-four hours the hangar where I had left my plane was banked by two feet of sand that had drifted into a cowl around the large folding doors. Taxiing the plane in a howling wind out to the runway the next day was excruciatingly slow work. One wrong turn of the ailerons, or an incorrect touch on the brakes, and the wing tip would rise and flip the plane onto its side. A tail dragger is notoriously difficult to steer on the ground. We crabbed laboriously along the taxiway, the plane pulling and shuddering like a thoroughbred horse. The crosswind placed incredible strain on the plane's undercarriage, stressing the control cables tight as piano wires.

I was forced to take off using the width of the taxiway, a distance of less than a hundred feet. The plane reared into a buffeting headwind, clearing the sandbank at the edge of the taxiway by inches. Free of the desert the plane shot up on the gusts, then north into a cerulean sky towards the city of Windhoek.

The farther inland we flew, the larger the sand dunes loomed below. Mountains of sand heaped up into massive shapes, like prehistoric humpbacked mammals lumbering across the desert. Spumes of blowing sand crested the dunes, driving the Kalahari farther and farther into the centre of Africa. Crossing our route, serrated canyons fingered the desert. Here, the earth's crust, untouched and hardened over five hundred million years, held primordial secrets of creation. Nothing stirred apart from the wind. An ancient light hovered over the land, hinting at the origin of things.

We flew for two hours with no visible sign of life below. I noticed with amazement that Krystyne was drinking the last of our bottled water.

"Hey, you're drinking our emergency supply," I remonstrated.

"I know, I know," Krystyne replied, "but I'm terribly thirsty. I'll replenish it once we arrive in Windhoek."

"If we go down in the desert, you've left us with less than twenty-four-hours' supply." She shot me a guilty look. She knew a two- or three-day walk out of the desert with inadequate supplies of water would be disastrous.

"Just one more sip, and then I'll stop," she said, taking a long swig from the soft plastic bag.

"Okay, but we agree in case of an emergency, what's left is mine?"

"Scott, don't be like that," she said. "I'm stopping."

"Fine. We'll share what's left and die together."

"Scott!" She hastily replaced the cap.

The engine thrummed steadily without a miss, its low-pitched rumble the constant purr of a large jungle cat. After so many hours of flying, the engine's harmonics were familiar; the slightest variation in pitch had me scanning the gauges, for oil, temperature, fuel mixture, the manifold pressure, the engine RPMs. The engine ran hot over the desert, the gauges hugging the upper limits of the safe operating range. At forty-three degrees centigrade, even at seven thousand feet, the engine cowlings had to be left open at cruise to provide extra ventilation.

I glanced over at Krystyne. Leaning forward to switch on the instrument lights, I caught her distinctive scent above the warm workings of the cockpit. There was something satisfying about our companionship, the two of us alone in the glow of the instruments, flying over the Kalahari at night, closer and closer to the city of Windhoek.

———————

Windhoek means "windy corner" in Afrikaans. The sun rides high over the clean streets lined with trees and flower beds. Brightly painted trams travel the main thoroughfares amid the easy flow of well-ordered traffic. Policemen in full uniform stand on old-fashioned kiosks under yellow and green umbrellas, directing cars with the unflappable efficiency of school matrons. Pedestrians, courteous and unhurried, amble past the storefront windows talking and laughing. The city, efficient and neat, reflects a strong Teutonic sense of discipline and order.

Namibia's small population of 1.6 million people appears to have successfully made the miraculous transition from a virtual police state to a democratic system based on law and order. In comparison with other African countries, the mix of races seems to live in harmony. Perhaps independence served as a welcome salve for past grievances. On closer examination though, we discovered that prejudices still linger in the breast of the German population. Trapped in a time warp, this curious minority resents the transfer of political power to the blacks. Bitter comments surfaced from the woman providing bed and breakfast, from the white shopkeepers, and from the owner of the aircraft hangar. Given the chance, they were all eager to share confidences with outsiders. The apparent calm of Windhoek disguises a racial bitterness familiar in all the parts of Africa where power has been ceded to the majority.

Krystyne and I sat at Roxy's Restaurant wondering whether Serge Pétillon would show up for our designated rendezvous, set a month and half earlier in Nairobi; we had not heard from him since. He was to fly in from Harare, spend eight days with us exploring Namibia, and return to Swaziland once we reached Victoria Falls.

We needn't have worried. Within minutes of the appointed hour, Serge, hunched like a boxer, sauntered into view. Dressed in a leather jerkin with a red bandana around his neck, unshaven and tanned, he looked like a bad man in a Sergio Leone film. He carried a small canvas bag of personal effects and a camera slung over his shoulder, nothing more.

Excited by our reunion, we settled around a table, ordered beer, and swapped tales of our adventures since parting in Nairobi. Serge's experiences in Swaziland had us regretting that we had flown over that country without stopping. He suggested we return with him, but our route was north from Namibia back to Kenya, and Swaziland would have been too great a diversion. We spread the map of Namibia over the table and discussed our plans to fly into the Kalahari Desert. Several rounds of beer later, we were still at the table; the afternoon shadows lengthened into evening and the brightly coloured streetlights danced before our eyes. Somehow, by then, it no longer mattered that we had lost the day.

We had to reorganize the plane to fit Serge's large frame into the rear seat. A third person required a major reconfiguration of gear, which at first felt like an invasion of personal space. The cockpit had become our intimate home, every corner familiar and useful, so the disruption seemed brutal.

Our immediate destination was Sössusvlei, in the Namib Desert, site of the world's largest sand dunes, where an Italian couple ran a unique ecological guest lodge called Kala Kuena.

It was a short flight from Windhoek, hot and bumpy. We flew at less than 350 feet above ground, in and out of thermal draughts that gusted off the semi-desert. Krystyne and I, accustomed to turbulence at low altitudes, readily traded a rough ride for the scenic view of volcanic rock sweeping beneath us. Serge, however, immediately became airsick—hard on his Gallic pride—which forced us higher into calmer air.

Our pre-arranged landing site at Sössusvlei proved irritatingly elusive. Under the glare of the desert sun, there was no hint of an airstrip anywhere in sight. We circled around, certain of our bearings but unsure whether or not to land. Serge was miserable, uncontrollably sick; we had to land.

I had obtained Sössusvlei's landing coordinates in Windhoek by telephone prior to departure. Unless I had transcribed them incorrectly, they placed us directly over a dried salt bed, probably an ancient desert lake, with no visible markers indicating a runway. I lowered the flaps, reduced the speed, and hoped the surface was as hard as it appeared from the air. We touched down and the wheels rolled on the baked surface as if it were concrete. Once the engine was shut down and the instruments switched off, we opened the doors of the cockpit and emerged into a furnace of hot air. The silence was eerie.

There was no sign of life. It seemed as if we had landed on the moon. Even with sunglasses, the horizon danced before us in a giant mirage that wriggled and squirmed under the blinding sun. We stood round the plane, overcome by heat, wondering and waiting. I rechecked the coordinates a third time against the GPS instrument and determined that we were within a hundred yards of the designated meeting spot. I speculated that, under such extreme temperatures, our engine would probably not start due to vapour expanding in the fuel line. We might be stuck on this salt pan until nightfall.

Then, Serge, who had recovered, pointed to a ribbon of dust rising on the horizon. "Our ride," he said weakly, although the vehicle appeared to be headed away from us.

"Why do you suppose they would ask us to land out here in the middle of nowhere?" Krystyne asked. "Shouldn't we try to get their attention?" I carried flares in the back of the plane; however, I was reluctant to use them unless it was a real emergency. Flares were hard to replace, and I might need them on my return flight to Canada.

"Let's give it a minute," I said. "We can always chase them in the plane," I added, having forgotten my concern about starting the motor. As I spoke, a Land Rover slowly swung round towards us. Within minutes we were shaking hands with the Italian driver, Angelo, whose wide grin split his dust-covered face.

"Sorry I'm late," he said breathlessly. "We suggest you leave your plane here for security reasons." He wiped his brow with his forearm, merely adding more dust to the mixture of sweat and chalk caked on his forehead.

"We wondered about this landing place," I replied. "We thought we'd been given the wrong coordinates."

"It's the right place all right. Nobody knows your plane is here, so it's safer than back at the lodge." He swung our bags effortlessly into the Land Rover. "We've had problems in the past," he added. "Once we found a plane's ailerons serving as a roof for a mud hut. Out here the plane remains out of sight. Now, are we all set?"

We clambered into the Land Rover and set out across the salt bed, winding around a two-mile depression that had been created by flash floods. Angelo drove like a wild man. The battered old Land Rover lurched from side to side, raising a tornado of dust. By the time we reached Sössusvlei we were sheeted in white dust; not even a shower and swim could eradicate the taste of it.

Kala Kuena had six one-room *bandas* a short distance from a large salon and dining room. The buildings were constructed from local stone and red earth, perfectly camouflaged from less than two hundred yards away. Inside, the spaces were attractive and cool in contrast to the scorching heat reflecting off the desert. We were the only paying guests, apart from Alberto, his wife, Maria, and their friend Alessandro Leospo, a professor of archaeology from Turin University. They welcomed us as if we were family.

After dinner we sat on large cushions outside on a deck under the stars enjoying the cool night air of the desert. Professor Leospo, dressed in white linen, rubbed his bare feet while he drew on his pipe and talked about Africa. His massive wave of white hair and thespian voice carried the authority of a university don.

"Professor, you are no doubt familiar with the Egyptian Museum in Turin," I ventured.

"Of course," he said. "Turin holds the most important collection of Egyptian antiquities in the world outside of Cairo—little appreciated, except by a few Egyptologists. Have you visited it?"

"Yes," I said. "Unfortunately, the museum was undergoing renovations at the time and much of it was closed, but what I saw was impressive."

"You must go back again," the professor insisted. "It holds incomparable treasures, rarely seen." He lapsed into silence, lost in thought, gazing at the beauty of the night sky.

Serge asked the professor why he was in Africa. He shifted onto his side, tucking a lumpy cushion under his hip before speaking.

"Ah, Africa," he said wistfully. "Everything started here." For a moment it seemed as if that was all he had to say. "You see, Africa is the oldest continent on earth, the place from which all others have drifted in a series of great tectonic shifts." The red glow of his pipe invaded the night. "Africa is our genesis, from the first solidification of rock to the first signs of animal life. Human evolution started not far from here only five million years ago. Just think about it." He lapsed back into silence. "Africa is our heritage. We are all descendants from the 'African Eve,'" he finally added.

"Who?" Krystyne asked in a whisper.

"The Old Testament speaks of Adam and Eve and yet all mankind is derived from an African Eve—our evolutionary mother. Every living person can be traced through genetic DNA to a single African woman who existed approximately 150,000 years ago. This African Eve of course was not the only woman alive then, but all other lineages, except hers, subsequently became extinct."

"I know some people who would be upset to hear that," said Serge dryly.

Professor Leospo ignored him and continued. "The first *homo sapiens* only left Africa 100,000 years ago, and yet their direct antecedents were wandering the African continent five million years previously. Anthropological findings in Laetoli, Tanzania, and Turkana, Kenya, date back as much as three and four million years ago." He leaned back on his pillow, and looked up at the sky, adding, "You ask me why I come to Africa? I come here to learn more about myself."

The professor stopped speaking again, and the rest of us remained silent. The Southern Cross lay on its left shoulder, its stem pointing south towards the pole. I wondered if it had the same navigational use in the southern hemisphere as Polaris, the pole star, had in the north. Or was its presence purely romantic?

"Why do you think Africa is in such a mess?" Serge asked. "Are there historical or cultural reasons that can explain the apparent hopelessness of Africa today?"

Maria, who had stepped into the lodge, now returned with a bottle of wine in her hand. The professor leaned forward to oversee the refilling of his glass in the half-light that poured over us from the open door. She left the bottle within reach of Serge, whose enthusiasm for red wine was only barely disguised. Then she turned and re-entered the lodge, leaving us to the stars and the professor's musings.

"Yes, of course there are reasons," he replied. "Many reasons arising directly from the geological characteristics of the African continent. People forget just how large Africa is, and yet less than 10 per cent of the continent is highly fertile. The rest of Africa has a thin level of soil that is incapable of sustaining more than a few planting seasons. The sun burns the land, while the rains fail or come in floods, washing away the topsoil, which means that even subsistence living is difficult, which in turn adversely affects population density. We think of Africa being populous, but Africa's population is less than a quarter of most northern countries. Only the Great Lakes area, the highlands of Ethiopia, parts of the Congo basin, the Nile, and a thin strip of Northwest Africa have ever had land capable of supporting more than nomads and pastoralists."

The old man shifted over to his other side and then pulled the cushion up under his arm. "Population density is critical to what we term civilized development," he said, still fussing with his cushion. "You see, the concentration of people encourages 'specialization' and 'specialization' leads to innovation. Societies living at subsistence levels cannot afford the luxury of innovation; they are conservative by nature, devoting their energies to survival." He stopped to relight his pipe, fumbling through his pockets for matches.

"Doesn't disease have as much to do with the lack of development as social structure?" I interjected.

"Yes," he said. "But these things have always been connected. The tsetse fly and the malarial mosquito bred largely in the few fertile areas of Africa, so that even areas capable of sustaining large populations were constantly afflicted with disease."

"Africa carries the curse of Cain," I noted.

"Yes, I'm afraid so. The afflictions of Africa are eternal," he said, nursing his wineglass in the palm of his hand. "Just as Africa's population began to exceed the critical three per cent annual growth rate in the eighteenth and nineteenth centuries, the continent was devastated by the slave trade. The Congo alone lost over nine million people to slavery. Both the East and the West plundered Africa of its people during the slave trade. And today the continent is reeling under the curse of AIDS."

He paused and then added, "Africa carries the world's soul in its bosom, and yet it has become the repository of our worst nightmares. While it preys on our conscience, we in the so-called civilized world pay it little heed and are therefore doomed to carry a burden of guilt."

A meteor streaked across the sky and plunged below the desert, leaving a showering tail of light. Serge pointed. "A shooting star," he said. Its sweep held us watching, as if for an instant we had caught a glimpse of creation, something that went far beyond the earthly concerns of Africa.

Krystyne's head slid onto my shoulder. The long days flying, the soft night air of the desert, and the intonation of the professor's voice lulled her to sleep. She seemed vulnerable, her breathing regular against my side, her shawl tucked under her chin like a blanket.

I still remember that evening so clearly, the night sky pinned with stars, the magic of being close to Krystyne, with Serge and the professor, our presence unknown to the outside world. I no longer cared about worldly ambitions, Toronto, or what the future might hold. I was utterly content to be there, under the heavens, in the middle of Africa, for us the centre of the universe.

Our time in Africa had only reinforced my personal conviction that the West has to lend serious help to Africa. The continent represents our human heritage, the birthplace of our soul. Existing efforts to provide aid by the Western world are hopelessly inadequate; ignoring Africa puts us in danger of losing our humanity.

The professor stuffed his tobacco pouch into his trouser pocket and rose stiffly to leave. With an exaggerated bow he bid us good night and disappeared down the rocky path to his cabin. Alberto and Maria had gone to bed, leaving Serge and me staring into a field of stars. Krystyne's breathing had slipped into a light snore.

"What do you think of the professor?" Serge asked me.

"He's somewhat theatrical," I said. "Most of what he said came straight from John Reader's book on Africa."

"I think he's a phony," Serge declared in a dismissive tone.

"Oh, come on, Serge, that's a bit strong. This continent is full of odd characters claiming a special affinity with Africa."

Serge remained unconvinced, stating, "He's probably not even a professor. It seems everyone in Italy is a *dottore* or a *professore*."

The next day we borrowed the camp's Land Rover and drove thirty-five miles south to see the giant sand dunes of Sössusvlei rising three hundred metres above the desert. Massive dunes, streaming pennants of sand from their curling crests, they advance sixty metres a year across the Namib, driven by the prevailing winds of the desert.

Our vehicle laboured over the soft sand in its lowest gear. Deep purples, reds, and oranges contrasted brilliantly under a tungsten sun. There was no sign of life apart from the faint traces of scorpions' tracks in the sand and a lone oryx, circling in doubt, not far away from us; the morning sun pulverized the land. It would be easy to lose our direction through the maze of dunes looming high above us. In three hours our tracks would disappear, blown over with sand. We pressed on, conscious of time, ready to retrace our route.

We returned to the lodge by two o'clock and were packed and ready to leave, having had a swim before heading to the plane. Alberto and the professor were on an excursion in search of fossils. Our departure was overseen by Maria, who scolded us for the short stay.

"You could spend a week here and not see everything," she said convincingly.

"I know, I know," I replied. "But we want to reach the Angolan border and we're short of time."

"Ah," she said, remonstrating, "time is all you need in Africa."

———————

Our next landing was at Swakamund Airport on the Atlantic coast. The airport had no defined runways. Blowing sand obliterated all runway markings so that planes landed anywhere, near the windsock, blown ragged by the wind. Pilots broadcasted their compass bearings to conflicting traffic as they approached, a procedure fraught with the potential risk of mid-air collision, and yet takeoffs and landings occurred regularly without incident.

To our surprise, the few hotels in Swakamund were full, even though the shops, the streets, and the hotel lobbies seemed empty. We managed to arrange lodging at our taxi driver's house, in a sparsely furnished room belonging to his daughter. Serge was billeted with the driver's brother, who lived above a rambling antique store filled with old books and Nazi memorabilia. The brother was an odd character who seemed obsessed by the ghosts of former German occupation.

We had dinner that evening in a small restaurant whose German owner was an ex-submarine commander who served in the resistance movement in Namibia at the end of World War II. He and his compatriots had fought a guerrilla war against the South Africans. He rambled on and on in a thinly disguised racist rant about how the country had declined ever since independence. It was a relief to finish the last of our wine and stagger out into what appeared to be a ghost town, empty of people and cars. The town's residents were either sleeping or hiding behind closed shutters. Only a few mangy curs circled aimlessly outside locked doors, searching for something to eat, but the pickings were slim. Dogs are generally unloved in Africa, and rarely fed. Their fate is to forage through garbage heaps, along with Africa's other unfortunates.

Swakamund was the last place where we knew we could purchase fuel for the plane. A couple of settlements in northern Namibia might possibly have had fuel in two-hundred-litre drums; otherwise, there was car gas, usable in an emergency. Charlie Foxtrot Whisky Mike Juliet could fly on car gas, though it was not recommended—over time it destroyed the engine seals. The desire to locate fuel had us studying maps late into the night, but it was obvious that if we continued on to Angola, we might run short.

By this time, the three of us had become old hands at travelling together. Our schedule was flexible and we had adjusted to each other's interests and idiosyncrasies. Krystyne and I had virtually adopted Serge as family, while he had the good grace to treat us as contemporaries, even though we were considerably older.

We flew north along the Skeleton Coast, skimming fifty feet above the white foam of Atlantic breakers. The ocean pounded an utterly deserted coastline, desolate, except for the countless shipwrecks lying broken on the beach. What accounted for these abandoned hulks, half-buried in the sand? Was it some gravitational pull on sailors along that stretch of coast, devoid of lights and other navigational aids? A one-degree error over sixty miles equates to a mile off course—being only a few degrees wrong in this part of the world could drive a ship onto these unlit beaches on a dark night.

We turned inland and flew over the strange geological rock formations that formed the Mount Brandberg foothills; furrows of rock, like thick corduroy, rucked up against the desert as if a giant comb had scored the rock, exposing veins of oxidized minerals, ochre, rust, mauve, orange, and green—a Jacob's coat thrown over the land.

Serge was in the co-pilot seat, anxious to photograph it all.

"Can I open the window?" he inquired.

"Sure," I said, "but twist the speaker behind your head so you won't drown the intercom." He unlatched the window tentatively while I banked into a right turn so that he could have a clear shot at a herd of oryx below. A manic tear of wind through the window had Krystyne busy rescuing loose objects whirling about the cabin.

"How long must we keep the window open?" she demanded. Serge kept snapping pictures.

"Only another minute," I volunteered. It was the closest the three of us ever came to a disagreement.

The worry over fuel continued to nag. I hoped to purchase some at Namutoni Camp, midway to the Angolan border, but each time we circled for a photograph we used more fuel, and flying at low altitudes required a richer mixture—which increased the burn rate of fuel per hour. Serge's photographs might yet prove expensive.

On approaching Namutoni Camp we sighted a recently prepared gravel strip, which almost guaranteed a supply of fuel. Sure enough, there were three two-hundred-litre drums stored in a shed at the camp. The plane could take only 120 litres. Since once a drum is opened the buyer owns it, this would mean leaving eighty litres of precious fuel behind. As a result full tanks came at a hefty price, but one we were happy to pay.

We flew over the mouth of the Kunene River, which ran along the Angolan border disgorging silt into the Atlantic Ocean. Over a million years, the Kunene River had managed to carve a gorge two thousand feet deep into the landscape. Erratic gusts of wind ripped through the canyon, forcing us higher into gentler air that blew down from the purple haze of the Muchimba Mountains.

———————

Epupu Falls, on the Kunene River, had the only landing space we had sighted from the air since taking off from Namutoni Camp. It had an eight-hundred-foot strip, terminating at a cliff face that rose a thousand feet above the runway. I flew in low over the strip, twice, feeling uncomfortable about landing there. Was I losing my nerve? It was hot, and Serge was having another bout of airsickness. I toyed with a third pass. The strip was a thousand feet above sea level, which meant the air was thinner, and the plane was fully loaded. Take-off would be tight—even more dangerous than landing. I decided to look elsewhere.

We circled Epupu Falls and spied a flat piece of ground two miles to the east, dotted with small scrub acacia, with enough space to land. The wheels touched down on the baked soil, and we stepped out into the blast of sunlight; nothing stirred, above the warring sound of cicadas.

I left Krystyne and Serge with the plane, setting out on foot to Epupu Falls. Serge was still intent on taking photographs.

"Don't wander too far from the plane, Serge," I suggested, not wanting Krystyne to be left alone.

"Yeah, I'll be close by," he mumbled, disappearing into the scrub. Krystyne settled down to read under the shade of the plane's wing.

Within a couple of miles I came across a small encampment of English students from Oxford University. They were on a charity fundraising expedition. Dropped by a helicopter six hours earlier with only a compass, minimum supplies, and a radio in case of emergency, their challenge was to find their way back to civilization from "one of the remotest parts of Africa." The sooner they returned home the more money they raised.

Their surprise at seeing a white man jogging past their makeshift bivouac was audible. Suddenly, "remotest Africa" seemed less daunting; indeed, anticlimactic. They served me tea and I furnished them with coordinates, which may well have assisted them to raise hundreds of pounds in lieu of wandering around for days in that poorly mapped area of Namibia.

At Epupu Falls I persuaded a truck driver to take me back to the plane, where Krystyne and Serge were entertaining three bare-breasted Himba girls. Serge had discovered them huddled under an acacia tree, terrified by the sudden appearance of our plane. Krystyne, looking up from her book, had been amazed to see Serge skipping towards her with the giggling Himba girls in tow. His comic behaviour had intrigued them, displacing a shyness that had quickly evaporated and turned flirtatious. They were crestfallen at the truck driver's refusal to invite them back with us to the small village at Epupu Falls.

The Himba, a sub-tribe of the Herero, originated from Bantu migrations of central Africa over a thousand years ago. A remote tribe, they traced their origins through a matrilineal line to a single female ancestor. They followed a traditional nomadic lifestyle, with a social structure based on "age set," the demarcation of which could be determined from the female headdresses and the hairstyles of young girls, ranging from the common *erembe* to the elaborate *ekori* goat-leather wreaths worn by brides celebrating marriage. The Himba had remained friendly and outgoing, maintaining their original customs, unaffected by the few whites who had made contact with them over recent years. The women rubbed their bodies with a mixture of ochre and ghee, the butter fat from goat's milk. Unabashedly sensual and provocative, they wore only a loin skin around their middles and decorated themselves with seashells and coiled bracelets of beaten metal. Handsome, well fed, and carefree, they were ready to engage in trade—crude carvings or shells in exchange for safety pins and ballpoint pens.

Serge managed to make friends with the Himba in spite of the barrier of language. This he overcame with his camera and his unique ability to communicate through mime. Krystyne and I marvelled at his natural grace. We speculated as to his possible attraction to a

Himba girl, as there were many that were eligible and friendly. However, Serge, intensely private, left us to our imaginations, providing no hint of personal interest beyond the superficial contact that led to dozens of photographs.

When it came time to leave, I taxied the plane in error into a termite hill. Termites are the most numerous of living creatures in Africa, over one hundred million years old. Their houses are amazing structures, like concrete poles rising as high as fifteen feet from the ground and designed with a network of passageways and chambers to control the temperature for the whole colony. The termite hill I struck was just below the front cowling, and therefore out of sight from the pilot's seat yet high enough for the propeller blades to hit the side of it, scattering red earth and stone like a pinwheel throwing sparks. There was a sickening screech of metal scraping concrete as I struggled to cut the fuel supply and limit the damage. The next hour we spent filing the leading edges of the propeller blades to render them serviceable, while a clutch of Africans gathered to watch, intrigued by what they believed was *muzungu*, or white man's, magic.

As we flew east towards Zambia, we crossed the Caprivi Strip, one of the oddest territorial boundaries in Africa, a long ribbon of land reaching into the heart of the country. The Germans in Namibia, at the turn of the nineteenth century, had hoped that the Zambezi River would provide a route to the Indian Ocean. In the European scramble for Africa, Germany claimed the land all along the river, only to discover that it was impossible to navigate. However, they kept the land. The Caprivi Strip divides the African Lozi Kingdom which had controlled the upper Zambezi for centuries, so Lozi tribesmen, still loyal to their king, remain separated by the present-day borders of Angola, Namibia, Botswana, and Zambia. The Lozis still argue for the reunion of their territory, but the world has greater concerns than the restoration of an ancient African kingdom and so the territorial anomaly remains in place.

The Caprivi Strip leads to Victoria Falls, locally known as the "smoke that thunders." Its cascading roar can be heard from a considerable distance, but it remains invisible until one actually peers down its gorge, cut deep into black lava rock. The swirling mist feeds a host of wildflowers that bloom on either side of the falls— creating a miniature rain forest that covers both sides of the gorge, unchanged since Dr. Livingstone's first visit.

We spent our last evening with Serge on the terrace of the Victoria Falls Hotel, a century-old colonial masterpiece. The scars of rocket fire were still visible on the wall above the veranda, a reminder of the Zambian (or what was then northern Rhodesian) rebel activity during Ian Smith's struggle for unilateral independence in the 1960s. The hotel sits on the edge of the gorge, like an aging dowager, complete with full-length portraits of British royals.

Serge expressed concern about his future as we chatted over wine and the distant sound of drums. He had no real future in Africa, and yet there was little to draw him back to France, other than his aging parents. In spite of his independent manner, he seemed vulnerable, a man who valued our friendship more than we had realized. We talked late into the night and exchanged promises to meet somewhere soon, but our thoughts remained heavy at the prospect of parting.

―――――――――――

With Serge gone, Krystyne and I were alone again, startled at the luxury of what seemed unlimited space in the cockpit. We had flown five thousand miles, looping around the southern part of the African continent in a little under a month. Our route home to Nairobi was east over Zambia, crossing Zimbabwe, formerly southern Rhodesia, south of Lake Kariba, to Malawi. Beautiful, spacious farms with painted barns, manicured paddocks, ponds, and gardens surrounding elegant colonial houses slipped below us, one after another, hour after hour. Seen from the air, the farms all seemed identical: at a respectful distance from the white owner's house there was always a haphazard collection of mud huts with tin roofs, housing black farmhands. It seemed clear that here as elsewhere in Africa the whites had cultivated the prize land, leaving very little for the black population. It was a situation designed to foment future revolution.

On the flight into Blantyre, Malawi, thunderclouds caused us to divert again and again from our direct course. We had not been able to get a prior landing clearance for Malawi, which I suspected might be a problem. Forty miles west of Blantyre, I radioed the tower for landing instructions, and they requested my clearance number. I requested permission to land without one.

A long silence followed while the controller checked with Lilongwe, the capital of Malawi, for instructions. Finally, I was asked how much fuel remained on board—a sure sign they planned to refuse us entry. I replied that I had enough for two hours' flying time, sufficient to return to Harare, in Zimbabwe. Another long delay ensued as we approached uncomfortably close to Blantyre airport without instructions. Predictably, I was instructed to leave Malawi airspace immediately and return to Harare. Trying one last time, I requested permission to land at Blantyre in order to sort out the problem more easily on the ground. Technically, I needed their permission to land unless it was an emergency. To my surprise the Blantyre tower acceded to my request. Once we were on the ground, a long debate ensued over our illegal entry. I steadfastly maintained that we had received their permission to land, and we were allowed to go on our planned route but nevertheless, a countrywide notice was sent to all airports in Malawi, advising them of our whereabouts. This notoriety dogged us through the country, and airport officials treated us with suspicion.

The flight up the shores of Lake Malawi was calm, the mountains reflecting purple and green shadows over the glassy water. We spied what appeared to be a lodge from the air and landed on a grass field beside a dirt track and then walked a mile through open bush to the shore of the lake.

In a clearing we found a miserable collection of daub-and-wattle huts. Naked children stood staring at us as we picked our way past discarded fish heads and corncobs, scattered along the path that terminated at the lodge. Our room had no electricity or mosquito nets and it was almost certainly here that Krystyne contracted malaria, which would break out several months later in Toronto.

Before dark we strolled down to the beach and paddled an abandoned dugout onto the lake to be free of mosquitoes and the pungent smell of garbage. A flaming sunset against the purple mountains was as beautiful as any we had seen in Africa. The wind rose in nervous gusts, so we inched back to shore, barely afloat, and scrambled onto the warm sand as the evening shadows masked the land. African women gathered up their washing and their children and slowly trudged across the beach, leaving us alone in the gathering darkness.

Over the next two days, we flew seven hundred miles into Mbeya, purchased fuel from missionaries, crossed Lake Manyara, and circled the Ngorongoro Crater. The rains had washed out the roads leading to the crater, so it was empty of tourists. I lowered the nose of the plane over the rim and glided into the crater, one eye on the airspeed indicator, the other calculating the turning radius of the plane. As we swooped overhead, masses of game schooled left and right, away from the roar of the engine. Birds flocked into angry clouds from the marshes below. We circled twice around the inside perimeter a hundred and fifty feet above the floor of the volcano, and then swooped in an arc over the northern rim of the crater and headed for Lake Magadi on the southern border of Kenya.

We were back in familiar territory, flying up the Rift Valley, over the N'gong Hills and into the wide plain south of Nairobi. Wilson Airport lay immediately ahead, just as we had left it, almost a month and eight thousand miles earlier; the controller's voice came across unchanged, the Flying Doctors Service ground staff ran out to guide us onto the ramp. It was as if we had never left, all was familiar. Shutting down the engine we sat in the cockpit, silent, not moving. A wave of melancholy rushed in, for this was our last flight together in Africa, and the realization was hard to absorb. We remained there, seated in the cockpit for what seemed a long time, listening to the unwinding noise of the gyros, while Stanley, the mechanic, stood outside, patiently waiting for instructions.

PART FOUR

14

Waiting for Twilight

OUR RETURN from South Africa to the Nairobi Club and the Flying Doctors Service colleagues at the hangar was poignant for us since we now had less than a month remaining in Africa. The April rains had arrived warm and sweet with promise. Nairobi was in flower again and the aging vestiges of the city's beauty had broken through its poverty and neglect. We found it comforting to walk along the same streets, among the markets and shops, passing familiar faces in the crowd. How easy it would be for us to slip permanently into Nairobi life. After two years, Krystyne and I had reached a crossroads; either we stayed and built a life in Africa or returned to our family and roots in Canada. The answer was difficult, but it was time to go.

The remaining weeks were dogged by the loose ends of departure. Krystyne planned to fly to Paris and stay with a friend for a week, and then drive with her to Tangier. I would remain in Nairobi and prepare for the long flight home. I wanted to fly over West Africa, across the Sahara and the Atlas Mountains into Morocco, to meet Krystyne in Tangier. This was a longer and potentially more dangerous route than flying north to Egypt via Ethiopia and west to Spain, but it allowed me to complete the circumnavigation of Africa, a goal that I had set myself before leaving Canada.

The evening of Krystyne's departure we drove along the Mombasa Highway to Kenyatta Airport, and Krystyne sat gazing at the sweep of the Nairobi plain, quiet at the prospect of separation. It was only a temporary goodbye, but the silence was heavy. She knew enough about flying over West Africa to have misgivings. I hesitated before reassuring her.

"Hey," I said. "I'll see you in Tangier. You know I'll get there." But her look burned into my memory, only to reappear over the flights ahead, flights across some of the most remote parts of Africa. Later, I came to regret treating her concern so lightly.

Choosing the West African route forced me to face reality. I hadn't realized how politically unstable West and Central Africa were. The odds of having my plane impounded on the whim of a corrupt official were high. The distance and remoteness of the territory meant there would be nowhere to land for nine to twelve hours, flying non-stop, and no means of rescue available in the event of an emergency.

On the positive side, the jungle of West Africa would be free from interference. A lone aircraft flying at ten thousand feet would hardly attract much attention and, on the ground, soldiers, rebels, and thieves were unlikely to steal a plane they were unable to fly. No, mechanical failure and African bureaucracy would be my only enemies.

The political uncertainties of West Africa were varied: Uganda was safe, but the next country, Zaire (since 1997 renamed Congo), was a mess. Once across Zaire, I would have to refuel in the Central African Republic, where the infamous Emperor Bokassa had ruled from 1965 to 1979 and had eaten his ex-generals, a supply of whom he kept in a freezer. Nigeria was listed by the United Nations as a "no go" country, and the former French West African countries, Côte d'Ivoire and Senegal, while politically safe, were rife with crime and lawlessness. Advice from the flying fraternity at Wilson Airport was consistent: take the safer, familiar route north to Europe. But I remained fixated on West Africa—even though it was clearly a gamble.

My departure from Nairobi was postponed several times. I still required overflight clearances for most of the countries in West Africa, but my telexes, faxes, and telephone calls had produced no reply. And there remained the test flight with Paolo, an Italian pilot from Wilson who had toyed with the idea of accompanying me back to Canada. Paolo was charming, independent, and available, but his flying reputation at Wilson was checkered—every serious pilot flying in Africa had a flying incident recorded in their logbook, but some thought he had a few too many. Still, I liked him, and he supported my idea of flying west across the Congo. We agreed to a test flight over the weekend. As it turned out, he was unable to fly to Canada with me, but he helped me with the preparations for the trip.

We headed for Lamu, the Muslim settlement on the coast. Paolo had business there, which turned out to be a beautiful Muslim girl-friend whose family disapproved of their relationship. The instruments and the long-distance fuel system functioned perfectly on our flight; the plane was ready. The weekend in Lamu turned out to be a brief respite before the big flight home.

We spent an unforgettable evening together with a few other guests on the veranda of Peponi's Hotel in neighbouring Shela. Candles flickered in the muslin-soft air that whispered in from the Indian Ocean; staff, barefoot, padding amongst us, served drinks, while we sprawled on cushions talking late into the night; hushed tones under a panoply of stars; a remote corner on the edge of the African continent, at peace and unreservedly civilized.

My thoughts wandered to the eight-thousand-mile flight home, over jungle, desert, and ocean. There would be physical dangers, of course, which didn't really concern me; it was more the prospect of failure, the possible need for rescue, in the face of advice not to fly the western route—that, and Krystyne's anxiety, had me restless.

———————

The African goodbyes, of course, were wonderfully genuine. The staff at the Nairobi Club extracted promises from me to return; Jim's secretary requested I send her mother a washing machine from Canada; Michael, the taxi driver, pleaded for money to repair his car; the hangar staff actually invited me into the tea room for the midmorning break. Mike Gerber conveyed a sense that he was truly sorry to see me go, and the pilots and the nurses . . . so many good-byes. Leaving seemed perfidious.

I could look back at the Flying Doctors Service with satisfaction. My contribution was modest, though not insignificant. In Africa it seems that nothing can be added and nothing taken away—changes for the better, somehow, remain elusive—but then, I knew that from the start. No matter what lay ahead, I would retain an interest in Africa and remain committed to the Flying Doctors Service. In that sense, our time in Africa had served as my apprenticeship. I had acquired humanitarian skills beyond those of running a business.

I considered the Flying Doctors Service project a success, except for my inability to win over the Society. Their behaviour defied logic, the vagaries of their motivation underlining human frailty—something I would never underestimate again. Still, in spite of their recalcitrance, there remained much to be pleased about. The morale of the pilots, nurses, mechanics, and hangar staff was high at the time of my departure. The Flying Doctors Service was a better or-ganized, self-contained unit, under one leader with a new medical centre. I was satisfied I had done my best.

The morning of my departure, Nairobi was bathed in pristine light. Clear skies promised an easy flight. I sat on Runway 14, waiting for final clearance, filled with mixed emotions. The plane laboured under the extra weight of fuel in the ferry tank as the takeoff roll ex-tended the full length of the runway before the wheels lifted from the asphalt. At seven hundred feet above ground I made a right turn over Nairobi Park and headed for the N'gong Hills. The tower signed off as I watched the familiar landmarks slip away behind me—the Nairobi skyline, the Kibera slums, the army barracks, and the monastery.

I cleared the escarpment and flew in a wide arc over the expanse of the Rift Valley. I'd flown it so many times before. Nothing could touch its beauty, austere and grand. A nostalgic pang somewhere deep inside had me wondering if I would ever fly this valley again. I was on the verge of a promise—to return one day. How could I do otherwise? I was leaving so much behind, so much tearing at the heart. I needed time.

Layered ridges of the Rift Valley, shimmering in newborn grass, swept beneath the plane. A flash of red, the telltale sign of the lone Maasai guarding his cattle, slipped from view. A giraffe lifted its head uninterestedly as I swung low over the acacia trees veining the valley floor. Under my right wing, Longonot Crater lay wreathed in cloud, majestic and imperial. Slowly, I climbed to nine thousand feet over the Oloololo Escarpment and passed high above the terraced hills that sloped all the way down to the shores of Lake Victoria, leaving Kenya, and two years of memories, in my wake.

Lake Victoria lay like a sheet of tin under a thick blanket of cloud. The third largest lake in the world, it serves as a border for Kenya, Uganda, and Tanzania. I struck out across its wide expanse and gradually lost sight of land. I would have little chance of survival if the plane went down amongst hippos and crocodiles in the water below, but the plane's engine thrummed dutifully on. Large clumps of Nile cabbage rafted over wide stretches of the grey water below, distorting the sky's reflection.

Uganda's Entebbe International Airport, scene of the famous Israeli rescue of hostages held in a hijacked plane on July 4, 1976, lay directly in line with the setting sun. I lowered Charlie Foxtrot's nose and flared onto the shimmering runway. Just as I touched down, a loud explosion occurred at the back of the plane. The tail wheel shot pieces of rubber and aluminium across the asphalt. The airplane swerved from side to side on the verge of a ground loop, until it came to an abrupt stop midway down the runway. Two thousand pounds of extra fuel was too much for a tail wheel at forty-five pounds' tire pressure. On the flights from Canada to Africa, fuel consumption over nine to thirteen hours had lightened the plane prior to landing. Nairobi to Entebbe was only three hours, leaving the plane a thousand pounds over gross weight on touchdown. The strain on the small wheel was three times normal.

Since I was unable to taxi off the main runway, the controller declared a full-scale emergency. Fire trucks, with sirens screaming and flashing lights, transported excited helpers to the plane, which they physically lifted off the runway onto the grass. There it lay, abandoned, but safely out of the way of incoming traffic.

Several hours later, I found a Belgian aircraft mechanic, Cousin Joles, in a hangar at the north end of the field. He helped me remove the damaged tail wheel, which he pronounced unserviceable. The rim was cracked and, in his opinion, would not survive another landing. He had no spare parts and no further suggestions. It seemed a dismal start to the long flight home.

I placed a call to Jim Heather Hayes at the Flying Doctors Service, who promised me another tail wheel by morning, and, true to his word, he scrounged one from the graveyard of old planes adjacent to the Wilson Airport tower. A Mission Aviation Foundation plane, scheduled to fly into Entebbe the next morning, agreed to deliver it to me.

In the meantime, I invited Cousin Joles to join me for dinner. A typical old Africa hand, Joles was a rough diamond whose hard life had left him bereft of spirit and money. Twenty-eight years in Uganda would take the spring out of any man. Just surviving the Idi Amin period, when the country was awash in blood, was no mean feat. Joles recounted how at one point he was placed before a firing squad to be executed. An unexplained diversion saw the soldiers wander off, leaving him blindfolded and tied to the post. Finally, a stranger untied him. On another occasion, he was robbed, beaten, and left for dead in his own house. Life was so unstable in Uganda in those years that just staying alive became a full-time occupation. Still, it never occurred to him to leave. Where else was he to go?

Africa was all he knew, and he was far too old to start again else-where.

Early next morning the Mission Aviation pilot strode across the ramp carrying my replacement tail wheel tucked under his arm. "You mean you let a problem with a tail wheel prevent you from flying?" he cracked as he handed it over to me—a prescient joke, since it was the wrong size. I had no choice but to bully Cousin Joles into repairing the old one, even if it was a temporary fix.

I was now three days behind schedule. Joles helped me manhandle the plane into position for takeoff. "If the tail wheel collapses, just tie a spade to the tail of the aircraft," he said. "The blade will slide along the ground, and it may even work better than what you got now."

My course was northwest towards Lake Albert, over the Ruwenzori Mountains, and across the vast jungle of Zaire, an area so remote and so wild that there was no place for an emergency landing within fifteen hundred miles. The consequences of mechanical failure would almost certainly be fatal, and my ears remained tuned to the slightest stutter or hesitation of the plane's engine. I watched the oil pressure and temperature gauges like a hawk. To my relief they remained firmly centred in the green. Crossing Zaire's jungle would be dangerous enough, but first I had to cross Lake Albert and the Ruwenzori Mountains, a flight that posed its own particular challenges.

The Ruwenzori Mountains, or Mountains of the Moon, were first described by Ptolemy in 200 BC as the source of the Nile. He was nearly right; the source of the world's longest river was eventually discovered in 1937 by a German explorer, Burkhart Waldecker, who placed the Nile's rising in the swamps of Burundi, known as the Kasumo, "the Gusher," by the Tutsi tribe. This enormous fetid swamp sits four degrees south of the equator and contains a small plaque with the words "Caput Nili" (head of the Nile) marking the site of one of the nineteenth century's most sought-after mysteries. And yet Waldecker's discovery has generally been attributed to John Speke, who in 1862 incorrectly proclaimed the Nile's source to be Lake Victoria.

By mid morning the build-up of towering cumulus cloud loomed ominously dark over Lake Albert, covering the Ruwenzori Mountains, which rose dramatically on the western shore to a height of fifteen thousand feet. Thunderstorms formed regularly and unexpectedly from the cauldron of moist tropical air crossing the lake and rising up the eastern face of the mountain range, where it was rapidly cooled by the lower temperatures at higher altitudes. It was a classic recipe for sudden and violent storms.

My storm scope indicated a spray of electrical discharges of considerable intensity, with only a narrow space between two giant thunderstorms on either side of my flight path. As I approached the lake, the sky darkened, and heavy rain beat loudly against the windscreen, obliterating all visibility. I had no idea that these two thunderstorms were colliding into one large unpredictable weather system covering the entire lake. The rain was so torrential, I feared it might block the air intake and suffocate the engine. The plane laboured against the sudden, sharp downdraughts. The storm scope indicated the thunderstorm was narrow, less than thirty miles wide. This meant that if I could punch through, the sky would be clear on the other side—but it promised to be a rough ride, lasting fifteen to twenty minutes.

I banked the plane into the darkened cloud, tightened my shoulder straps, scanned the instruments one more time, and prepared for the worst. Instinctively, I threw a quick glance out the window at the large spars connecting the overhead wings to the fuselage, a design feature of the Cessna 180 that permitted the wings to take on considerable G-force stress. The real question was not the plane's strength but my ability to keep control of it while flying through a thunderstorm.

Time for speculation ended; it was too late to turn around. I was in the thick of the storm, and I remembered the old flying adage "Never turn in a thunderstorm; keep the wings level; punch straight through." Turbulent draughts took hold of the plane as if it were a toy, one minute shooting it 2,500 feet per minute high into the air, the next plunging it down towards earth at a frightening rate.

Lightning pierced the thick cloud repeatedly, strike after strike. The sky became a series of highly charged electrical flashes, like a strobe light, temporarily blinding. I kept blinking, only to re-create the same disorienting flashes that turned the world into fields of exploding light.

I was on the verge of losing control of the plane. My attempts to correct the sharp vicious rise and fall of the wings with the stick were ineffectual. The sudden wrench of the ailerons threatened to snap the control cables. How, I wondered, could any plane take such a hammering without breaking up in the air? Sudden changes in the plane's attitude had the stall-warning horn bleating constantly. My seat belt was strapped so tightly across my chest I could hardly breathe.

I abandoned the stick and flew on the pedals. Touching the stick was out of the question, only the pedals had a chance of correcting the unpredictable swings of the aircraft. Lateral gyrations of a wing caught in a sudden explosion of updraughts threatened to flip the plane. I was in the funnel of the storm; outside the cockpit the world had gone dark as pitch. I heard my voice through the intercom cry out, "Sweet Jesus, see me through this!"

The deafening noise of the storm was psychologically debilitating. I fought against an insidious sense of hopelessness, of resignation: I was doomed. The plane was about to flip into an uncontrollable spin; I had committed a major error in judgment. I knew that. What was I thinking flying into a thunderstorm?

The cockpit was alive with flying objects that had worked loose and become a hazard. The first-aid kit struck me in the back of the head with a tremendous whack. I felt a warm trickle of blood finger its way beneath my shirt collar.

Outside, the rain turned to ice pellets that beat against the plane with the ferocity and noise of gunfire. Two loud reports in quick succession, like rifle shots, recorded lightning strikes that slammed into the fuselage. I had no idea where I had been hit or what damage had been inflicted. A strong smell of burning electrics rose from below the instrument panel, although I could see no flames or source of smoke. I had lost control of the plane.

My hands no longer on the yoke, I watched it jerk back and forth violently on its own, placing unreasonable stress on the cables controlling the ailerons. I feared even minimal attempts to control pitch would cause the elevator trim to snap. The loss of a control cable would end it all. Suddenly, the right wing received such a violent upward jolt it turned the plane completely on its side. I was in danger of entering a roll and flying upside down. I countered with opposite rudder and, to my utter amazement, broke through a wall of thick cloud into the royal blue of a clear, unmarked sky. Skeins of mist rose from the Zaire jungle that stretched for a thousand miles ahead, green and lush under the hot tropical sun.

I had crossed the Ruwenzori mountain range and the raging storm was now behind me. The cockpit was a total mess. A mineral water bottle had burst, spraying the instrument panel like a garden hose. The nauseating smell of fuel escaping from the vent of the ferry tank permeated the cabin. An opened package of wet shortbread biscuits lay scattered across maps and papers strewn on the floor. Critical information for the remainder of the flight—my fuel calculations, projections of wind direction and strength, my two sets of maps, topographical and instrument—lay in a heap around the fuel pump. Restoring order to the cockpit without an autopilot was slow and tiresome work, absorbing the next hour of flight.

Still, I was alive, chastened and thankful. The plane's engine droned on as if nothing unusual had taken place. Behind me the storm scope painted a terrifying crescendo of electrical crosses, as the two storms converged into an intense vortex of electrical and turbulent power, discharging its anger over Lake Albert. I was lucky, really lucky, to have squeezed my way through. Never again would I intentionally fly through a thunderstorm.

The remainder of the flight seemed absurdly easy. If there was danger, it was disguised beneath the brilliant green jungle, which stretched unbroken to the horizon. The routine tasks of navigating and fuel management seemed trivial and familiar. I was beyond the range of normal radio communication, having last reported my position to Kinshasa on the HF radio. No one really cared whether or not I communicated—I was on my own, of no interest or concern to a soul within a thousand miles.

Eight more hours and hundreds of miles of flying lay ahead over the thick green jungle, flat as an ocean, hugging the curvature of the earth, without a sign of human habitation. In truth, danger lurked below. A crash landing into the jungle canopy was far more dangerous than crashing into the desert or ditching at sea. An engine failure, and I would plunge into the treetops, the light frame of the fuselage crumpling like paper. The wreckage, dripping aviation fuel, hanging in the thick foliage, a hundred feet above a dark, inhospitable jungle floor, would be invisible from both the air and the ground. Any hope of rescue would be unrealistic. Over the desert, one could attempt to land safely and make contact by radio. Ditching at sea, while problematic, was still preferable to crashing into the jungle—better not to think about it.

———————

The city of Banqui in the Central African Republic was my next stop. It offered its own peculiar difficulties—African bureaucracy, restless, undisciplined, armed soldiers, and a rundown airport. My idle speculations about crashing into the jungle, desert, or sea vanished before these more real, immediate, and intractable challenges.

I felt uneasy the moment I touched down. Perhaps it was the horror stories I'd heard from pilots at Wilson, of being held captive there. The country's reputation for murder, rape, and corruption hardly inspired confidence. The place had an eerie look to it. I taxied up to a dilapidated building surrounded by soldiers at the east end of the field, and as soon as I shut down the engine an uncivilized crowd pressed in against the windows of the plane. I hardly managed to close the cockpit door when a gun went off, and the crowd fell back in disorder, unsure what had taken place.

Two soldiers sauntered over to the plane and accompanied me to the airport building. I was ushered into an airless room packed with more soldiers, one of whom demanded my papers, which I duly gave him. They were passed from hand to hand to a man sitting behind a desk. I was instructed to pay an extortionate landing fee of $100, more than three times the normal charge. I objected, holding up my landing clearance, the only one I had for Central and West Africa, but to no avail—the fee had to be paid.

I inquired about purchasing fuel, but my request was ignored. Instead, they demanded to know why I was in the country, where I was going, and who owned the plane. A cold air of hostility permeated the room. Again, I inquired about fuel and was told I could have it in the morning. My instincts were to press for fuel right then and there, regardless of the cost, and leave Banqui immediately. I produced another hundred-dollar bill as inducement. A brief argument ensued, and then I was informed that drums of fuel would be available within the next ten minutes.

A lengthy conversation in a tribal language I didn't recognize filled the room, animated and discordant. No one person had seemed in charge until I offered the money for fuel. The men parted and a smaller, older man with a poor complexion and bulbous eyes leaned forward and took the cash. He shoved a pencil in my direction and demanded something that was totally incomprehensible. He became agitated and kept pointing to the plane, and suddenly I realized he wanted me to file a flight plan, even though there seemed to be no radio communication in the tower and no controller on duty.

Outside, jeeps filled with armed soldiers careered back and forth on the narrow strip of asphalt road adjacent to the airport. One vehicle, for no apparent reason, was racing up and down the active runway, the soldiers firing shots into the air. Once the fuel drum arrived, the same crowd pressed around the plane again. I was offered no help to hand-pump fuel up into the wing tanks. Two soldiers were assigned to watch. It turned out their reward was the residue from the drum: less than five gallons, once my tanks were full.

I clambered into the cockpit, started the engine, and taxied to the runway threshold, followed closely by a jeep full of grinning boy soldiers. The vehicle stopped alongside me, beneath my left wing. I hesitated, not sure of their intentions. Then suddenly it occurred to me, they wanted a drag race down the runway.

I was stunned by the recklessness of the idea. I went through the takeoff checks automatically, my mind churning, trying to determine a course of action beyond that of getting airborne as quickly as possible. I glanced over at the jeep of grinning soldiers, all with rifles. Suddenly, a more sinister thought took hold: what if, the moment I was airborne, the plane presented an irresistible target?

I applied full throttle, heart pounding, hands sweating on the yoke. The jeep was uncomfortably close to the plane. As I roared down the runway, the jeep pulled ahead, swerving towards the centre line directly in front of me. I edged over to the side of the runway, slowly gaining speed but not wishing to overtake them before getting airborne. The moment the wheels left the asphalt I banked sharply, ninety degrees to the right, hoping to present as small a target as possible, staying low, opting for speed over altitude. I heard no shots over the roar of the engine at full throttle and within minutes I was clear of the airport, cruising over the sprawling slums of Banqui.

I turned due west into the white-gold streaks of the setting sun; the compass slowly settled on 282 degrees, west by north; the cardinal point of reference, almost directly in line with Toronto, seven thousand miles to the west. A sense of weariness overwhelmed me. I estimated I had five more hours of flying, most of it in darkness, before reaching the city of Douala, in Cameroon. The land below was already in shadow.

The jungle canopy crawled beneath me; the only evidence of my progress was the throb of the motor. But gradually the jungle thinned, and scattered settlements emerged along the banks of entwining rivers. The telltale smoke of cooking fires signalled human habitation below. In the half-light I could see conical grass-roofed huts hugging the river's edge. For many miles I followed the largest of these rivers, the Sanaga, which drains the Adamawa Highlands, a river that meanders a thousand miles from the northern savannahs of Cameroon into the Gulf of Guinea.

A thin blanket of cloud slid over the last rays of sunset, leaving the cockpit with only the soft amber light of the instruments. Occasionally, isolated flashes of lightning flickered far off on the horizon. The plane droned steadily into the approaching night, gauges firm, airspeed indicator recording 125 knots true, in calm air. The dim glow of the compass needle remained fixed to my magnetic course, and the green-lit numbers of the satellite GPS recorded my progress. I had flown a total of fifteen hours since leaving Entebbe.

The topographical map placed Mount Cameroon only twenty miles north of Douala Airport. It is a mountain into which many an unsuspecting pilot has crashed over the history of flight in Africa. At fourteen thousand feet, it is the fourth-highest mountain on the continent, rising straight out of the Atlantic Ocean. Its looming hulk now lay ahead of me, imprinted on the darkness through flashes of lightning from a distant storm.

I peered through the windscreen to line up the runway lights of Cameroon's only active runway. The outskirts of the city streamed beneath me in a fantasy of electric light and street fires. On final descent, I could see the silhouettes of people running, darting in and out of the shadows next to the runway. I was too tired to care. I yearned only to put my feet on land and my head on a pillow. The tower informed me the airport was out of fuel and unlikely to have it within the next ten days—a huge problem that would have to wait for morning.

I awoke the next morning in a sweat, tangled in a sheet on an iron cot in an airless hotel room. A large cockroach inched its way along the rim of the sink's faucet, three feet from my pillow. Absent-mindedly, I watched its progress as I tried to calculate the amount of fuel left in the plane: one hour and twenty minutes' flying time, or less. I faced some unenviable choices: I could fly into Lagos, considered a dangerous airport; retrace yesterday's route back to Yaounde, Cameroon, which would drain every drop of fuel, assuming I had no headwinds; or head south into Equatorial Guinea, hoping to find fuel in a country that was off the beaten track.

I leapt out of bed, washed, dressed, and descended the stairway to the lobby. The male receptionist lay stretched on a broken couch in his underwear, drinking beer. The hotel was particularly shabby in the cold light of day, and there was nothing to eat or drink. I paid the bill, grabbed a cab, and made straight for the airport to find the airport officials decidedly unhelpful about where to find fuel. In Africa, I reminded myself, self-reliance and patience are prerequisites to survival.

I crossed the tarmac to the plane, started up the motor, and tuned into the local radio frequency for planes flying into Douala airport; local traffic would almost certainly know where to obtain fuel, assuming it was available within an hour of Douala. Before long, a South African pilot reported his position inbound, and within fifteen minutes Tim Clark had swung out of the cockpit of his Cessna 206 and was unloading cargo.

He informed me that my best option was a forty-minute flight to Malabo Island, which belonged to Equatorial Guinea, not far off my intended route. Malabo had fuel in drums, but he warned me that I might encounter difficulties persuading the owners to sell it, since he believed it was used to facilitate illegal smuggling in and out of the island. Flying into Lagos was out of the question; if I landed there, he said, my plane would be impounded. Yaounde had no fuel. All of Cameroon was out of fuel because of an argument between the airport authorities and the minister of finance over the payment of an extraordinary tax on fuels—essentially, a dispute over kickbacks.

So, Malabo was my only choice. Within fifteen minutes I was airborne, fully aware that I was committed to finding and purchasing fuel, since once there, I would not have enough to leave the island.

On the flight across the Bay of Bonny, I heard the voice of a Canadian over the radio, piloting a helicopter for Mobil Oil's offshore rig. The distinctive "eh" gave him away. I asked him about Malabo, and he said the place was bad even by African standards, and not to leave the plane unattended.

My heart sank as I approached a potholed runway at the end of which sat a tin-roofed shack half-hidden by encroaching jungle. The place looked utterly rundown. The windsock had blown out, leaving only a rag hanging limp in the humid heat of mid-afternoon. I taxied up to the end of the runway and cut the engine in front of a weathered sign hanging above the lintel of the doorway with the word "Malabo" written on it in faded script. Slouched in the entrance was a disagreeable-looking character with long sideburns and a dirty wool toque; he wore a sullen look. He watched me step out of the cockpit and approach the building.

"*Buenos días,*" I said, assuming Spanish was still spoken on the island. "*Quiero comprar gaz por mi avión, por favor,*" I continued.

He regarded me with sullen contempt, and said laconically, "*No hay benzene aqui.*" He didn't move as I approached closer.

"You speak English?" I asked weakly, but he remained silent. I squeezed past him and entered a dingy room littered with soiled papers, layered in dust. The place appeared to be abandoned. "*Dónde es el capitán?*" I tried again, as I stepped back outside. He merely shrugged his shoulders uninterestedly. I gave up, returned to the plane, started up the engine, and taxied back down the runway to a battered hangar whose folding doors were left half open.

Three men were huddled around a drum of burning garbage outside the hangar. I told them I was here to pick up fuel, and demanded to speak to the boss. One of them jerked his head towards the rear of the hangar, where I found a large African, dressed in Western-style coveralls. His name was Emmanuel, his English limited, and he steadfastly maintained there was no fuel for sale. A long and protracted negotiation followed.

Price was not the issue. I needed the fuel regardless of cost, and as a result I was charged three dollars a litre for an opened drum of two hundred litres—easily the most expensive fuel in Africa. It came with no pump, no funnel, and no strainer. I was handed a bucket and, using my T-shirt as a strainer, I hand-lifted forty-nine pails of fuel up and emptied them into the wing tanks. In the meantime, a growing crowd of onlookers pressed in around me menacingly.

It was impossible to make payment for the fuel without a dozen eyes observing the transaction. Within minutes a tall African wearing a baseball cap, dark glasses, and torn jeans squeezed through the crowd and demanded a landing fee of $150. The crowd pressed closer, excited by the prospect of large amounts of money changing hands. The landing fee was outrageous; however, I felt it wise to pay and get out of there as quickly as possible.

I turned to climb into the cockpit, only to be faced by a second demand: this time, it was a "navigation fee" of $250. That was too much; I refused to pay. The crowd threatened to turn nasty, squeezing between me and the plane. Drenched in sweat, rattled, and angry, I realized I was at an impasse. I stalled for time.

"Who authorized navigation fees when there is no radio, tower, or controller?" I asked. "Where is the boss? I want to pay him directly," I insisted. They remained nonplussed but unwavering in their demand for more money.

In the distance I heard the sound of a chopper approaching. The Canadians I had contacted earlier by radio? I took heart that help was near and that together we might find a solution to an increasingly dangerous confrontation. The helicopter landed and Bill and Wayne, both from Alberta, introduced themselves. Neither could speak Spanish. Although they were supportive, we were outnumbered; there were approximately thirty of them to three of us. Bill suggested we try and contact Mobil's Spanish-speaking representative, Hernandez, who lived somewhere on the north end of the island. It was a reasonable plan, so I set off down a path that collared the shore in search of Hernandez, while my new-found friends stayed with the aircraft.

After several inquiries, I found Hernandez asleep in a hammock underneath a grove of palm trees on the beach. Unperturbed at my interrupting his siesta, he led the way back to the airport, single file, in silence. Within seconds of his arrival, the atmosphere of the crowd changed; brandishing a stick he flailed left and right, raining incredible blows with fury on the crowd while screaming abuse, until it scattered like a pack of curs. He clearly enjoyed the confrontation, considered it sport, even refusing a tip. Hernandez waved goodbye and ambled back down the path to his hammock as the helicopter rose in a swirl of dust and I took off on a six-hour flight to the city of Abidjan on the Ivory Coast.

———————

When I arrived at Abidjan, a young African, Liberté Tchande, or "Freedom" to his friends, sidled up to me, hoping to provide taxi service and advice as to what was available in Abidjan. He drove me to a hotel and we arranged to meet later that evening, giving me enough time to bathe and catch an hour of sleep.

Abidjan was lively—more so than any city in East Africa. Excitement and the promise of wild drinking filled the air; young men cruised the streets in rusted cars, on bicycles and on foot, flirting with girls gathered around the street bonfires. The starless night was drowned in firelight and the deafening music of portable radios; the young were high on drink and drugs. The city was in a mood to party.

Freedom drove a Volkswagen that had lost its muffler and shook like an old-fashioned washing machine. We inched our way to the centre of town, past young men running, arms extended with half-empty beer bottles held high; prostitutes peered in through the car windows, "Darlin', darlin', you want it, I got it." Banter, insults, and screams, intermingled with rude gestures, ended in rejection and finally indifference.

Freedom mumbled something about picking up his girlfriend at home. We drove for half an hour over mud tracks until we reached a creek bed, at which point we had to get out and walk. The night was ink-black and the unlit path so crowded at times we had to stand single file, waiting for others to pass.

Eventually, we arrived at Freedom's house, a red mud hut with no windows and the ubiquitous corrugated tin roof. The place smelled of sewage. The warm glow of a kerosene lamp shone on his younger sister, sitting idle on the front stoop in order to escape the sweltering heat inside the hut. Freedom's mother sat perched on a wooden box in her underwear at the back of the room, sewing in the half-light. Making no effort to cover herself, she mumbled that Freedom's girlfriend, Phoebe, had left twenty minutes earlier with friends. We retraced our steps to the car, while Freedom assured me that a search for Phoebe would not be in vain. My patience was running out. I needed something to eat. Freedom insisted Phoebe would be nearby, and sure enough within ten minutes we found her dancing with friends by a large bonfire smack in the middle of the road.

She and her two girlfriends bundled into the car, and we returned to the centre of town through a series of narrow mud streets until we came to a small nightclub, Le Colibri, next to the local jail.

The club was crammed with Africans sitting around on sofas and pillows on the floor. A live jazz group was led by a blind African, who played an electric organ and crooned the sweetest music. The crowd was relaxed under the smell of hash and cigarette smoke that curled thick as fog under a ceiling of intimate conversation.

Freedom and Phoebe quizzed me about Canada. Was the country as rich and the jobs as plentiful as they had heard? I confirmed that advancement did not rely on corruption or political connections. Yes, life was good in Canada for those with determination and talent. They listened, wide-eyed, attentive to every detail. Canada, compared to Abidjan, was paradise, milk and honey. The only trick was to get there.

Our conversation was interrupted by sudden applause that swelled into a roar as a female singer pushed through the curtain onto a small stage at the back of the room. Dreadlocks hung below her waist. She was in a skin-tight dress—a dead ringer for Eartha Kitt, and while her sultry voice was not pure, her antics around the stand-up mike as she sang a rendition of "Fever" warmed the audience.

Later, she was joined by a comedian whose impersonation of local politicians escaped me, in spite of Freedom's frantic effort at translation. A delighted crowd threw coins at the pair, which the man caught with amazing dexterity.

We moved next door for something to eat: samosas and beer. Questions about Canada continued in earnest, although I became impatient with the subject. I was more interested in Abidjan and their lives in Africa than in promoting dreams of Canada that were beyond their reach. We stayed for a while and then drove back through the city to Freedom's house for a late-night beer. The streets were even more crowded than earlier; the city had no plans to sleep before dawn.

Back at the mud hut, I sat on the only chair, waiting for a beer, while Freedom and Phoebe fussed over the lighting of the kerosene lamp. The place was empty. Freedom's mother and sister had disappeared. I was given a warm beer while Freedom slipped out to get some smokes. I was tired after nearly ten hours of flying and I decided that, when Freedom returned, I would ask him to drive me back to the hotel. My thoughts wandered as I sat in the flickering light, hardly aware of my surroundings. Without warning, Phoebe appeared in front of me and lifted her dress over her head. Her white underclothes contrasted starkly against her glistening black skin under the kerosene light, and this startled me as much as her unexpected performance. Moving with the feline grace of a panther, she never took her eyes off me as I stood up from my chair.

"Take me to Canada with you," she pleaded, moving closer. "I work for you in Canada." She came round the table slowly approaching me, arms extended. Instantly, the whole evening became clear: Freedom and Phoebe had dreams of Canada and saw me as transportation. I was surprised by the revelation. Undeterred, she arched her back and effortlessly removed her bra, revealing her breasts riding high and full. I turned towards the door, feeling awkward at the misunderstanding I had unwittingly encouraged. Retreating, I stammered something about the difficulties of Canadian immigration, work permits, the long cold winters, leaving her confused and defeated.

Out the door, I rounded the corner of the hut and, in the blackness of the night, bumped into Freedom, the devious architect of this mischievous plan. He was casually smoking a cigarette, leaning against the wreck of an old car. We drove back to the hotel in silence after I cut short his attempts to reintroduce the subject of Canada. Hopefully, he would not blame Phoebe for the evening's debacle. It was clear to Freedom that something had gone badly wrong with his plan, and that the flight to Canada had gone up in smoke, but by the time we reached the hotel there was little acrimony. We were friends, evidenced by the genuine warmth of our good night and goodbye.

What twist of fate had Phoebe confined to a life of poverty, through circumstance beyond her control, from which she yearned to break free? Here was I, returning to the security and privilege of Canada. What justification, I wondered, had I to fly off to a life of opportunity, leaving her and Freedom despairing for what lay beyond their reach? These fleeting thoughts left me uneasy.

———————————

Next, I faced a twelve-hour flight across the southwestern corner of the Sahara Desert from Abidjan to Dakar, Senegal. It took an hour to climb fourteen thousand feet altitude. It was important to monitor fuel consumption carefully and maintain high altitudes in order to burn less fuel. Fuel and navigation were serious preoccupations when flying long distances across the desert. I calculated compass variations and theoretical waypoints, which I recorded with precision on my map.

Undulating dunes gradually displaced the few tufts of dried grass and sparse scrub along the coast. The plane's ground speed slowed to less than ninety knots, bucking a headwind that swept over the Sahara into the Gulf of Guinea. Within two hours I had lost all radio contact with the outside world. I inched farther and farther inland, over miles of empty desert.

Five and a half hours on, the sky darkened into the red haze of a sandstorm swept aloft by the warm Sahara wind. Visibility faded away. The smell of sand permeated the cabin. Particles of grit collected in my eyes, nose, and teeth. I worried the air filter might clog and starve the carburetor. Instinctively, I reached for the bottled water to stave off dehydration from the high altitude and dry air. The horizon disappeared; I was flying on instruments, without radio contact. What had started as an easy flight had become more demanding; reference points beyond the plane's wing tips were reduced to a swirl of reddish sand.

I continued for another two hours flying in the semi-darkness of the sandstorm. Small grains of sand eddied in behind the fuel vents and the sky turned darker and darker red. Suddenly, the alternator warning light on the instrument panel flashed an emergency: an electrical failure had occurred. Was it the alternator, voltage regulator, or an electrical short somewhere behind the instrument panel? The plane's electrical system was draining the plane's single battery—a battery that was no longer receiving a charge from the alternator. The instruments, radio navigation lights, and ferry-tank fuel pump were destined to fail within the next few minutes.

My immediate concern was fuel; everything else was secondary. I had seventy-five gallons in the ferry tank behind my seat, enough to keep me flying for nine hours; however, fuel was useless if I could not pump it up into the wing tanks. The fuel pump installed two years ago by Dave McDevitt, my mechanic in Toronto, was electrically driven. Was there sufficient power left in the battery to drive the fuel pump?

I could rely on the plane's engine, whose electrical power was generated by a set of magnetos independent of the battery; the engine would carry on to Dakar, as long as it had fuel—lots of it.

I shut down all the electrics, hoping the battery still had sufficient juice left to power the fuel pump. The familiar tick-tick-tick of the pump indicated fuel flow for approximately three minutes before it slowed and then fell silent. It was impossible to gauge just how much fuel had reached the wing tanks. Meanwhile, one by one, the navigational instruments toppled onto their sides in a grotesque game of broken statues—even the gas gauges keeled over and died. Only the heading and horizon indicator, both driven by air pressure, continued to register the plane's progress through the red haze of sand.

I had to quickly establish priorities, estimate the amount of useful fuel remaining, and record the time and my exact position on the map. My GPS contained a small internal battery that permitted me to verify my exact position, critical for dead reckoning. For a limited time I would be able to compare my hand calculations to the GPS—as long as its battery held power.

I reworked the fuel calculations a second time only to realize that I had insufficient fuel to reach Dakar—and I was past the point of no return. The shorter distance lay ahead. It would be a cruel irony to run out of fuel and crash in the desert with seventy gallons sloshing six inches behind my neck. The fact that I had no emergency hand pump to push the fuel from the ferry tank up to the wings was an issue to discuss with Dave McDevitt, back in Toronto. I tried to think of a clever way to avoid the impending fuel crisis, but nothing came to mind. I could hardly abandon the flight controls and let the plane slip into a spiral dive. The only option was to fly higher, lean out the mixture to use less fuel, and hope for clear visibility ahead.

An hour later the GPS's internal battery ran out of power. I was 450 miles from Dakar, with insufficient fuel and no further means of verifying my position. I had to make a decision. I could fly due west until I reached the Atlantic coast, then proceed north until the fuel ran out, or continue straight across the desert, hoping for clear weather and somewhere to land. I opted for the coast and the slim possibility the sky might clear near the ocean, permitting an emergency landing.

Flying west with no visibility meant I might miss the coast and continue out over the Atlantic. I descended to three thousand feet and peered out the windscreen—nothing. I would have to rely on time-and-distance calculations and then descend to five hundred feet over the water.

Within two hours, the sky gradually began to clear. A faint tracing of narrow rivers winding through the mangrove swamps indicated I was near the coast—no place to land a plane. I turned north, expecting at any moment that the engine would quit, as I zigzagged east and west along the coastline. The engine purred without a tremor. Unlike the case in most flying emergencies, which require a quick decision, this time there was ample time for mind games to romp in and out until, suddenly, in the distance, I sighted the faint outline of the city of Dakar.

Dakar's international airport sits on the tip of a five-mile peninsula that forms a large crescent bay to the west of the city. My calculations had the plane already out of fuel. Should I fly directly across the water to the airport, or take the additional ten miles around the bay? I decided on the longer, safer route around the bay, fully prepared for an emergency landing on a road or public square. What I really needed was a lucky break.

Unable to communicate with the Dakar International Airport, I flew straight for the tower, three hundred feet above the ground, at right angles to the main runway, and wiggled my wings up and down, indicating distress. Soaring past the tower window, I was conscious of startled faces peering at me, just as the engine coughed, caught, coughed again, and then quit. The remaining fuel had sloshed to the other side of the tank in the emergency rotation of the wings, starving the engine. My heart pounded as I wheeled into a tight glide and descended towards the main runway, wing tip to wing tip with another plane on final descent. The controls felt leaden. I remember the wide-eyed, incredulous look from the other pilot, less than thirty feet across from me. Having received a clearance to land, he had no idea where I had come from or what was happening. I made no attempt to give way. We were on converging paths, both headed for the same runway—only I had no power, no communication, and no choice.

The controller, realizing an accident was imminent and unable to communicate with me, instructed my neighbour to overshoot, which permitted me to land unobstructed. Ironically, the pilot of the other plane turned out to be a French Canadian, resident in Dakar, undergoing his final pilot's exam. He told me later that his instructor was more frightened than he was, and he maintained charitably that I had helped him pass his examination, because he had remained cool under the pressure. We spent the evening together, stumbling through the smoke-filled bars of Dakar, swapping tales about flying, Montreal, and Africa.

15

Tangier

THE AERO CLUB OF DAKAR is the second-oldest flying club in Africa but, unlike the Aero Club of East Africa (the oldest), Dakar's facilities are basic: a box-like building with linoleum floors and cheap furniture. A small maintenance shop sits at the back of the hangar, with a few spare parts and a set of basic tools—of course, no spare alternator. The place was to be my home for the next three days.

Albert, the African mechanic, undertook the task of trying to rebuild my defective alternator, fabricating replacement parts by hand—ingenious work, though progress was slow. Constant interruptions from pilots had him setting down tools, missing deadlines, and cursing. I became increasingly restless. First, the drill press broke, then the compressor failed, the wrenches and sockets of the correct size were missing, small carbon pieces were too intricate to fabricate, and spare parts were nowhere to be had in the country. Rebuilding an alternator was an ambitious task, one that ate up the hours.

Frustration turned to despondency, and then—this was typical of Africa—just as the limit of my tolerance had been reached, cause for hope surfaced from an unlikely quarter. Albert found a substitute part in an old Cessna in the back field. A small-sized carbon washer retrieved from the shaft of a defunct alternator served to turn the copper brushes of my alternator. True, it was a temporary fix, like the tail wheel, not likely to last, but enough to get me to Tangier, perhaps even to Europe.

I was three days behind schedule and unable to communicate with Krystyne, waiting in Tangier. I had lost her telephone number in the shambles of the cockpit following the storm over Lake Albert and the mad scramble out of Banqui. I knew she would be anxious. Still, there was little I could do but press on and try to find her once I landed in Tangier.

I turned north across Mauritania into the Western Sahara over miles and miles of empty desert. Tawny yellows, blood reds, earthy browns, and black protrusions of lava rock surfaced through waves of fretted sand. I never tired of flying the desert; the subtle play of shadow and light; the sensual cresting of dunes, endlessly advancing, driven by the prevailing wind; spumes of sand drifting across the land. I had walked the desert, ridden and flown over it. I sensed its movement, like a mariner on a long passage at sea. Immersed in its haunting beauty, its emptiness, I had come to understand its moods, its capacity to reach a man's soul, and yet at the same time eliminate all record of his passage over its endless sweep of sand. The desert gripped my imagination, appealed to my nature.

Gradually, I sighted the Atlas Mountains rising like the backbone of some giant mammal from the flatness of the desert. I trimmed the plane for a slow descent into the cradled city of Marrakesh. Unstable air burbled over the leading edge of the wings, cross-buffeted and confused by the katabatic gusts that blew in cold from the Atlas snowfields high above me. I reduced speed to lessen the stress on the controls. Marrakesh lay sprawling below, pinned to the desert by the flickering lights of minarets pointing to Allah, and the fading light of an evening sky.

Marrakesh held so much of North Africa. Gone were the black-skinned women, beautiful in dress, figure, and stature. Muslim women covered in bui-buis flapped like stricken crows through narrow streets, avoiding eye contact. Men sat cross-legged sipping tea, smoking opium through elaborate glass pipes (*nargilas*) discussing local politics, business, and endless family feuds. Mischievous young boys ran through the back alleys, trading insults with their elders. Tropical black Africa, lying only a few hundred miles south of the Atlas Mountains and the Sahara Desert, was another world, entirely different to North Africa.

I took a room in the Hotel CTM on the edge of Place Djemaa el Fna, the old city's main square. Spine-tailed swallows swooped over the night skyline as crowds began to form in the square. Groups of men huddled together to watch with mild amusement the tired entertainment of tricksters, snake charmers, acrobats, storytellers, and other crazies competing for attention and paltry sums of money.

Slowly, the square underwent a transformation; wooden stalls were erected and fold-up tables and chairs were arranged into portable outdoor restaurants. Food cooked on propane stoves filled the air with dark greasy waves of smoke that billowed over the crowd. Strings of light bulbs powered by portable generators swung drunkenly on makeshift wires, casting crazy shadows over the walls of the square.

The noise and confusion of people milling about the square and the smells of cooking goat, shish kebabs, fish, sausage, and spicy sauces permeated the air. Competing cooks offered discerning buyers samples of their fare. Harassed proprietors rushed from stove to table overseeing the cooking, soliciting customers, and chasing away gangs of small boys intent on stealing from the heaping plates of food.

I drifted with the horde, pushed and shoved along the narrow spaces between tables, when suddenly a propane canister exploded under a nearby stall, sending flames and sparks shooting into the night sky. Several of the cooks ran screaming through the panic-stricken crowd like wild dervishes, djellabas on fire, and their friends in hot pursuit beating them with rags in an effort to smother the flames. A common occurrence apparently, and so the brassy squeal of horns, the beat of the drums, and the wailing supplication for customers continued without interruption. The incident was seen as less competition for the sellers of food and drink.

As the evening progressed the square degenerated into a manic frenzy of noise and bargaining where solicitations to man's basest predilection lurked in the shadows behind every corner of the kasbah.

Early the next morning I explored the labyrinth of souks behind the square; a maze of hidden alleys snaking through the market. Handmade crafts fashioned from leather, fabric, wood, and copper were thrust under my nose by obsequious vendors eager to sell and refusing to take no for an answer. Carpets, antiques, and furniture piled high to the ceiling. Proprietors employed their children, their deep, brown, languid eyes imploring, "Just look . . . come in . . . no need to buy. . . !" The Arab trader, emotional and clever, relentlessly pursuing the customer, was in stark contrast to the black African whose usual rejection by a buyer left him despondent, a mere victim of fate.

———————

Only one more long flight remained to reach Tangier and Krystyne. On the horizon, the purple loom of the Atlas Mountains delineated North Africa's Mediterranean flank. The jagged edge of the desert gave way to ancient rock as I climbed fifteen thousand feet and flew for hours over the snow-capped range. The craggy peaks gradually gave way to a sea of yellow gorse, tugged and torn by gusting winds that swept down the rolling foothills to the Mediterranean Sea. Small villages huddled in the shadows; a faint necklace of light laced the narrow valleys in the approaching darkness. I coasted into a large open plain, down to the airport runway, and into the arms of Krystyne whose deep relief lent poignancy to our few days together in Tangier.

———————

Tangier is a strange city, locked in its past with little argument for the future. Occupied by Romans, Vandals, Byzantines, Arabs, Berbers, Fatimids, Almohads, Spanish, Portuguese, British, and French, the city has seen it all. Established as an "international zone" shortly after the turn of the nineteenth century, Tangier pursued a degenerate path. The city became Europe's playground for the sexual and financial proclivities of those on the fringe of society, providing what was demanded of it and sometimes more. Eventually, it became too much, even for Moroccans. The city lost its independent status in 1956 and never recovered its reputation or interest.

Krystyne was staying at Barbara Hutton's palace, which had been purchased in the 1990s by Toronto friends of ours. Situated on the edge of the kasbah, a network of narrow alleys barely wide enough for two mules to pass, the place was a jewel: a wedding cake of Arabic carvings, every inch of wall and ceiling carved with intricate design. Swirling vine and leaf motifs in wood and plaster bordered the doors, windows, and walls. Cool breezes wafted between corridors, and shafts of sunlight cascaded over the antique tiles of exquisite courtyards. Fountains spouted into pools of water, reflecting shadows onto the walls and ceilings; the palace was a museum of Islamic architecture and culture. No one else was there; it was ours for three days.

Tangier was our farewell to Africa. A different Africa from the one we knew, for sure, almost a different continent. The excitement of exploring new territory held our interest, though it came with the knowledge that soon it was all coming to an end. There was the fear that, somehow, we were leaving more than Africa behind; more than the savannahs of the Masa Mara, the geography of the Rift Valley, or the northern deserts of Kenya; something more intimate within us— new-found sentiments, innominate but clear. We had grown closer in Africa, without realizing it, and now there was resistance in the uprooting. We always knew leaving would not be easy, but faced with the moment, it pulled against our instincts.

————————

Krystyne and I drifted through the souks and cafés of Tangier, climbed the cobbled streets around the mosque, wandered past the sad-eyed donkeys, and stepped into the rug merchant's cave for sweet tea and negotiations. Arm in arm we strolled along the quay of the harbour, past the rusted Panamanian cargo ship bound for the Black Sea, up the long cut of worn marble steps to the outdoor market smelling of fish and tobacco. And all the time the hours ran out the days, carrying us like a tide towards departure. Those last nights, sitting out on the open roof overlooking the Grand Souk, had us wondering about loss, and all that we were leaving behind. There is always loss.

I remember we were drinking brandy and it was late. Somewhere in the distance a baby was crying. In the courtyard below, a cat scuttled after some nocturnal prey. The city never slept, but that night its movement seemed far away. "Do you think life exists somewhere out there?" Krystyne asked, pointing to the heavens. The air was soft and warm.

"Almost certainly," I replied, "though maybe it's only our souls, drifting with the sidereal motions of the constellations. Or perhaps, it's more a sense of faith, that anything is possible, within and beyond our imagination." How else to describe those spiritual feelings under the late-night galaxy of the stars? There are moments in one's life that remain in memory, perhaps forever, and our last night there, together on the rooftop of Africa, was one of them. I never wanted it to end.

Our time had finally run its course, irretrievably gone. The emotional wrench of departure pulled at the gut. Africa had become our personal reawakening, a catalyst, our romantic touchstone, lifting us beyond the mundane routine of our previous life. Africa had somehow changed everything, taken hold of us stealthily, like a pathogen. Seduced by its idiosyncrasies we had grown tolerant of its bureaucracy, corruption, and poverty; the continent had reordered our personal values. We had let slip our North American moorings and, unknowingly, imperceptibly, drifted into new territory. Africa's overwhelming physical presence, massive in scale, hauntingly beautiful, had worked its spell and captured our imagination. And now that we were leaving, its sensual and mysterious workings, with all its confused emotions, still gripped our hearts, like a lover who refuses to be so easily discarded.

Krystyne drove me to the airport. She refused to fly across the Atlantic with me. I busied myself with the mechanics of the plane until it came time for us to part. We spoke of reunion in Toronto, only eight days off, ignoring the seven thousand miles it would take me to fly over Europe, across to Iceland, Greenland, Baffin Island, and home; flights, through good and bad weather, with carburetor icing, and the threat of ditching into Arctic waters. Headwinds precluded the southern route home, via the Azores. Not enough fuel even with the ferry tank.

Krystyne would of course miss the night flights, the beauty of the northern lights drawing curtains of magic across the Arctic skies; the limitless horizon of floating pack ice, dotted with icebergs, majestic cliffs of ice drifting on black leads of open water. She would have to forgo the austere beauty of the Greenland ice cap, the snow desert of the North (a graveyard of planes that misjudged the height of its eleven-thousand-foot icefield). Later, I would relate my flight over the tip of Greenland, where I saw the blue-green glaciers calving into the Uummannarsuaq fiord.

She would probably not be sorry to miss the tricky landings at Narsasuaq (Bluey West One), Nuuk, and Iqaluit; my seven days of flying would be far from straightforward, but then we both knew that, no use pretending. I watched her wave, hands growing smaller as the plane rose and banked into the morning sun over the Mediterranean. I could see her scarf fluttering in the wind as if she intended to lift off and join me. Her image stayed with me, sacred, over seven thousand miles of flying, only to reappear unexpectedly on the sea ten thousand feet below, or under the starboard wing, or over the horizon at the close of day.

There were moments of tension flying alone. Carburetor and airframe icing along the coast of Iceland threatened to pull me into

Arctic waters; storms covered the Greenland ice cap in blizzards of snow; ice pellets pockmarked the leading edge of the wings and elevator. And through it all, Charlie Foxtrot, my sole companion, remained loyal, dutifully at work, keeping me airborne.

At Nuuk, Greenland, I paused for twenty-four hours following a thirteen-hour flight from Iceland, nerves on edge, exhausted. I walked through the town that evening, up the hill overlooking the harbour, to the Catholic Church, aflame in the Arctic sun. I thought of attending Mass—a thanksgiving of sorts. The church door was locked, and as I turned to leave, the priest came to the window. I told him I had come on the off chance of attending evening Mass. As it happened, he was holding a vigil for Pentecost, which normally includes a Mass. However, it requires at least one communicant in addition to the priest, so together, we celebrated Mass, far from the Saturday-night carousing of the town, the sounds of which floated up the hill in the crisp evening air. Far out to sea a small fishing boat clocked its way up the coast, under a mackerel sky that slowly turned rose and purple as the sun dipped below the horizon.

Then, of course, there was the unforgettable, sweet, redemptive thrill of touching down at Iqaluit, the first landing on Canadian soil. Although I was still fifteen hundred miles from Toronto, the landing in Canada was a triumph. Only one more eleven-hour flight, driven by a north wind, over James Bay, across northern Ontario to Georgian Bay and down into the Toronto Island Airport and, suddenly, I was home.

I taxied over to the Shell Aero Centre ramp and walked across the tarmac, into the mechanics hangar. Sure enough, there was Dave McDevitt, working on the stripped-down fuselage of a Cessna 172, just as I had left him two years ago, tools spread out all over the floor. Hardly raising his head, he said, "You're back!"

Somehow, I expected more than this, in view of the distance flown, and the time away, but then he was busy, and his work was behind schedule. I left my gear in the plane and walked over to the island ferry, with only my headset in hand, ready at last to start my new life in Toronto.

Epilogue

OVER THE TWO AND HALF YEARS of our African odyssey, I flew twenty-three thousand miles over desert, jungle, snow, and ice, and twice across the Atlantic. In addition, I circumnavigated the African continent. These were the flying markers I had set out for myself, over and above my assignment with the Flying Doctors Service . . . and yet, so much more had taken root. Our time in Africa left Krystyne and me with insights beyond normal experience, and discoveries about each other that might never have occurred with the press of business, family, and friends in Toronto.

Though, as so often happens over time, Africa seems to have faded into our past, strangely removed, memorable but distant. How could it be otherwise? Images of life in Nairobi keep resurfacing, and the yearning for Africa remains, always there, sacred and unforgettable, but it comes less often, only to reappear unexpectedly, like a half-remembered face in a crowd, or the discovery of a forgotten photograph.

I remember sitting one evening at a dinner party, next to a woman who said, "Tell me about Africa." I looked into her eyes, but found I couldn't speak the words, they simply wouldn't come. How was I to describe the beauty of the Rift Valley drowned in early-morning mist? How to tell of the majesty of Longonot, or flying across the

Kenyan Highlands, bathed in the purple streaks of an African sunset? How was I to convey the silence, the wonder of the desert, remote and harsh, the camel herders and warring tribes of the Northern Frontier?

How, indeed, to explain the corruption, crime, and poverty that poison African society, while at the same time giving it a human face? And should I have even tried to persuade her of the West's moral obligation to Africa, without appearing clumsy or rude? Would those inquiring eyes have understood the tragedy of it all, might she really have cared?

What possible interest could she have had in the politics of AMREF, the dedication of the Flying Doctors Service nurses, or the dangers pilots face, risking planes and lives flying into dirt strips for Africans who place so little value on life? Would she have comprehended the enormity of the human cargo of lives, struggling to survive the Nairobi slums, the desperation of the sick and starving in those ghettos?

Perhaps I could have teased out some interest in the soft seductive beauty of the Indian Ocean, nights with friends drinking under the stars; I might have described for her the subtle seduction of Muslim eyes, dark and secretive over the veil, or the sight of ancient dhows plying the monsoon coast with spices and small arms from distant shores.

Or should I have simply recounted my love for Africa, already slipping into memory, leaving so much behind. All the struggle, the heart-rending cry of Africa, stripped of its people, wealth, and culture, despoiled and impoverished. I looked at her apologetically and repeated, to her quiet astonishment, several times over, "My heart is Africa . . . it's over there in Africa."

Glossary

ADF	automatic direction finding
AME	Aircraft Master Engineer
askaris	guards
bandas	cabins
belly	part of fuselage
boma	thorn fence
bwana	mister or boss
CIDA	Canadian International Development Agency
dukas	shops
ekori	goat-leather wreath worn by Himba brides
erembe	goat-leather wreath worn by unwed Himba girls
ETA	estimated time of arrival
GPS	global positioning system
HF	high frequency
IFR	instrument flight rules
ILS	instrument landing system
jambo	hello
karibu sana	welcome
kazakazi	monsoon (from the North)
kikoi	sarongs
kuzi	monsoon (from the South)
LED	light-emitting diode

luggas	streams
m'ganga	witch doctor
makuti	grass roof
manioc	plantains
manyatta	small settlement
matatu	privately operated bus
MEA	minimum en-route altitude
mugumu	fig tree
murram	mud
muzungu	white man
nargilas	glass pipes
ndege	bird or plane
toto	small baby
Tusker	Kenyan beer
ugali	porridge
VHF	very high frequency
white gold	ivory
yahudi	silver beads
yussr beads	prayer beads